THE MIS-ADVENTURES OF A SEA WYFE

by ley liberson.

Ley LiSeison,

Aug 2016

ISBN 978-1-4092-0247-9

On an ancient wall in China
where a brooding Buddha blinks,
deeply graven is the message
it is later than you think.
The clock of life is wound but once
and no man has the power,
to tell you just when the hands will stop
at late or early hour.
Now is all the time you own
the past a golden link,
go cruising now my brother
it is later than you think.
Anonymous

This book is for my Aunt/Godmother, who introduced me to libraries, my mother who gave me the love of live theatre and Trevor, who provided the real adventures from the theatre of life.

PART ONE
CHAPTER ONE
'SEA MANDALA'

What am I doing sitting in the middle of an ocean in a life raft? I am sure that there are better things to do with my time. I have been here for five days now. Five long, hot, boring days. Our water is rationed and my mouth tastes foul. I say "our" water, as at least I am not alone in this situation. The one I love most is with me and as hour slowly follows hour, we draw closer together in our love. Trevor is worried that I am only here because he persuaded me to go sailing. Not so, I went of my own freewill. I shut my eyes to go back in time to remember how it all started. After all it seems that I have plenty of time.

* * * *

When I first met Trevor I never thought that there was seawater coursing through his veins. This did not become apparent until we had bought and refurbished an old cottage, got married and seemed to be enjoying a fairly standard lifestyle. Then one Sunday morning, looking from the bedroom window, he casually said, "I think I would like to build a boat." This triggered very little reaction from me, as previously he had produced some quite unexpected suggestions and they had usually faded away as the sunset. He had spent a little longer on exploring the possibility of giving up work and becoming self-sufficient. We visited the library and browsed through tomes on growing one's own food, keeping a Dexter cow, how much acreage is required to produce all one's needs, etc. (This was before the advent of BBC TV's sit-com "The Good Life".) The final outcome was that we applied to the council for a small allotment, continued with full time work and spent most of our weekends digging, planting and finally producing some edible food; usually all ripening at the same time when it was at its cheapest in the shops. Actually the most interesting thing that we dug up was a rusty pistol.

I digress. The view from our bedroom window was of the Cattewater in Plymouth Sound, where a variety of boats hung onto their buoys and moved with the wind, current and tide. In fact it was about 25 yards from our house to the water's edge. At that time I did not even know anyone who actually owned a boat, but obviously Trevor did. So there followed a season of reading, looking at, and visiting and of course talking, boats. In between we continued with our respective jobs, dealing with our joint eight children, running our home, meeting friends and let's not forget the regular attendance at the allotment.

Things became a little more serious when Trevor arranged a weekend visit to a friend's boat moored in Cornwall. Complete with backpacks and via British Rail, we arrived at the delightful village of Charlestown, found the boat, plus the Skipper and went on board. Once there it became very serious indeed, as it became obvious that he had forgotten to tell his wife that they had guests for the weekend. After the initial shock, she took it in her stride and a good time was had by all. For me the really serious stuff began when we got ready to retire for the night. The boat was of an open plan design and we were each allocated a single bunk or a hammock. Just before lights out, Martin, the skipper, produced a galvanized bucket, which he set in the middle of the floor. We were to use this if nature called in the night. Evidently he did not approve of lavatories on board.

For me the next shock was to discover that this boat was built of concrete. In the midst of all these knowledgeable boat type people, for once, and unusually, I kept my mouth shut. I knew that they were joking and that I was the fall guy. Technical discussion followed and I suddenly realized that it WAS a concrete boat and it FLOATED. As I was to later discover, this is not an unusual method of boat building and the first one was built over one hundred years ago. In fact they became popular in the Second World War when barges for the Normandy Invasion were built this way.

In our situation it seemed the most suitable method, as it did not necessitate a large financial commitment. The materials could be bought as and when required, but before we began even thinking of building we needed plans of a suitable boat. Here again our weekend friend helped out. He suggested that we take the lines of his 30' vessel and loft them to build our own. The lines are in fact the plans of a boat, scaled down. Therefore we needed to bring them back to actual boat size, and that is "lofting". The next problem was where to do this marathon task. Hire a Church hall or Boy Scouts' Hut? Not a bit like that, this is where I could make my contribution. At that time I was Training Officer in a large factory where we boasted a good-sized canteen. So one weekend The Boat Building type husband and me, not forgetting rolls of plain wall paper, measuring tape, sello tape and quantities of marker pens, moved all the tables and chairs and began to loft the lines of a 30' yacht. For me this was an unexpectedly interesting exercise; most definitely hard work but a fun thing to do together. At the end, dirty but fulfilled, we climbed into the car, surrounded by rolls and rolls of paper and staggered home.

While all this was happening we also had to find a site. We needed somewhere close by and we didn't want to spend a fortune. Remarkably we discovered that at the end of our tiny village where the Naval Cable Depot stood, was a miniscule piece of land just outside the Depot fence. It would be perfect for us. A 'phone call to the Dock Yard and for the princely sum of £5. per year, we rented our own building site. The best part was the beautiful contract that we received. It was in parchment, in the name of the Queen and boasted seals, ribbons and very impressive signatures. I only wished that I still had it.

I will not bore you with the finite details of the boatbuilding project but will just explain the technique. (Those of you with no technical disposition just move on).

Trevor first made a rough wooden boat shaped frame in sections. These were cut out on my kitchen floor and then assembled on the site. This was covered with two layers of weld mesh and ¼ inch thick steel wires, both horizontal and vertical, strengthened it. Another two layers of weld mesh were added and then the whole structure was pulled together and secured with wire ties. These ties were pushed through and fastened every four inches and the very last one was made of gold! In fact they numbered about one quarter of a million. Then the wooden frame was removed and the boat was plastered with Ferro cement. As we were both working full-time, the boat took five years to build.

During this time life continued; I had promotion at work and Trevor changed jobs a few times. The kids were growing up fast and sometimes furiously, and a couple of grand children arrived. It was in fact a very full and fun time for us both. There were a few lows but not too many. Trevor had the philosophy that to complete this marathon task he must do something towards it everyday. Even if he came home from work late and tired, he would visit the boat and do just one job. Sometimes it was only to add a dozen more ties.

This caused the first real low. One evening he penetrated his eye with a piece of wire. At first he thought it was just a small injury but as the evening progressed it became clear that this was not so. We visited the Eye Infirmary where it was washed out, examined and he was sent home to return the next day, Sunday. This he did and it was found that he had pierced through all, but one layer of his cornea. They kept him hospitalised for five days. Fortunately no permanent damage was done. But obviously more care was to be taken. He was told that if ever he had trouble with that eye, he was to bypass any Doctor and go straight to hospital.

At this stage I think I should say that the thought of this boat actually sailing, and more to the point with me on board, did not cause me much concern. It seemed light years away. In retrospect I should have done two things. First gone sailing on someone else's boat and secondly visited more boats to see how they differed, particularly in the layout "down below". I guess at that stage I was still saying "down stairs". Anyway Trevor was progressing well and we were approaching the day of plastering.

You will visualize that by now we had an enormous boat shaped birdcage. In fact we had become a tourist attraction. People visiting our village on holiday were returning each year to watch progress. I even think that we should have sold tickets. All this attention was often irritating, as Trevor would be summoned by a "Hello there." He had to climb up out of the boat, peer over the top, and answer a barrage of questions; usually including, "I thought you were breeding parrots in there."

He usually managed to keep cool and often invited some of them home for a cup of tea. These were usually of the female variety and more often than not, young. Up until this point Trevor had done the entire work by himself. I had of course, helped out, but what with my demanding job, the house, cooking and let us not forget the allotment, it really was a one man show.

Being an amateur boat builder is OK, providing you build with care and use good materials, and we found that Bruce Bingham's boat on concrete boat building was excellent. However, when it comes to the plastering, the professionals are essential. We had heard of a good team and they came and inspected, gave it the seal of approval saying that the lines were "true and fair". They fixed a date and gave us a list of requirements –
twenty friends,
numerous buckets,

one concrete mixer,
spades,
water to the site,
working gloves
rope
bags of cement and sand
and most important of all NO BEER ALLOWED ON
THE SITE. As the Gang leader said, "keep your party
'til the evening".

The great day arrived and we allocated jobs to
everyone and the fun began. Concrete was mixed, a
bucket brigade hauled it up into our weld mesh hull
and the Ferro cement was pushed through the holes,
from the inside. The Plastering Gang just stood
around and watched, sometimes offering advice but
generally looking on. This went on for what seemed
like hours.

We had a quick break for sandwiches and soft
drinks and at about 2pm we were told to stand back.
Our friends slowly drifted away and it left the Gang
and Trevor and I. In front of our eyes this rough, wet,
concrete mess gradually turned into a lovely
streamlined hull as these talented craftsmen skimmed
the cement, even and smooth. It looked perfect to us,
but they still continued until they were satisfied. This
was in the month of March and we were experiencing
a magnificent spring. We had been advised that the
concrete must dry slowly and this time of year was
perfect. It was all over except for the cleaning up and
of course the evening festivities.

At 7 o'clock a very different looking crowd
assembled in our local pub. All squeaky clean, well
maybe a little cement under some fingernails, and

11

ready to enjoy ourselves. We had beer, wine and Cornish pasties and this was my first experience of the generosity of sailing friends. They had gladly given up their Saturday in some cases the only rest day of their working week. One had appeared from the depths of Cornwall. He'd heard the jungle drums telling him of the plastering party and just had to be there as Trevor had helped him with his boat many moons ago.

Another very special friend had driven across the country to collect our ferro-cement as Trevor had injured his back. Their enthusiasm was great and we gladly paid our friendly Publican and everyone went happily home. Instead of doing the same, Trevor and I strolled through the village to the site and there in the moonlight, stood and admired our boat. The first stage was completed and now would begin the fitting out, making the mast and boom, rigging and sails and lots more besides that I did not even know about. Next day, Sunday, arrived bright and sunny and very, very hot. In fact it developed into a mini-heat wave. Never heard of in the English month of March. How the devil were we to dry this monster slowly?

The Skipper, I suppose I can call him that now we are halfway towards a proper boat, spent all day rigging up a simple sprinkler system. Needless to say, I was back working the allotment!

As this is supposed to be fun to read, as well as informative, I will not go into the details on how the rest of the boat was competed. Sufficient to say that it was, thanks to Trevor's incredible hours of hard work and that she floated!

CHAPTER TWO
LEARNING TO SAIL

By the early Summer of 1981 "Sea Mandala" was on her mooring and nearing completion She was a double ender, rigged as a gaff cutter, painted very dark green, her deck was cream and her sails were in the process of being made. These were to be tan coloured in keeping with her traditional appearance. Below, there was a galley (kitchen), a navigation area, the main living/sleeping quarters, a hanging wardrobe with two drawers, and separated by a water tight door, a small area in the bow, which housed the ropes, fenders, spare anchors and sails, etc. and a toilet. No galvanized bucket for me!

She also boasted a wood burning stove. Trevor reckoned this was to keep us comfortable during the very unreliable British Summers. In fact, I think it was to keep him cosy during the long cold months while he completed the fitting out.

At this stage I was becoming familiar with the boat's layout, getting used to the motion while she was on her mooring and even beginning to grasp some of those strange nautical expressions. My annual holiday was fast approaching, when Trevor suggested that I book myself on a sailing course for the first week of the holiday. He felt that under the heading of "a husband should never teach his wife to drive", sailing was in the same category. Also he felt that I should experience one on a boat of similar size. This was suddenly becoming serious stuff. I investigated the local newspaper and found one that was for absolute beginners, five days on a 32' yacht, either daily or one could sleep on board. A telephone call later and I had reserved my place. Captain Gordon explained that he liked four students, and I made the fourth. We had to bring suitable clothes and a packed lunch. It would be Monday through Friday and would begin at 9 am and finish at 6 pm on each of the five days. I would attend on a daily basis. The die was cast.

The holiday period arrived and my colleagues were happily packing sun tan oil, bikinis, finding their passports and collecting travellers' cheques. I was shopping for sailing gear that took the form of bright yellow oilies and Wellington boots. Let us not forget the seasick tablets. That weekend I lay awake worrying as to what I had let myself in for. But as sure as night follows day, the Monday morning arrived, very grey and very windy. "Never mind," announced the envious skipper, who had to go to work. "It's obvious that you won't do any actual sailing, the weather's too bad. You'll probably tie knots and things, talk about safety and generally get used to the names of everything." With those cheerful thoughts he dashed off to work, packed lunch in hand. "See you tonight. Can't wait to hear all about it." The door banged and he was gone. I tidied up, changed into trousers, tee shirt and sweater. Put on my deck shoes and packing the waterproof trousers and wellington boots, struggled into the stiff jacket and was on my way.

Once at the Marina I discovered that I had forgotten my packed lunch. With a rush of adrenaline I bought a pack of white plastic looking sandwiches and assuming that my Instructor type host would be providing coffee, found the boat. There she sat, white,

14

absolutely pristine as if she had just been unwrapped. I was greeted by Captain Gordon, climbed on board and met my fellow students. All males. A Doctor, a Finance Controller and an eighteen year old student. Over a cup of tea our experience was checked. Both the Doctor and the Finance guy had been on a couple of flotilla holidays in Greece and the youngster had dinghy-racing experience. So much for the absolute beginners' course!

Even though we were in a sheltered Marina, the wind was still making itself felt, but the rain had stopped. We were shown around the boat and then were each given a length of rope. With this we practiced a couple of, and I quote, "absolutely vital knots." We would repeat these and others each morning, until we could tie them in the dark. As we practiced and the wind howled outside, I thought that at least Trevor was right, and there would be no actual sailing today. My mood lightened.

The ropes were replaced and we were given a lecture on the fact that on a yacht, everything, and I mean everything, must be returned to its proper place. Nothing must be left out to be lost or trodden on, as on a sailing vessel safety comes first and things happen so quickly that everything must be to hand. This was to be the safety aspects Trevor had spoken of. I now felt completely relaxed, although I had by now completely forgotten how to tie the bowline. Perhaps we'd get another cup of tea. With that in mind, I was thrown into panic when our Instructor announced that we would soon have the sail covers off, the engine on and go sailing. We were shown how to remove the sail covers, properly folded and stowed of course. How to turn on the engine and untie the warps securing us ashore. Before I had time to worry, Captain Gordon was gently going astern and motoring out of the safety of the Marina.

Within the shelter of the Bay we each took turns to steer the boat. It did not have a wheel, but a tiller. This is a long stick at the back of the cockpit and quite comfortable to sit at. When it was my turn I found it devastating to have to push this tiller in the opposite direction from where I wanted to go. Of course this was not a problem to the experienced three. My ineptitude did not seem to be a problem to Captain Gordon, he was very patient and understanding, but it certainly was a problem to me.

By now we were in the open sea and so were several other boats. Because of my lack of experience he left me at the helm much longer, while the others did complicated things like hanking on the foresail. Thankfully, my turn came to an end and the sails were hoisted, the engine turned off and we were sailing. The boat leaned over at an alarming angle and we were shown how to reduce sail and make everything much easier to handle. There followed an hour of confusion on my part while we tacked, luffed up, gave way and even gibed. Finally we found a little cove and anchored for lunch. A lovely respite, but spoilt for me by the fact that the afternoon was still to come. It did, being a repeat of the morning, until we turned for home and once again tied along the dock.

My legs were like jelly, but we hadn't finished yet. Everything was to be checked and secured. Sail covers on and decks washed down.

At last "time to go home," as Zebedee would have said. No, not yet. We were all called below, given a reusable clipboard of the British Isles, marker pens and listening to BBC's Radio Four Shipping Forecast, marked the relevant weather features on our boards for the next day.

We packed our bags, not forgetting our piece of training rope, and departed for home. I felt as if I was walking on cotton wool and my head was in a whirl. Trevor was waiting for me as I staggered in through the front door.

With an enormous smile on his face he asked, "How was it?

"You were wrong." I replied, "We did go sailing."

"Wonderful," he said, "How was it?"

There was a pregnant pause. "I hated every minute of it!" I emphatically answered.

I got through the following four days, became a little more comfortable with the motion, learned how to row and drive the dinghy with the outboard motor. We did a man overboard drill, learned more knots, became a team and developed a love/hate relationship with the skipper.

Given my time over again I would do the same, as I am sure that if I had been left to learn the basics on our own boat, it would not have worked. In hindsight given the choice, I would have preferred a complete beginners' group and perhaps a female crew, or at least one other woman. I did learn a lot, and also I learned a lot of tips that we were able to use on "Sea Mandala".

As we completed our last afternoon, we each had ten minutes with our instructor. I was told that as a complete novice and in my forties, I had done very well. I would soon become a useful crewmember and as we owned our own boat, providing I sailed regularly on her, I would probably become more skilled than the other three. As I pondered on this, it was driven home to me that, yes, "we did own our own boat". It was no longer Trevor's project it was OUR BOAT.

As I write this, having since sailed over 45,000 miles, I realize Captain Gordon was a very wise man when he suggested that it was possible for me to become more skilled than the others. I only hope that they have had as much fun as I have.

CHAPTER THREE
SAILING, SAILING AND MORE BLOODY SAILING

At last the day arrived when "Sea Mandala" should go to sea. Very wisely Trevor decided that this was the time to use his beefy sailing friends, as everything was untried and if anything went wrong he would need experience as well as muscle. He also decided he did not want me anywhere near on this occasion. A very wise decision, as we had witnessed too many men who scared the pants of their wives by taking them out in the wrong circumstances or in bad weather.

Anyway a group of enthusiasts leapt aboard and disappeared over the horizon. Evidently they just pottered around Plymouth Sound, adjusting this and tweaking that. It seems all had a good time and the exercise was repeated on several occasions; various adjustments having been made and I guess a quantity of ale consumed.

Came the day when Trevor decided we would go sailing together, just the two of us. It was a bright sunny Sunday with a gentle breeze and the forecast was good. We rowed out to the mooring, tied the dinghy astern and Trevor explained that we would drop the mooring ropes and motor out of the trots, not raising the sails until we were in the open sea. The trots are a long row of mooring buoys and each boat ties to a buoy on the bow and one on the stern. We were just about in the middle of the row. Clear so far? He showed me how the engine was started, also how the gear lever worked and how to stop the engine. Quite different from my training yacht of course.

With the engine purring nicely, he dropped the bow and stern moorings and putting the engine in ahead, began gently to pull away.

"Try to do everything slowly," he advised.

Slowly being the operative word. THE ENGINE HAD DIED. We did not seem to be going anywhere. He began investigating. We were not going anywhere indeed; there was a mooring rope around our propeller!

At this stage there was no diving gear on board. A stiff drink was called for and at 10 o'clock in the morning we downed a much needed whisky and soda. There was nothing we could do it being Sunday and everyone else seemed to be actually sailing. We did a few jobs on board, had lunch and waited for the intrepid cruisers to return. About 3.30pm a boat came past, coming to our assistance by loaning my frustrated skipper its diving equipment. In no time at all the problem was solved but it was too late to go sailing. Never mind, "Tomorrow is another day," as Scarlet O'Hara would have said. But in our case tomorrow was work as usual, so we had to wait for the next weekend.

The next weekend came and we went sailing. In fact we began to sail every weekend and I slowly became familiar with the boat and all her ways. She was a complete contrast to my training yacht. She was heavy. Being a gaff cutter, she had four sails as against the two I had become used to and because of this there were lots and lots of rope. Some called sheets and some halyards and some even called warps. Only men could have thought all this out.

All this did not pass without incident of course. We had our adventures like all sailors do. Nothing too horrific but to me as a beginner often quite disturbing. I remember sailing down the Fowey River and suggesting to my skipper that we turn on the motor, take down the sails and give ourselves plenty of time to get ready to anchor as we normally did. But no, he felt that I was getting more experienced and we could leave it a little longer this time. The wind puffed up and we accelerated, heeled over and went like a train. I could now see all the little boats bobbing on their anchors. Surely we should now take down the sails.

On we went. The tiller became very heavy for me to control. This was not fun anymore. At an alarming rate we began to pass the first of the anchored boats and then the next and the end of the estuary was in sight.

"Go up into the wind," shouted the skipper. "This bloody sail won't come down, it's jammed."
With my heart racing I did, and the problem was eventually solved.

I began to notice that each weekend we were usually the last to arrive at the various anchorages. God alone knows why, we left early enough in the morning.

There were in fact two problems. One was that "Sea Mandala" was a very heavy and slow boat, even under full sail with her topsail flying. Secondly, Trevor loved to sail. To suggest turning on the motor was absolute heresy. The combination of both meant we were anchoring, while everyone else was sitting in the cockpits, clean and on their second G and T. We came to an agreement that if our speed dropped below two knots we would turn on the engine.

During all this I must say that Trevor was very patient. We did not go out in bad conditions, he explained things time and again and he only swore at me three times a day. Nevertheless I still did not enjoy the actual sailing.

Our holidays loomed and we decided to sail to the Channel Islands. He reckoned that living on board for two weeks and sailing everyday would help me to become more proficient and eventually overcome my fears. I didn't think that I had any fears, only a dislike of the motion and the angle of the boat when sailing. Anyway we stocked up with food, water and fuel and packed both our bikinis and foul weather gear. Knowing the English weather anything could happen.

Our first leg was from Plymouth to Salcombe; we had a gentle wind, sailed the whole way, made good time and I thoroughly enjoyed myself. We anchored, cleaned up and went ashore for a meal and slept like babies. The next morning it would be up bright and early. We set the alarm clock for the early shipping forecast but did not need to hear what the man said. We could see the thick fog through our portholes. Never mind, a lovely day in Salcombe, actually this was more my idea of a holiday. Next morning all was clear again and we set off. This trip was to be my first night passage.

Learning from my limited experience I had begun to prepare some meals well in advance. At the beginning of a voyage when the going was bumpy, the last thing one wanted was to spend time below in the galley. I had discovered that I was not a sick sailor but a queasy one. We had a very enjoyable sail and I took my night watch with instructions from the skipper that if I was in doubt to call him. Not to hesitate just give him a call. This I did, but not too often. I soon began to pick out the port and starboard lights around me but gauging distances I found difficult.

In these early days we had little in the way of electronic equipment. We had electric lights, with oil lights as a back up. A VHF radio, a depth sounder and a trailing log to tell us how fast we were going. Trevor used a sextant for navigation; this was pre GPS days although some boats did boast Satellite Navigation equipment. We also had a Radio Direction Finder, which helped us with navigation. All very basic stuff but normal for that time. We did, however, have an automatic pilot. This wonderful piece of electronic equipment took all the hard work by doing all the steering. We called it Fred and he was our faithful third crewmember.

The holiday in these islands was almost uneventful. The gears stuck and we could not go astern; at a crowded fuel dock of course. The mechanic type skipper soon fixed this. While sailing between islands we heard on the VHF that there was a small ships' warning and that all boats should make for harbour.

The winds were certainly getting stronger so we made for the island of Guernsey. It began to blow and we called the Marina to see if there was a berth available.

My word, this was truly beginning a real holiday,

actually going into a Marina for a night. Think of all that fresh water and electricity. The reply came back that the entrance to the harbour should be avoided as several boats had had knock downs and a flotilla of small sailing dinghies were having trouble. My wonderful Skipper did a quick about turn and took us to a nearby island, anchoring on the sheltered side. In the safety of this position it seemed as if the wind had suddenly been turned off and the violent seas were calm once more. At least one of us seemed to know what he was doing. The holiday continued without many more adventures and fourteen days later we arrived back home, tired, sun tanned and I began to decide that sailing was perhaps not so bad after all. Summer ended and the cold autumn evenings began to draw in. We continued to sail at the weekends and were glad of our little stove. Finally the Skipper reluctantly agreed to "put the boat to bed". The sailing season was over.

Once more I could spend my weekends with family and doing all those things that normal people manage to enjoy on Saturdays and Sundays.

Trevor decided to take an evening course and learn Spanish. So I guessed that Spain would be on our itinerary one day. I was already committed to evening classes where I was teaching adults to read and write.

Later I was to regret that I did not make more effort to join Trevor in his language class. Trevor was also continuing with a Yacht Master Course. Needless to say I was making regular visits to the allotment. "Sea Mandala" just sat on her mooring looking very tranquil and pretty.

Once Spring arrived we continued our sailing weekends and that summer we were to venture to Brittany in France. Very serious stuff for me. We now owned a life raft, old but recently serviced. The skipper began to realize that a traditional boat was OK but with only two people to sail her, life on board could be made easier. The autopilot was certainly valuable and now we decided to dispense with our hank on foresail, going for the roller furling variety. This meant, no longer did one of us (usually the skipper) have to struggled to the bow in all weathers and put the sail on by hand and pull it up and down while balancing there. We could have one that was a semi permanent fixture and it would roll in and out as required, and we could do all this together from the cockpit. It still needed our muscles of course, but heady stuff. I think that we were still definitely the slowest boat around.

We ventured out most weekends and my tanned face and arms were the envy of my colleagues. Some sails were good and some bad. During our Easter break we went to the Scilly Isles. A gorgeous trip and our actual time there was idyllic. We returned home via Falmouth and some distance out our engine broke down. The mechanic type husband who is very good with engines, was not so this time. So we put all the sails up and sailed to Falmouth. There was very little wind and even that began to drop and drop, and we got slower and slower and it got later and later. We arrived at Falmouth Harbour and had to tack to get what little breeze there was managing to make the anchorage by midnight. We had been sailing for over twenty-four hours and my bed seemed very inviting. Dream on Ley, this was not to be so.

"What's to eat?" asked Trevor.

"Bread, cheese, pickles and tomatoes?" I replied hopefully.

With disgust Trevor announced that after all the energy he had expended, he needed some real food, good and hot or he would never sleep. I gave him a cup of hot chocolate and quickly heated up a tin of beef stew, threw in the contents of a tin of potatoes all to be eaten with crusty bread. I was so annoyed with him I did not bother to talk or even look at him. When I did with a piping hot bowl in my hand, he was fast asleep. In hindsight I sometimes wonder how our relationship survived this time.

In August we made our trip to France and the coast of Brittany is very rugged indeed. The weather was not perfect but it was fine for sailing, if a little cold and you liked that kind of thing! By now we were beginning to talk about sailing for longer periods of time but with full-time employment, talking about it was all that we could do. Perhaps we would win a Premium Bond or even a Lottery. My feelings about sailing were slowly changing, I still did not get a buzz from the actual sailing but I did enjoy visiting other places in company with our own "home". Rather like snails, we were slow but carried our house with us.

Work wise, I was now Training Manager for my Company and during this period there were changes at my place of work. We were taken over by one of our competitors and six hundred people were made redundant. Fortunately not me. I had the dubious honour of being promoted to Training AND Personnel Manager with no increase in salary! Nevertheless I was lucky, I still had a job.

Six months later the surprise came. Out of the blue, the Company decided to change the structure of the Organization. It would be divided into separate Units each with its own backup services and some positions would be redundant. An overall Personnel and Training Manager was no longer viable. I was to join the ranks of the unemployed, but with a reasonable amount of Redundancy pay in my Bank Account and as a Manager, three months' salary.

The company rules were that I could leave immediately or work to the end of the day! I telephoned Trevor to ask him if he would like to go sailing for a year and promptly burst into tears. I had commenced with this Company in 1974, when my marriage had broken up, starting as a lowly Training Clerk in the Training Department. Graduated to Training Officer and then Training Manager and was awarded a Fellowship in the Management of Training. I represented the Company on a variety of local committees, helped with the beginning of a Government Youth Training Programme for the unemployed and hopefully helped some of the people to progress through their chosen occupations. Now it was over, and so abruptly and not even time for goodbyes.

Now a full-time wife and homemaker again, I did not have too long to feel sorry for myself, as unexpectedly, I was asked to participate in a Course being run by our Local College of Further Education.

This was for Military personnel who were being retrained for their new careers in Industry. They were studying for positions in Safety, Personnel or Training and as my knowledge and experience was quite up to date, I could fill in for the lecturer who was unfortunately in hospital. This did not effect my redundancy payment nor my three month's salary and I was now paid a handsome amount by the hour for the new work. It all seemed to be too good to be true.

Meanwhile we decided that we would plan for an absence of one year, rent out the cottage and cruise the Mediterranean. Sounds easy if you say it quickly enough. We could see ourselves ready in about six months time. We informed the family, all of whom were involved with their own careers, families, houses, spouses, and partners or were just fancy free. They all received our news as if it was quite a normal thing to do, and said that they looked forward to free holidays in the sun.

There followed some very hectic months as I prepared courses, ran the home, become heavily involved with getting the house ready to let and making lists. On the boat I learnt how to prepare wood, rub it down and varnish. Trevor was still working fulltime as well as preparing the boat with a view to a year's cruising, getting charts and pilot books and lots more besides, all of which I have now forgotten. Would you believe it, we still had the allotment?

I took time off to visit my mother who lived in Canterbury and told her of our plans. She also took everything in her stride and I was so grateful to her reaction. I am an only child and she has brought me up single handed, never making any demands of me, just giving me her full support and encouragement. With everyone having such a laid back reaction to our decision, I began to think that I was the only one who thought that it was a monumental decision and needed to be agonized over, especially in the wee small hours of the morning.

Finally Trevor left his job, I completed my contract with College and the house let. We had managed to stick to our six month time frame. It was actually six months since I had been made redundant and the decision made. So with all the farewell parties over and the good-byes said, we were ready the day before our agreed deadline. There seemed little point in sitting on our mooring, twiddling our thumbs. We went ashore and bought some fresh bread and fruit, walked passed our house and along the beach and as we got into our dinghy we saw only one person, who casually said, "Are you off then?"

"Yes."

"Have a good trip." he shouted, as he walked away.

What an anti-climax, I just sat in the dinghy and felt quite disappointed. I had really thought a full orchestra would have struck up and a choir sung. After all I was sailing away from everyone I knew and loved, leaving my pretty cottage and for me, going into the great unknown.

There was no turning back. We climbed aboard, stowed the last few things and as a seasoned sailor I dropped the moorings and we were on our way.

CHAPTER FOUR
A VERY EVENTFUL BEGINNING

If I remember correctly we had sailed for the first twenty-four hours with good weather and no problems. We kept three-hour night watches. We were planning to sail to La Coruna in North West Spain and that should take about three and a half days. It was quite an anxious time as these seas are full of traffic. We needed to always be on the lookout for other vessels and some of them were mighty large.

The pattern began to be repeated the next day, the winds had been favourable and we had not needed to use our engine. Our faithful Fred was steering us and Trevor was plotting our position with the sextant, and we kept an hourly log, our position duly entered on the chart. Sometime during the second day Trevor decided to run the engine to top up our batteries. This was our only means of producing electricity. At that time weekend sailors did not consider the need for wind generators or solar panels. In fact solar panels would have been a waste space in the UK. I think that we were definitely still thinking, weekend sailing. He asked me to start the engine, which I did. I put it in ahead to give us a little extra drive while the batteries were being charged, when suddenly there was a loud bang and it stopped. We looked at each other in amazement. Trevor removed a panel to expose the engine, nothing obvious; he removed the engine box. I remained in the cockpit being the eyes on this occasion, as there was still a lot of traffic around us.

He came up to join me. "We have a problem," he announced. "The coupling bolts have broken and bent the prop shaft."

"What does that mean?" I asked.

"It means we can't use the bloody engine," he retorted.

"Can you mend it?" I asked.

"Not this time," was his immediate reply.

What could I say? There seemed no answer to this one. The wind was still blowing steadily and we were making good progress under sail. Really nothing seemed to have changed.

There was a long silence and then Trevor said, "As I see it we have three options." There was a pregnant pause. "We can turn around and go back to Plymouth. We can detour to Brest to get repairs but I haven't got detailed charts for that area. Or....." There followed an even more meaningful silence. "Or.... we can go on under sail. After all we are a sailing boat."

The decision was mine. But I knew the answer that was expected of me.

I didn't give myself time to agonize over the decision, "Let's sail on".

Did I really say that? Sailing with no engine. Yes I knew that's how the old sailors did it, but they didn't have huge tankers and cruise ships all over the ocean.

During my night watch I analysed my reasoning. If we had gone back to Plymouth, I felt that I would have found it almost impossible to leave again. Going to Brest was going out of our way and I did not fancy new Harbours without a chart. It really only left the third option, and after all it would not take us long. We had done nearly two days already.

In the early hours of the next morning the wind began to drop. Until by daybreak we had little or no wind. The sea became glassy calm. We took down all the sails because the constant flapping and banging as we rolled in the lifeless sea became really annoying.
"Sea Mandala" just sat there like a big fat duck on a pond. Even the log line hung absolutely straight beneath our stern. Our biggest concern was other traffic so we kept a very close watch and with our VHF on channel 16, were prepared to hail any vessel that looked as it was heading our way and hadn't seen us.

We fished and ate, with no fear of seasickness in this weather. Night followed the day and in the morning our situation was the same but the skies were darkening and looking extremely ominous. The barometer dropped dramatically and then the wind began to blow and blow and blow even more.

Wearing our safety lines, we put out a fraction of main and genoa and let the wind take us. Trevor plotted our course and if this direction of wind continued we would be heading for Gijon on the North coast of Spain, nowhere near our original destination.

The seas were getting enormous and the skies were still black. The main came down. Waves were building up behind us and sometimes they looked like a mountain chasing us. The genoa was rolled in, and to my surprise we sailed along on our rigging. So perhaps all those pieces of rope were useful after all. Trevor got out our storm trysail and storm gib, which we managed to raise, giving us a little stability. Together we sat in the cockpit, roaring along with mountainous seas behind us. Occasional green waves broke into the cockpit. How long this lasted I cannot remember, sufficient to say that it seemed to go on forever. It continued through the night and we seemed to rise up on the waves and go down into the troughs. Once we saw another boat in a trough while we were perched on a wave. Trevor called him on the radio and he said that this weather stretched as far as Gibraltar. We had one knockdown, but 'Sea Manadala' came back upright like the lady she was. Very gradually the winds eased and the seas finally got less and we were able to put up some more sail.

Trevor plotted our course and we were definitely heading for Gijon. He studied the charts and gave me the estimated time of arrival. This was going to be considerably longer than our planned three days. Although the winds were lessening the seas were still enormous. This meant that when I went below to get something to eat, I was thrown every which way. I will leave the picture of me using the loo to your imagination. We continued on our course and once again the winds got less and less.

On the EIGHTH day we neared our destination, but Murphy's Law meant that late evening, as we were in sight of our landfall, the wind nearly died. We just managed to make the Harbour Entrance before dark, but not knowing the depth and with no engine we decided to play cautious. We had had enough excitement; we would anchor outside and await daylight.

We ate supper and I decided that after eight days, I wanted to be really clean again. I boiled the kettle, filled a bucket and removing all my clothes started to wash. The first surprise was that I looked considerably thinner, great. The next surprise was an enormous knocking on the hull. This was ridiculous; we were alone out there. It reminded me of the Tony Hancock sketch when he was piloting a plane and heard someone outside knocking on the wings. The intrepid skipper poked his head outside and there was a little rowing boat, with two young men buried under a pile of lobster pots. Trevor's Spanish lessons paid off as he found out that they were concerned because we were not in the Harbour. He explained our predicament and that we had no engine.

"No problema Senor," was the smiling reply.

They took a line and towed us into the Harbour, and casually juggling a few fishing boats, tied us alongside. By now I was fully clothed, if not clean, and extremely grateful. They would not take any money but reluctantly agreed to accept a bottle of wine. We went to bed and slept like logs. The next morning we discovered we were in a large town, busy and bustling. Numerous fishing boats surrounded us and on the dock, cobbled stones led us to a small Police Station. We reported in with our papers, became legal, and explained our situation. After much head scratching and struggling to understand each other, we were given the name of an engineer and most important of all, his phone number.

We had some Spanish money with us so we bought provisions and using the small change made the phone call. Trevor struggled with the phone in one hand and a dictionary in the other. His classes hadn't covered such words as prop shaft, bent and bronze.

Nevertheless there must have been some success as it was agreed that the engineer would call early on Monday morning. We had a very restful weekend although we soon discovered that we were to be a bit of a tourist attraction. This old-fashioned gaff cutter with a British Flag nestling amongst their fishing fleet was worth a look.

Again it stretched Trevor's Spanish as we were asked loads of questions. Fortunately we realized this would stop once Monday arrived and everyone would be back at work. Sure enough Monday arrived and with it the engineer. The problem was explained, and after much discussion with a now well-thumbed dictionary, a solution found. He would arrange for a boat to tow us to a wall, where we could tie along side. We would wait for the tide to go out, and then Trevor would remove the prop and the bent end would be cut off and the rest of the prop shaft removed. Of course a bung would be made to fill the hole, before the tide came in again. The engineer would then make the new shaft. A price was agreed and off he went.

In preparation Trevor removed the gearbox and sure enough at the appointed hour, a boat arrived and swiftly, we were tied along the good said wall. The tide went out and so did the prop shaft and with much banging the bung went in. Then everyone left and we watched the water rise again. No leaks from the hole, all was well. Not so, as we slowly rose up the wall and the sea surged a little, we saw that the wall was in bad condition. There were spikes and rough stones. In fact it was not a good place to wait for the return of the engineer, which would probably be at least three days. We would have to be towed back to our original spot. Before this could happen a small launch came along side and a very dignified gentleman asked if he could tie alongside us. He explained that he was from the local Yacht Club and they had watched what was happening and would like to invite us to sit along their dock, while we awaited our repairs. Their launch would tow us and of course, there would be no charge as we were guests at Gijon Yacht Club. Oh yes, we must feel free to use their clubhouse and take any drinking water that we required. What could we say, but "Yes, please, and thank you very much." No sooner said than done and from then everything went magically. Even the engineer arrived on time and we reversed the process and were functional again.

The prop shaft was made from stainless steel this time. In fact that had been Trevor's original choice, but the mechanic making it in England had suggested bronze as more suitable.

Many years later we heard a very funny story about a bent prop shaft. Our friend Brian somehow managed to bend his while he was in Venezuela. Having extracted it he took it to an engineer and explained he needed another one made. This was very difficult as Brian had little or no Spanish. Anyway all seemed to be understood and he called back to collect it in one week. Lo and behold there was a beautiful new shaft waiting for him. But there was one problem. The engineer had made it exactly as it was, still with the bend in the end! Another week later and the job was put right. Brian dined out on the story and even wrote it as a letter to a magazine and later won the letter of the year award. I guess every cloud has a silver lining.

Thinking back to that happy time, I realized that we were lucky to have the backup oil lamps as without the ability to charge our batteries we would have been sitting in the dark. We were also glad of the enormous batteries that Trevor had installed; they had taken us this far without any means of topping them up. Let us hope that we had not damaged them. We cleaned the boat, collected water and did the laundry, explored the town and made use of the Yacht Club. We met many lovely people and I personally wished that we could stay there and never go sailing again. We made our first visit to the Bank and drew out some money; in those days we used Euro cheques. In fact it was a very happy time.

Finally it was time to leave. We spent our last evening with our new friends in the Yacht Club. There Trevor checked the weather forecast and there was no reason to linger any longer. Back on the boat with a contented sigh Trevor fell into a deep sleep, I lay beside him wondering and worrying as to what would happen to us during the next leg of our sailing venture. Finally I did fall asleep and very early next morning we slipped away.

CHAPTER FIVE
SAILING'S OK, BUT ARRIVING IS BETTER

Of course I did get used to sailing again and there followed a period of exploring new towns, experimenting with new foods, moving on and in fact I do not remember any more very bad weather. It seems that we just had day sails and anchored wherever it looked interesting. We had a pilot book that was very useful. It gave us loads of information with little diagrams of harbour entrances, depths of water and what to expect to find in each anchorage and town. Of course we used our charts but the book gave us vital detail. We made regular 'phone calls home, and eventually gave everyone an address to write to. This was to be a town that we hoped to reach in about two weeks. No Email in the mid- eighties. We had been sailing for about two months and felt it was about time to collect our mail. Exciting stuff.

We arrived at the town to collect the good said letters; we were going to use the Poste Restante system at local Post Offices. On cue we were there, the Post Office was there, but the mail wasn't. We waited a week, then another week. Still no mail. Eventually it arrived, but we had learned our lesson. We needed to give a much longer time frame.

My daughter was acting as our Agent. She collected the rent, dealt with the Bank and acted as our mailing address. At this stage we did find our Banking arrangements very frustrating. Usually only one Bank in a town dealt with Euro cheques, but we were noticing most Banks and shops had the sign that Visa was acceptable. We would have to look into this.

We seemed to stop at every port or harbour and loved exploring every new town. As we approached them and dropped our anchor there was always an element of excitement. We began to see boats that we had met before and it was nice to catch up on gossip and information. Of course we must not forget book swapping. With no TV on board, books became an even more vital commodity.

There did not seem to be any Marinas but we usually managed to tie alongside docks or swing to our anchor. We took detours up rivers and life was really idyllic. Finally we reached Portugal. Our first shock was that although we had thought the language very similar to Spanish, this was not so. So we bought a Portuguese/English dictionary and this has become the pattern with every new country we visited.

Our original plan was to go through the Gibraltar Straits and into the Mediterranean. But as we left Portugal and got nearer to the Rock we began to hear from other cruisers that once inside the Western Mediterranean, the Spanish coast there was very "touristy" and was getting spoilt for cruisers.

Discussion time. We finally decided on two things 1) We were enjoying this lifestyle and 2) We would like it to continue for longer than the planned one year.

How could we fund this? After more discussion Trevor suggested that we backtrack a little and go into a large Marina in Portugal. In fact, at that time, it was the only Marina in Portugal. There he would try and get some work with his original trade – engine repairs. This would give us some extra funds and from there we could possibly go to Madeira, Azores and even further. Perhaps I would find some work too. We scanned the Pilot and decided that Vilamoura looked interesting. About turn and Vilamoura Marina here we came. There followed a very pleasant time, for me anyway. We actually spent five of the winter months there. Winter in the Algarve was delightfully warm and I remember wearing shorts on Christmas Day. Trevor did find work and he also ran an evening class in Celestial Navigation. In fact he too seemed to enjoy himself while making money. I didn't find work until the last month but it brought in a few more pennies. We made lots of cruising friends and began to realize that people who had the "get up and go" mentality were a lot of fun. Also one didn't wait for introductions, time was too short, they could have sailed away by tomorrow. So friendships began to develop fast and furiously. The international community was stimulating and one could have lovely cockpit evenings over a bottle of local wine or beer.

Of course one of the best experiences was making friends with the locals and finding out about their culture and lifestyle.

We also used this time to reflect on the sailing performance of "Sea Mandala". She had remained a very slow boat and was quite heavy to handle. As a gaff rigged boat she carried a tremendous weight above the decks. We had a lot of rope and blocks and her mast was a heavy telephone pole and the boom was also made from solid wood. During our slow meandering along the Portuguese coast we had seen some small traditional barges, these were gaff rigged, but loose footed. Loose-footed means that they had no boom. Trevor had been giving this a lot of thought.

Each country has its own regulations and Portugal is no different. After a period of three months any visiting boat must sign out and sign into another country before they can return. One can, in fact return the same day. We decided to use this time to remove the boom and have a trial sail to the Spanish border, sign in, and go up the river Guadiana and see the effect. At least we could not get into too much trouble there.

The boom was removed, lashed onto our side deck and off we went. This certainly did make a tremendous difference to our performance. So the boom was deposited on shore and Trevor reckoned that we had lightened the weight by about 150 lbs. The bonus was that the trip was fantastic and the little Spanish village that we found by the river was gorgeous. It was like stepping back in time, no cars, tiny shops with unusual foods and a bakery with fantastic bread. We had to place our order as they never had any visitors and they only made the required number of loaves each day. Sadly we left but vowed we would return.

In the Marina we made more friends, exchanged a great number of books and most incredible of all, there was a large air-conditioned cinema, which showed English films. On a Sunday evening they had a midnight movie. I will always remember the night that we went with friends. It was a hot, balmy night and we walked to the cinema, sat in wide, yellow leather seats and with an audience of twelve watched "Passage to India". What a treat.

It was during this time that I began to question the accommodation on board "Sea Mandala", not discussing it with Trevor, but during the time I spent on my own. Making up a bed in the salon every night began to be a chore, having to wash at the kitchen sink or in a bucket in the cockpit was hardly ideal. We had no refrigeration and although this did not present a problem while in the Marina, it made catering difficult while under passage or at the tiny anchorages. Also we both were beginning to realise that a 30' boat is quite small by modern cruising standards. We had limited space inside but more important, with such a short waterline and even minus the boom, we would never be speedy. We didn't want to set records but it would have been nice to arrive sooner, rather than later! There was nothing we could do about it; we would have to settle with what we had. Just think, the alternative would be working again in England and after all, this was a period of just putting our toes in the water and seeing if the lifestyle suited us. We could always think about changing the boat when we returned and once back in the UK, we knew that it would certainly be a long time before we would be full-time sailors again.

Time was approaching when we should start cruising again, so with a quick lift out, a couple of coats of anti-fouling paint and we were ready to go. It was interesting that during our stay in Portugal VAT was introduced. No problem for us as we had already become used to it in the UK. The first time that we made a purchase after the big event our invoice was stamped with the date one day before VAT was introduced. The next week and another purchase, the same thing happened again. The penny dropped; being unfamiliar with the system, our friendly shopkeeper made all transactions at that date so he would not have to cope with complexities of the new system. We often wondered if he is still doing it?

CHAPTER SIX
OH DEAR, SAILING AGAIN

Once again I had a case of the tummy wobbles at the thought of actually sailing again - would I every get used to it? At this time Trevor was never aware of my inner thoughts and feelings. It was not because he was particularly insensitive; it was a case of it never entering his head that anyone could not love the art of sailing and I felt that I couldn't tell him. I am not feeling sorry for myself, as I loved the actual lifestyle once we arrived at our destination and knew that the sailing was the means to the end. We signed out and I must warn you that at that time the Portuguese Bureaucracy was unbelievable. Four different officials had to be located and visited and the appropriate stamps obtained. We always had to visit a Doctor who just stamped the papers and never even looked at us, let along examined either of us. So much for health legislation. At last we were on our way and heading for Madeira or rather Madeira's sister island of Porto Santos.

The forecast was good, but once we were about ten miles off shore, the seas became lumpy and the wind blew and I felt ill. Looking at Trevor's face, he was not feeling so bright either. Perhaps we had just lost our sea legs. By sunset the wind abated and the seas went down. I think the trip lasted about four days, was finally very comfortable and we saw little traffic. Visibility was always good and Trevor was able to take regular sun sights and plot our position. One day he said that we should soon see signs of the island and within half an hour we saw a small point of land on the horizon. I was always impressed with his skill in getting us there, taking sights was often very difficult but at least now that we had left England we usually had the sun to help him.

We arrived at ten in the morning. We anchored making sure that everything was secure, collected our papers and rowed ashore. As we approached the shore the waves were breaking and landing would be very difficult and very wet. We opted to go alongside some steps by a wall. Easier said than done, the seas went up and down, and the surface was covered with green slime. We made it. We went into the town and found the Police office. This island being Portuguese we expected the same pattern of long and tedious signing in. Not a bit like it. The official greeted us, made us welcome and suggested that he took us into the Bar next door and introduce us to the local wine. Then and only then, would he stamp our passports and deal with the obligatory paperwork. This was more like it.

We stayed on this island for about three weeks. It was flat and very arid but the people were extremely friendly. I joined the woman at the water pumps to do my washing, by now I was quite expert at hand washing in cold water. I did know one thing, next time I would equip our boat with dark sheets and dark towels, no more white tee shirts and certainly nothing that required an iron. You have to realise that sometimes water is not always easy to come by and also finding and carrying five-gallon containers, via the dinghy back to the boat, becomes quite disenchanting. One never wastes water and to leave a tap running while cleaning one's teeth is unheard of. If the seawater was clean we used it for washing up and for cooking vegetables. Our diet changed and we ate more fresh food, and fish became a large item on our menus. In fact it was in Porto Santos that I first tasted fresh tuna. I saw them on the market slab and the rich red flesh looked nothing like the tinned anaemic variety that I was used to. What a wonderful taste and texture. In most of the Butchers' shops the meat smelt decidedly "off".

There were two or three other yachts here and we enjoyed their company. One was a German doctor who had had his own clinic in Hamburg and another American couple were sadly visiting the island where their teenage son had committed suicide. We were discovering that this lifestyle was providing us with the most interesting people and certainly widening our perspective.

Having our fill of this interesting island it was time to move on to Madeira itself. At that time everyone was advised to go into the Marina as the holding outside was poor. Not a thought that pleased us as Marinas cost lots of pennies and anchoring is free. I think we were so naive at this stage of our cruising lives, that we never questioned statements like this. Trevor sailed single handed that day as I was feeling wretched with a sore throat; only later discovering that I had an enormous abscess on my tonsils. He says it was one of his most magical sails. He called me as we approached the entrance to the Marina and he needed help to tie alongside and with sails down, we motored in.

It appeared to be full to capacity, all the slips were occupied and yachts were rafted up side-by-side, along the walls. I saw one space. There was an enormous yacht which had no boats tied to it. At my suggestion we made for that one and I held out the mooring line and shouted to the crewmember to please take my lines. After some hesitation he did. Safely tied up, I disappeared below to continue feeling sorry for myself. Trevor began to take note and realized that we had tied up alongside "Flyer" which for two years running had won the Whitbread Race. It was obvious that everyone had been too inhibited to lie beside this beautiful creature. Trevor soon began talking to the skipper and apologized for my speedy disappearance by explaining my sore tonsils. The millionaire owner was horrified and said that he would never sail long distances still sporting his tonsils, and laughingly said, "You will tell me that she still has her appendix next." My skipper, who has neither tonsils nor his appendix, joined the laughing. Listening from my deathbed, I felt the first rumblings of my appendix playing up!

A quick visit to our German Doctor friend who we found nearby, several antibiotics later and I was nearly new again. (For the record, after sailing thousands and thousands of miles I still have a superb pair of tonsils and my appendix.)

We explored this beautiful island that is just a high mountain jutting out of the sea. The crop rotation is fantastic and channels of water, called lavadas, run all the way round and down the slopes. They grow lettuce and tomatoes in the shelter of banana trees and fruit and vegetables abound. Further up they grow hardier crops and at the top are the grazing areas. Walks are laid out and are graded for one's physical ability. The people are welcoming and very proud of their island.

The town was delightful and we bought local Madeira wine by the gallon, providing our own bottles. We sat in the local bars listening to their music, explored the markets, saw the sights as all good tourists should and Trevor had a haircut. Unfortunately he chose early closing day to try and get this done, and seeing our dilemma a friendly policeman took us, passing the closed shops and through a few back streets into a kitchen, where the hairdresser was performing her art on some local women. With big smiles she indicated that he was to be first and snipped away. In Portugal and these islands the man is definitely the boss. During our stay here we found many cruisers waiting to head to the Canaries and then on to the Caribbean. Their casual attitude to such an undertaking took my breath away. We met up with people on annual holidays and began to remember that we too were on borrowed time. We would try to stretch our money as far as we could but one day soon it would run out. The rent from our cottage was not quite enough to support our sailing lifestyle. It certainly covered our day-to-day living costs but any maintenance, marina fees, luxuries, etc., soon made a hole in our sailing fund. By the way for luxury read eating out once in a while or using a taxi!

CHAPTER SEVEN
BUMP IN THE NIGHT

Once more it was time to leave and our next passage was to be to the Azores. We read up on these islands and they sounded fantastic. We had already said our good-byes to "Flyer" as they had left earlier heading for Australia. The owner had had her refitted as a cruising yacht and was taking some of his original race winning crew, plus their wives, for a "thank you" cruise and then she was to be handed over to her new owner. Our Doctor left for the Canaries to await an Atlantic crossing. There was no reason left for us to stay, so as was the tradition on this island, we painted a picture on the harbour wall, clearly marking it "Sea Mandala" and gently sailed away.

This sail was very pleasant, light winds, calm seas and very little traffic. In fact once we left the island I only remember seeing one other boat. I can't remember how long we expected to take but it was to be quite a distance. It was easy to cook in these conditions and Trevor loved the smell of hot bread coming from the oven, we relaxed and read and listened to the BBC World Service. I even began to be interested in taking sun sights and fixing our position. The winds were light and we did quite a lot of motor sailing and our boomless boat was certainly an improvement.

Nevertheless it was going to be a slow trip to the Azores. In fact we began to be concerned about our fuel situation. If we were to continue motor sailing would we have enough diesel to get us there. I gave a silent chuckle, remembering the days and days that we had sailed engineless earlier in the adventure. We took our respective three-hour night watches and soon had only eighty miles to go.

That night we were still motor sailing and we changed watches as I was on from midnight 'til three. Trevor retired to sleep and I plugged into my talking book. We did not read at night as we felt we would lose our night vision. After the first hour I left the cockpit and went below to fill in the log entering the distance, wind direction, compass course and barometer reading. Remember we still had the faithful Fred doing all the hard work. I popped up and had a quick look around – nothing. I went below, made a coffee and decided to try the cake I had baked that afternoon. Another long look around and I settled in the cockpit with my coffee and cake. Great. Suddenly the boat seemed to rear up, lean over at a tremendous angle and then settle back down again. Apart from spilt coffee everything looked the same. I had a hurried inspection and there was nothing ahead, around or in the water. A startled Trevor appeared but he could see nothing. He had been thrown off his bunk and thought that I had collided with another ship.

We spent awhile looking and talking about it then deciding that whatever it was had gone. He started back down the companionway steps. Later he told me that he thought the salon carpet looked strange. He went down below and discovered why. He was ankle deep in water. His words were - "bloody hell, we're sinking!"

I was stunned into silence. His immediate action was to try to find out where the water was coming from.

He had built the boat and knew every nook and cranny but could not find it. Quickly we found that our manual bilge pumps were not able to cope with the quantity of water coming in. Particularly as I was the only one pumping, Trevor being occupied with more immediate matters. How stupid had we been, having all these manual pumps without the bodies to support them?

Decision time. Trevor told me to get the life raft ready and put it over the side. He would plot our position, send out a VHF May Day and put up a flare. This was done. The water got higher. I got the life raft in position but could not get it over the lifelines. The water got even higher. We swapped places and I retrieved the grab bag, our papers, my bag and the flare pistol with the extra flares and more besides. By now the lids from the bilge lockers were floating and I was in danger of putting my foot into the actual bilges and breaking an ankle. I too went on deck; once there I saw our life raft gently bobbing on the sea, it was nearly at deck level.

Trevor told me to get in and he passed me everything, then went below and got the five-gallon container of fresh water. We managed to tie our deflated dinghy behind the raft and at the last moment Trevor threw in our waterproof, cockpit bunk cushions. With one last look around he too climbed in. He stood with his back to me, still holding on to "Sea Mandala's" lifelines and head bowed. I did not know if he was crying, praying or what. I told him to untie the line holding us to "Sea Mandala" or we would be dragged under with her. He did and later told me that his delay was caused by trying to think of what he had forgotten. Too late, as by then we were drifting safely away. Our boat was still under full sail and still rapidly going down. In all, from beginning to end, it took about thirty minutes.

We sat there like refugees and had to get some sort of organization. The life raft was a Beaufort, which comprised two inflated rings, a single skin floor and a canopy, which had a flap, which could be opened or secured in bad weather. It was orange and designed for six people. Inside were several items including a pump and cans of water. With the pump we inflated the dinghy and tied it more firmly behind us. We could now only see the tops of Sea Mandala's sails. We tried to get some order with our meagre belongings and when we next looked, our home had gone.

Taking stock we realized that Trevor, who had been dressed for sleeping, was ringing wet and very cold. We wrapped him in a refuse bag that had housed our emergency kit. As I had been on night watch I was dressed far more warmly. Inside the raft was a sea anchor and we threw this over the side, as we did not want to drift too far from our reported VHF position. We both knew that there was little hope of anyone hearing our Mayday as we had seen little or no traffic in the last few days. We just rested until dawn.

With the light came the reality. We were alone out here and no one knew about it. This was before the time when a yacht would carry an EPIRB (electronic position indicator radio beacon.) We sorted through our belongings and checked what was standard kit in the life raft. I first noticed the plastic card. One side told us how to right the life raft if it turned over, sobering thought. There did seem to be a great number of sobering thoughts. The other side informed us that we should not eat raw fish, as one needed a large amount of water to digest this. AND not to put human waste into the sea as it attracted sharks. They did not tell you what to do with it. (This is your trivial pursuit question and the answer will come later.)

There was a torch with a broken bulb, a bailer, a length of cord attached to a quoit, a knife, six cans of water, small paddles, sponges, seasick pills and the rest I have forgotten. Our contribution included several tins of food and fortunately a tin opener. Two plastic cups and two bowls, spoons, a first aid kit, toilet paper, Trevor's knife and I guess many other things but 1986 is a long time ago.

Trevor made some decisions and the first was that we were in a survival situation and everything that we did was to lead to our being found. This sounds rather pompous now, but it didn't then and more important it worked. He worked out that we would each do one hour watches and during this, a complete look around would take place every fifteen minutes. This was based on his calculation of the speed of any passing ships. We would have one pint of water each every day and a tin of food between us every two days. We placed the bunk cushions on the floor and arranged everything around the circumference of the raft. There were little pockets and loops around the inside edge and things could be secured. We decided to use the cans of water first and not eat until the following day.

Trevor told me to find something in my bag and write down exactly what had happened, I quickly realized that this was in case we did not make it and the raft did. At least our family would know what had happened. Very sobering thoughts indeed.

The next problem was going to the loo (toilet). I was a very weak swimmer and the life raft acted like a lively trampoline, so sticking my rear end outside the opening and somehow getting a good distance out, was not appealing. We compromised by emptying the first aid box and using that as a chamber pot. At about midday I was on watch and saw a large ship sailing away from us. Trevor sent up a couple of flares and had to stop, as it was obvious that we were not seen. We could not afford to waste anymore precious flares. Those wretched sobering thoughts once more.

The day passed slowly and one interesting thing occurred. We had our one pint containers of water and we drank from the same can, never doubting that each would take only his share. Night came and the little light in the roof ceased to work. It had been powered by a salt-water activated battery. We continued with the same watch system and neither slept well as we disturbed each other with this trampoline effect.

DAY TWO. Very similar to Day One and we still had out our sea anchor as the wind direction was such, that we would not drift to land but out to sea The Atlantic Ocean is mighty big. The seas were calm but we had a sprinkle of rain and were able to test the water catching system. This was fine but the first pint was undrinkable, as it tasted of salt and rubber. At least we had a most welcomed wash. The next lot was OK giving us an extra drink. We shared a small tin of ravioli. For the record, cold and straight from the tin it tasted delicious. Night came again and we realized that the bunk cushions were a great help. The single skin floor became very cold and with condensation, would have been very unpleasant to lie on. Night came but no ships.

DAY THREE. No rain today but we seemed to spend a great deal of time talking. First of all Trevor was distressed because he felt that with his desire to sail, he had put me in this position. This was not so, I was over twenty-one and had made the decision to go sailing all by myself. Before we left the UK I had read the book "Survive the Savage Sea" by Dougal Robertson, and I was fully aware of what could have been in store for us. In fact the reason that we were towing our dinghy was from that book. Two boats are easier to see than one, and if God forbid, the life raft began to come apart we had an alternative. In fact a life raft does look very flimsy indeed. My only suggestion to life raft producers is, that sitting inside this miniscule piece of flimsy rubber, it would have been great to have seen "good luck" printed on the inside. Nevertheless it was amazing how quickly it had become our "home". I tidied up each day and generally behaved like a regular homemaker. It was on day three that we began to notice an interesting thing. Under our small home was the only shade in the whole ocean and many fish took advantage of this. Small fry, medium and large fish, a small shark and I saw a turtle. They all stayed there in absolute tranquillity until about three in the afternoon, and then as if we had rung a dinner bell, they began to frantically hunt, chase and eat each other. About an hour later calm was restored. In this strange situation we ourselves did nothing frantically, in fact we were calm and seemed to be drawn very close together. We talked about food, what would happen when the water ran out, what had hit us and then food again. Yet another day ended.

DAY FOUR. Food today and we decided to eat a small tin of ham. Not a very good decision as it lay in my stomach like lead causing me to bring up a lot of bile. I guess that I needed much more water to absorb this protein. Trevor insisted that I lay still as I could ill afford to lose any liquids. By now we were using our five-gallon water container. We discovered that this was not a successful container, as trying to fill the cups in the bumpy raft, it was impossible not to spill our precious liquid. We found ourselves saying that next time we would have a container with a tap or smaller vessels. NEXT TIME, we looked at each other in amazement.

At this time Trevor began to think that we would not be rescued. I was absolutely certain that we would be. Time would tell. Actually in hindsight we did have some macabre conversations. Who would die first? Would the survivor be able to lift the other to throw the body into the sea? Would one eat the other? We seemed quite calm as we continued to carry out these Hammer Horror type conversations. In spite of these the time was actually beginning to drag and although we had one book in the raft we didn't feel inclined to read it. People ask us if we had sex. Although we felt very loving and emotionally close it did not trigger any amorous interludes!

Watching the antics of the fish made us realize that we had no fishing hooks. Not that we fancied eating raw fish at this stage but we spent an interesting hour making some from phone cards using my nail scissors. It's surprising what one can find in a handbag. By now the wind direction changed and we were able to bring in the sea anchor. I was still feeling sick and we realized that ham was a stupid food to have eaten, as I needed a lot of water to absorb it and we had none to spare. Lesson learned. Night fell and day four was over.

DAY FIVE. Golden sun, brilliant blue sky and calm azure seas. Sounds like a holiday brochure. This day we began to tentatively talk about boats. What sort would we like, how big, the layout…. and before we knew it we were in the throes of deciding on boat number two. Trevor was still feeling uncertain of our rescue, when we both suddenly saw an immaculate cigarette packet floating slowly by! In this great expanse of sea we seemed so small and vulnerable and oh so low in the water. Aeroplanes were frequently flying overhead and later we discovered that they were from an American Air Force base in the Azores.

The day slowly passed and we were both thirsty, tired and I was still feeling queasy. The worst part of the whole enterprise was that five days without cleaning my teeth had left my mouth feeling foul and I'm sure smelling horrible.

Night came and I began to feel sick again. I lay down and Trevor took over the night watches. At 1 am he looked all around. Nothing to be seen but inky darkness and a million stars. At 1.10 I began to vomit, and as he emptied the first aid box/pee pot and now sick bowl, he looked up and saw a ship.

"Quick, pass me the flare pistol."

"Why?"

"Because there is a fucking ship out here".

Up went the flare.

"Pass me a parachute flare, it will be brighter."

Up went the larger flare, and its exhaust fumes filled the raft and nearly choked me. I struggled to get my head through the flap and breathe again. As I did so, we both saw a searchlight come on from the Bridge. Sickness forgotten, we just stared and stared, frightened to look away in case this creature vanished. She didn't disappear, but she didn't move either. Nothing to do but wait. What was happening? We sent up a couple more flares just in case she had lost sight of us. Much later finding out that we were clearly visible with our bright orange, fluorescent canopy. Also discovering that the Captain was busy radioing Head Office with his latitude and longitude in case we were pirates (This is part of Maritime Law against Piracy at sea. Before any rescue is attempted a call must be made). His engineer was in the process of changing the fuel, as they needed a thinner type for manoeuvring. We also wondered why they didn't send a tender for us. There was plenty of time to ponder on this. Eventually the ship began to approach us. Whow how big she looked!

She tried to come along side and her wash gave us our only heart racing time since we had sunk. Off she went again. She returned from another angle and gradually came along side our tiny vessel. So smoothly this time, a great piece of seamanship. I looked up and up and up at this huge monster, the hull streaked with rust, it seemed to stretch forever. Leaning over the rails were lots of brown faces with flashing white teeth and, as I watched and waited a ladder came rolling down. It seemed to be a very homemade ladder, with tatty rope, twine, pieces of bamboo and nylon cord. Trevor grabbed it and a voice shouted to come up. I was horrified, I couldn't climb this.

"Go on," encouraged the now Survivor type skipper.

And lo and behold I went up. As Trevor said later, like a rat up a drainpipe."

CHAPTER EIGHT
RESCUED

As I stepped on board I was embraced by a huge black giant, who wrapping a blanket around my shoulders, shouted, "Praise the Lord, you have been saved!"

I sat down on a bench realizing that my legs were very shaky and only then realizing that I had been rescued. I watched Trevor step on board and his legs actually collapsed. As he was helped to the bench, my black benefactor whispered in my ear "The woman is always stronger than the man."

I didn't care who was the stronger, we were safely on board and with a cup of tea in my hand, and I felt absolutely on top of the world.

The crew carefully lifted our life raft out of the water along with the dinghy. Then the contents of the raft were put into a bag and we were asked to check that they were all there. All around us were beaming faces. The ship began to get up speed and we were given bowls of minestrone soup with fresh bread. The finest meal that I could remember. The Captain came along and checked our papers and told us that they were en route to Genoa in Italy, a journey of about four days. We would be their guests until then. We would talk more in the morning. We were shown to the Owners' State Room, relished in showers and looked longingly at the beds. My giant was actually the Chief Steward, and he suggested that we had a light sleeping pill. No way, we would sleep the sleep of the dead. Telling us that his name was Hazard, he left with instructions that we were to call if there was anything that we needed and he still recommended a sleeping pill. We climbed into the inviting beds and both lay in silence but wide-awake until the morning! Hazard knew best.

Next morning our breakfast was brought to us on two trays. They were loaded down with tea and coffee, orange juice, cereal, egg and bacon, toast and waffles with syrup. Our shrunk stomachs could only cope with a fraction of this banquet.

We met again with our Spanish Captain and all our details were taken. There was an invitation to the Radio Room to phone our family. He also told us that he had contacted the British Embassy in Genoa with details of our rescue and the ship's ETA. We had passed muster and our meals could be taken in the Officers' Mess and we had the run of the ship. If we wished they would fill the small swimming pool for us. What hospitality.

During the course of our "cruise" we discovered that the ship was part of Fyffe's Maritime Division. Her name was Rio Cuyamal and the cargo was refrigerated bananas. The Captain was Spanish, the First Engineer Polish, and the Radio Operator was Chinese. The rest of the Crew was from British Honduras, which was the ship's port.

We only had the clothes we were wearing when we sank. I had a tee shirt, trousers, knickers and deck shoes. I also had the jacket, which I was wearing on that epic night watch. Trevor only had his underpants and a tee shirt. I guess our clothes smelled. Without being asked the crew provided us with a second set of clothes, even down to a pair of shoes for Trevor but the shoes were without laces and the jeans covered with oily stains. I was invited to use their washing machine and soon we were the proud owners of two sets of clothes. I was even given a brand new pair of y-fronts so that I could wash my knickers.

The four days passed very quickly. We were invited to view the bridge and during our conversations with the Skipper we realized that we had been so lucky to be found. There had been an amazing number of coincidences.

The First was that the ship should have delivered her cargo to New York, but owing to a Dock strike she was diverted to Italy. Secondly, the Captain was new and wanting to beat the sister ship also going to Genoa, he had decided to take another route, which led to us. Of course he didn't win the race and I quote, "I had to stop and pick up two idiots in a life raft."

The third and last coincidence was that the World Cup Football match was being played, and every time the ship came within range of land they would pick up a TV signal. On this night they picked up the signal from the Azores and leaving two on watch, everyone enjoyed the game. When it was over most of them went on deck and the Captain took the score to his two Watch keepers. As they chatted, one said that he thought he had seen a red light. The skipper felt that it was probably the red masthead light of a yacht. They all looked and they saw our second flare. You know the rest.

Life on board this busy ship was interesting. The crew was small and while sailing, they spent their time doing maintenance. The Engine Room boys were always wiping their hands with oily rags, so obviously found plenty to do. To me the bridge looked like Space Ship Enterprise and was always manned. To small boat sailors this was very confidence giving. The cook and stewards seemed to work hardest of all. There was a constant procession of glorious meals appearing three times a day. Bread rolls were cooked twice a day and I would hang around the galley waiting to catch one while it was still red-hot. Breakfast was served at 8am, Lunch at mid-day and Dinner at 6pm. Of course there was a heap of food in the refrigerators, as no one was expected to go from Dinner 'til Breakfast without a snack or two. With all this largesse, the sylph like figure that I had acquired in the life raft sadly began to fill out.

Our four-day cruise was coming to an end and we could now hardly wait to go home. As we approached Genoa, Hazard asked if they could pump up the life raft. Of course we said "yes." They may not have won the race but they were making sure that everyone knew that they had been involved with a sea rescue. As we approached the Harbour we were invited by the Captain to go up to the Flying Bridge. He felt that we would be interested to see the scene from up there. Quite different arriving on the deck of a tiny sailing boat.

We docked with a bustling scene surrounding us. Refrigerated lorries were standing by with equipment to speedily transfer the precious cargo. The Agent climbed on board with the news that a mini refit was scheduled here in Genoa. While this would take some days he had an invitation from Fyffes that we might like to stay on board as their guests and explore

Genoa. No thank you, we wanted to go home; we had reached our limit of excitement. He took us to town where we bought aeroplane tickets for that night.

Returning we found a worried Captain who explained that he had received no word from the British Embassy. He was puzzled I'm sure on our behalf, that no-one had come to see us. Our arrival had been at the exact time he had given them and he could not understand it. This perfect gentleman had been so kind to us, probably saved our lives and fully expected our Embassy staff to check that we were OK, did not need their assistance and I would hope, thank him. We phoned the Embassy. Trevor could only speak to a very junior member of staff. He was very angry, not for us but for our hosts. The official listened to him as he explained the situation.

Very casually the bored civil servant, type voice at the other end said, "If you want to, I suppose you can come around and see us but it is Friday." We declined but it left a very bad taste in our mouths. Much worse than the taste of the five days without a tooth brush. We profusely thanked the Captain but it was not the same as an "official" thank you from the British representative of our country.

We were asked by the Agent what they should do with the life raft and dinghy. There was nothing we could suggest for the life raft, but we asked if anyone would like the dinghy for their children. The Captain suggested that it would be much appreciated by the crew. In Harbour they spent many hours fishing from the ship's stern, with a dinghy they could explore the little inlets and have much more pleasure.

There was nothing left to do except retrieve our flare pistol and cartridges from the Captain's safe, collect our few possessions, climb aboard a taxi and shouting our thanks and good-byes, DRIVE AWAY. We reached the Air Port and surprisingly were whisked away and before we realised it we were on board. First on in fact. We were shown to our seats, champagne put into our hands and I sunk back into my spacious chair and stretched my legs with surprising leg-room. I looked around as the other passengers settling in. How beautiful they all looked. Almost like film stars. I turned to Trevor to comment on all of this when the penny dropped. We were in Executive Class.

I had asked for the first available flight home and of course taking me at my word the Agent had probably bought the only tickets left. Executive ones. I looked at Trevor in horror and saw his shoes without laces and the oily jeans. Then I saw the funny side and shared it with him. What the hell we were going home. We held out our glasses for a refill of champagne.

PART TWO
CHAPTER NINE
"BOON"

Summer of 1986 and we were safely back home again. Quite a culture shock. Suddenly we had responsibilities, employment to find, links to forge with our family and to prove to everyone that we really hadn't changed at all. We did however, dine out on our experiences but everything is short lived. The reality of it all was that if we wanted to buy another boat we had to work hard. "Sea Mandala" only had third party insurance so there was no money to throw around; we had lost our clothes, all Trevor's tools and worst of all, the memories of a year in our lives. There had been a visitors' book on "Sea Mandala" where all our new friends had entered their thoughts and addresses. That was gone, so we had no means of re-establishing contacts. All our photographs had disappeared together with our logbook and diary. Enough of feeling sorry for ourselves, we were alive, fit and had a purpose in life - to buy another boat. Trevor felt that, although less expensive, building one would take far too long – and he should know!

We moved back into our cottage and I spent many hours identifying with our treasures once again, and Trevor being the more practical and determined, immediately found himself a job. I spent a few weeks putting my seal on the house and replenishing my wardrobe using the now popular Charity Shops. It is amazing how quickly one's values change. I frequently visited the Job Centre and studied the Situations Vacant notices. Of course we had to re-identify with the family once more, one can't run away for over a year and expect everything to be the same. We had a brand new granddaughter to discover and one son had a lovely new girlfriend to meet. Careers had moved on but generally everyone seemed to be at peace with life.

One day the phone rang and the magazine "Practical Boat Owner" asked if I could write an article on our experiences in the life raft. Whow, how did they know about that? Actually I never did ask them. That was a challenge, their only request was that I should end it with advice on what we should have done or taken in retrospect. This I did and was delighted to find that they made no alterations and it appeared at the end of the year. That provided a bonus for us as many of our friends saw or heard of us via it, so we began to receive letters from sailing acquaintances via this friendly magazine. The skipper of "Cat Morgan" even sent us a lovely picture of the boat, correctly assuming that we had lost all our negatives.

That was a five-minute wonder and I had to get back to the serious business of job hunting. I had one proviso; this time I wanted a job that finished at 5pm. No more taking work home or mentally solving my work problems in bed. I was seeking a nice, simple job. I brushed up on my typing skills and began to apply for all the typist and clerk positions that I could find. Nothing. It appeared that I was over qualified.

During this time we were making decisions on Boat Number Two. It would be fibreglass, bigger, and most definitely have a separate sleeping cabin and proper washroom. For some obscure historical reason, toilet and washing facilities on a boat are called the "heads". It was far too early to make any more decisions; we would just work at saving our cash.

Trevor suggested that I try for jobs more suitable for my experience and reluctantly I did. I applied for a Training Manager's position with a Government Youth Training Scheme. I had experience of this as part of my previous job and loved the work with the youngsters.

At interview, I was told that the position had already been filled internally, but there were two vacancies for Training Co-ordinators. One in the office section and another in retail. Yes, I was interested. The outcome was that the Office TC slot was filled and I couldn't be considered for the Retail one as they assumed that I had no retail experience. I was about to agree when commonsense prevailed. Who had been born over a grocer's shop, grew up with the philosophy that the customer was always right, stocked shelves, served customers and added up the takings? OK, it was a long time ago but do we forget? I may not know electronic tills and bar coding, but I could learn. I got the job.

There followed a good time for both Trevor and myself. He changed jobs several times, each time chasing more money. I just got deeper and deeper into mine, loving every minute of. I was lucky that the Head of this Scheme was a woman with vision who understood young people. Briefly, under Government guidelines we taught young people retail skills, placing them in shops and warehouses where they could do some "real" work experience. This was carefully monitored by the TC's and each TC was personally responsible for twenty-five trainees. We visited them at work, liaised with the shopkeepers, they had periods of day release and we taught them ourselves at the centre, preparing them for a qualification. Many of them had had problems at school and never dreamed of obtaining a qualification. Training them in a "college" type environment they seemed to revel in their less formal surroundings, called us by our first names and were quite enthusiastic about getting a certificate. Of course we listened to all their dreams and woes, and fairly quickly I was made Head of this Retail Section. So much for my dreams of no responsibility.

Finally Trevor changed jobs once more and began work on a tunnel being built under a road in Cornwall. This paid big bucks. He worked incredibly long hours, sometimes doing a 20-hour stretch and going back four hours later to do a normal day shift.

To visit my trainees I needed a car so we decided to run only one. Trevor started work at 7am. So we would leave the house at 6.15am and I would take him to work one side of Plymouth and then drive to my workplace on the other side. I usually arrived an hour early but that was no problem as there was plenty to do. Reversing the whole procedure when he was ready to come home. Quite often it was in the middle of the night.

I guess you are beginning to wonder if this is really a section about sailing and the sea!! Just hang on in there and all will become clear. After all if you want something badly enough you have to work for it. Everything we did at this time was to add to our growing Bank Balance.

The first winter, Trevor joined an Amateur Radio Club. He had often thought that if we had possessed a ham radio we would have made contact prior to our sinking. Anyway next time we would have an amateur radio on board. (Remember all this is prior to mobile phones and email.) First of all one of us had to get a license. Trevor drew that short straw. All this time Trevor was also studying the Yachting Magazines and we often visited the Yacht Brokers. We were checking on availability and boat prices. Just for fun some weekends we would look at boats. Eventually we felt that we could seriously start to make a few offers.

One evening Trevor saw a boat advertised in a Yachting Magazine. 34ft, fibre glass and designed by Van de Stadt. It still needed some fitting out below. Sounded a possibility and most important of all the price seemed right. A 'phone call was made and the boat was to be seen in Scotland. We were in the furthest corner of the South West of England and this was in Edinburgh in the North. A British Rail night passage, including an excellent British Rail Breakfast and we were soon looking at the boat minus mast and rigging, perched in the owner's back yard. A long examination by the possible new Skipper, then over a cup of tea, an offer was made. The offer was eventually accepted and the deal finalized, Scottish style, with a handshake and dram of whisky. We heard the sad tale. The owner was converting a farm house, fitting out the boat, holding down a demanding job, raising two small children, had a beautiful wife from Thailand and disaster struck when dry rot was discovered in the house. Something had to go. Their loss was definitely our gain. His only sorrow was that he had intended to name the boat after his little daughter. It was Marie followed by a very difficult sounding Clan name. Trevor and I looked at each other. We couldn't even say the name, let alone spell it and no one would understand it on the VHF anyway.

We compromised. We glanced at his beautiful Thai wife who was named Boon.

"We will keep it in your family. We will call the yacht 'BOON'."

By mid-day the same day we were back on the train, arriving in Plymouth in the early hours of the morning and ready for work. We now had to earn the money to fit her out and buy mast and rigging. We would have to truck her overland; in fact there were numerous things to arrange. None of these mattered; we had a boat once again.

Trevor made one more trip to Scotland to arrange the transport and the boat was delivered overland to Plymouth. We could not get it trucked directly to our village of Turnchapel, as the one road into the village was too narrow. So 'Boon' was put in the water on the Barbican and towed over the Cattewater (which was named after one of King Henry Eighth's six wives,) where she, 'Boon' and not Queen Catherine, was unceremoniously picked up by a crane and put down in the local Boat Yard. Then the pattern was as before. Remember Trevor was working all day and sometimes half the night and so any spare time was spent fitting her out; making the mast and ordering sails. The hull and deck had been professionally built and the previous owner had only started the fitting out. This gave us the opportunity of deciding exactly how we wanted it. Within reason of course, as one is limited by size and shape. One thing I knew and that was I wanted a reasonably sized galley. It seemed to me that boats were designed by men and little thought given to the actual layout below.

'Boon' was a sloop, that is she had one mast and boom. She had a mainsail and a sail at the front called a genoa. Again we would have the genoa roller furled. We would carry a cruising chute for light airs and storm sails for bad weather, but I didn't want anymore of those. One went below via the companionway ladder behind which was the Volvo engine. To the right (sta'board) was the navigation area and to the left (port) the galley. Both were of identical size. You see what I mean, a galley needed to house a cooker, sink, possibly a fridge and cupboards to hold cooking and eating utensils and of course some sort of work top. The navigation area only needed an opening chart table; seat and any instruments could be fixed around and above it. Charts usually went inside the table. From there were upholstered seats either side, which could double up as bunks, then a table, which folded down, on its long sides. There were lockers beneath and above the bunks. Moving on there was a door to the heads and then to the sleeping berth. The sleeping berth filled the whole of the bow, double size with again lockers underneath and shelves above. Opposite the heads was a hanging wardrobe with drawers. Outside once more and we had a large cockpit with cockpit lockers and a tiller for steering. Nice and simple. After much head scratching I asked Trevor to shorten the port side bunk and extend my galley. It was very successful.

By New Year 1990 we realized that the boat would be ready in the spring. We needed to have sea trials and then hopefully we would be ready, mentally and perhaps financially, to leave that summer. Long discussions followed. We both agreed that we were ready but could we financially fund it. We did not want to let the house again. It had been built in 1770 and because of its age needed a lot of maintenance, or as we liked to call it, lots of Tender Loving Care. We were not living in what experts called "a desirable area" and we doubted that the rent would be enough to fund our trip. Decision time again. We would sell the house and invest the money, leaving enough in the Bank to cover our first year. Then the annual interest should be sufficient to fund us. By now Trevor was coming up for 63 and felt ready for retirement and a state pension was only two years away.

Trevor passed his Amateur Radio Examination together with the Morse code test. He now became G0MKO on the airways. It was quite a relief not to be constantly hearing the dots and dashes as he practiced.

CHAPTER TEN
AT SEA ONCE MORE

Our village now sported a small marina and it was great to be able to step on and off the boat via the dock. Come the spring and we started sailing again. What a difference from dear 'Sea Mandala', this one was light and easy to handle, the sails went up like a dream and of course we did not have to make up the bed every night. We had kept it simple and as yet we did not have a fridge.

We decided to make June our departure month, but first of all we must have a shakedown cruise and as we had a week's holiday at Easter nothing could be better. We would revisit the Scilly Isles. The forecast was right, the boat looked good and we felt great, so off we went. We decided to sail along the coast with no overnight stops going straight to Penzance. No silly little distances for us, we were seasoned travellers!!

We went into the lock at Penzance and after a supper ashore slept well. The next evening as the lock gates opened, we left. We motored to the point and almost immediately a thick fog descended upon us; there was the call of the foghorn ashore. Night had fallen and we could see nothing but around us we could hear the answering foghorns from neighbouring boats. We joined in the symphony with our own horn. We had no choice but to go back, but it sounds easier than it was. Through the grey mist we eventually saw Penzance but of course the gate was closed. We anchored and slept fitfully till morning. When we awoke it was still foggy so we once more slid through the gates.

The following morning was bright and sunny and off we went, soon we were sailing and enjoying the trip. All was well with our world. Trevor needed to visit the heads, so with a quick look around he left me. Some five minutes later I heard a bellow -

"Shit!!!" was the anguished cry from below. I dived down to see what had happened. He had been pumping out the toilet when an end had sprung off a pipe and the contents had gone everywhere. "Shit" was the operative word. I returned laughing to the cockpit; after all I was on watch. Trevor grabbed a bucket of seawater and retired below.

It was a wonderful time exploring a few of these beautiful islands; the sailing was gentle and unhurried, the weather perfect. Sadly we had to return home and go back to work. We had learned one thing and that was that when living full-time on board, one needed much stronger equipment. The toilet that was installed in the boat at the time of purchase was only fine for weekends and day sailing. For full time use, we must buy a superior model. Subsequently, my Aunt/Godmother wanted to give us a present for the boat and you can guess what we chose. In was a king among toilets. I gave thanks to her every time I used it.

At this time we invested in a satellite navigation system, no more sextant sights for us. Of course we still carried a sextant, who better than us knew about things going wrong.

So it continued. Putting the house on the market, finishing the boat and winding down our jobs. In fact one weekend our sat.nav. system failed and was returned to a workshop for repair. One of our grandsons was born during this period and as we held him for the first time, we wondered how big he would be when next we saw him. We were going to miss Jo's first smile, first word and the first few steps. But we were about to once more take our own first few steps into this big ocean and had so much to think about.

The time flew, but the sat.nav. was not returned. After many anxious phone calls the impatient skipper said that he was waiting no longer, and before we really had time to have regrets, we were untying our lines from the dock. At that exact moment Wally our faithful electronic whiz came running down the dock, threw the repaired item at us and we pulled away. I guess we still owe him the money for the repair. Once more we were attempting to head nonstop for La Coruna in Spain.

This time the sail was good with no problems; maybe that is where the expression "plain sailing" comes from. We stood our watches, listened to forecasts, reinstalled the sat.nav. and wondered at its accuracy. Rounded Ushant with all its traffic and on night watch I was amazed and horrified at all the ships surrounding me. There seemed to be red, green and white lights, small ships and enormous things that looked like brightly lit hotels everywhere. This time we had radar and it was very confidence giving to be able to plot the exact course of these monsters in relationship to my tiny yacht. I began to ponder on a very strange thing. All the time we lived aboard 'Sea Mandala' I thought of her as a boat, but 'Boon' seemed to be in the category of a yacht.

At last we came to our destination, La Coruna. It was dawn and the sun was just rising. We could see the Yacht Club in the distance and ahead were mooring buoys; we were to pick up one of these. We could also see the small Marina but not for us, we had to stretch our hard-saved savings. Trevor slowed down and pointed out the buoy he wanted, one that was fairly close in with less distance to row ashore. Confidently I stood poised with boat hook in hand; there was not a soul in sight just sleeping yachts, how peaceful and how I longed to be asleep myself. Then it happened, the engine stopped, and immediately we were drifting into a group of moored boats. I do not know how but my arm seemed to grow like Pinocchio's nose and over the stern I managed to hook a passing buoy. We quickly attached ourselves to it and tried to look as if we had intended to use that buoy all the time. Unfortunately there was no one around to appreciate my feat of seamanship.

We soon sorted out the problem and had a glorious week exploring this grand town with its cloistered town square, delightful small shops, wonderful bakeries and of course the services of the Yacht Club. There was no charge for using the buoys or the showers. Those were certainly the days. We 'phoned home and this time everything had gone according to the plan.

Time came for us to leave and once again we were sailing along the rugged NW Spanish Coast, it was early afternoon and the wind began to rise, so we put a reef in the main. On we went, more wind, so in went a second reef and a roll in the genoa. The wind was behind us, we were going like a train and the yacht was performing beautifully. The wind became even stronger so we rolled in even more genoa. Nothing happened. We went up into the wind and tried again, but it would not budge. The exasperated skipper went forward to see what the problem was. The roller furling was jammed. We had always carried our cruising chute halyard (a rope used to pull up the chute) fixed to the pulpit (the rails at the front) and on this occasion it had caught in the roller furling and it was not going to budge. We were stuck with it. Of course friend Murphy came too and the wind got higher and higher. We were going like a rocket. 'Boon' was handling this very well but the crew was not so happy. The wind speed indicator was registering 50 knots. We hurriedly dropped the main and Trevor took a flying leap down below to check the chart.

He called, "Finnesterre is nearby and if we round the cape, we can get in the shelter of the land and sort it all out". That was fine by me. We rounded the corner and it was as if someone had flicked a switch and turned off the wind. We undid the sail, moved the offending article and pulled it in again. We decided that we would anchor at Finnesterre and continue in the morning. On cue the entire fishing fleet seemed to leave as we arrived, but there were a few yachts sheltering from the increased wind. As I ate my supper I realized that I had always thought that Finnesterre was a spot on the shipping forecast and not an actual tiny town. I still had a lot to learn. Actually as I am retyping this in the year 2002, it has just been announced that because of any confusion as there are several Finnesterres, a decision has been made to change the name to Fitzroy. I feel as if I'm losing an old friend.

The summer continued with a few stops along this coast. The weather was fine and the scenery majestic. We enjoyed tranquil harbours and local food. We did not make the same mistakes as last time. We arranged for mail to be sent to Gibraltar and with our faithful ham radio we had contact with the outside world. We could still listen and transmit using the regular UK Net both morning and evening and if there were any problems at home we could be contacted via this service.

We did however make two sentimental journeys - one to Vilamoura Marina and the other to the river Guadiana. Both were delightful and in the Marina we saw some of our old friends, caught up with their news and of course they wanted a firsthand report on our disaster. We even managed another evening at the cinema. We found the river Guadiana completely unchanged it was if we were in a time warp. People were still tending a few goats, transport was by donkey and reeds were gathered at the water edge, dried and made into baskets and mats. We stayed for a while and finding that we could not get water ashore we were told to fill our buckets from the river letting them stand and as any sediment sank we would have clean, sweet drinking water. This we did and it was very successful until one morning we saw a bloated dead sheep floating by! So much for drinkable water. It certainly was time to move on. This time we were going to sail straight to Gibraltar with no more sightseeing. We had decided that we would explore the Mediterranean, after all there were so many countries there and also we had discovered that it was not necessarily wise to listen to others. Our philosophy was to be "to find out for ourselves or suck it and see."

A few days later we found ourselves approaching the Gibraltar Straits but no way were we going to get there. Strong winds and big seas, all on the nose of course, held us back. So we detoured to a little Spanish town called Barbatti and had a delightful interlude there. We met many new people all waiting for the weather to improve, explored, ate the "meal of the day" at several local restaurants and experienced a local fiesta when the Virgin blessed the fishermen, their boats and the sea for another year. This was followed by a firework display the like of which I have never seen before. British Guy Fawkes Night eat your heart out – you ain't seen nothing like it.

Eventually we made Gibraltar. Here we found our mail, had our new credit cards stolen in the post office system and used in a nearby Spanish town, made phone calls and had a recap on the situation so far. We had to await new cards and as our radar had been misbehaving we had that checked. We stocked up with food and decided to buy an Electronic Position Indicating Radio Beacon (EPIRB). This piece of equipment was appearing on the market, suitable for cruising boats and if one was in distress it could be activated and ships and aeroplanes would pick up the signal and report one's position. For Yachtsmen this had proved most successful but there had been a few incidents, the funniest was when someone was travelling back to his boat with the magic machine in his luggage, he stayed overnight in a hotel and somehow the beacon became activated. Its signal registered and the local police screamed along in the middle of the night to ask him to turn it off. At least he knew that it worked.

While staying on this little rock it was fun to discover the cruisers that we had been speaking to on the regular ham net. With very few exceptions they never looked as we had expected them to.

Gibraltar was busy and bustling and for me, not the most attractive place, but our time there was short and soon with little wind we were motoring out of the Bay surrounded by dolphins. This certainly was the life and I think I should spell Life with a capital L. Perhaps even Sailing with a capital S. On this happy note the engine died. Investigation showed that we had something caught around our propeller. What now? At that time we did not carry diving gear and looking at the seas around this harbour, Trevor was not keen to dive. In fact there was so much garbage there that it was not surprising that this had happened. Up went the genoa to give us some steerage and it looked as if we would have to sail back, then the eagle-eyed skipper spotted a small boat with Royal Navy Divers on board. It looked like a training party. We sailed over, explained the situation and six eager young sailors, all under diving training, were ready to dive in. One was chosen, down he went and with his knife cut away metres and metres of industrial polythene. He held it up triumphantly. We offered them beer but they declined, so with many thanks we turned on the engine and motor sailed away. As I looked back I was horrified to see them unthinkingly throw the offending material back into the sea.

Perhaps this was a ploy to get some genuine diving practice. A pattern was now established, with so many little harbours we would sail for a day and stop somewhere, go on the next day or stay much longer if the place appealed. As we had been warned, this part of the Southern Spanish Coast is indeed very attractive to tourists, but on our own boat we were able to anchor in little Bays and choose which towns to visit. If we didn't like a place we just moved on. We of course met other boats and their crews, thus enabling us to have firsthand information on suitable anchorages, good places for swimming and the best places to shop or eat and towns worth visiting. On a boat one makes friends with remarkable speed, there are no barriers like garden fences, and anyway they may be moving on tomorrow. Of course if they are not pleasant you can move on too.

Our British ham radio net gave us an excellent weather forecast twice a day and therefore we usually had good warning of any bad weather. I think I would like to say an extra special thank you to Bill, Bruce, Ernie and Rudi who manned this frequency. It also became clear that this beautiful Mediterranean had the darker side. Strong winds could blow up out of a clear blue sky and could continue for several days. Also it was beginning to be clear that most boats went into Harbour or a Marina for the winter months. Most sailed until the middle of November and then started again about March, weather permitting of course. So Trevor and I began to watch places carefully hoping to find our watering, or should I say wintering hole for those months? It was sailing around the beautiful islands of the Balearics that we found Mahon on the island of Minorca. This seemed ideal. It was well sheltered, it seemed an interesting town and as historically Lord Nelson had kept his Navy there, we felt if it were OK for him it would do for us.

CHAPTER ELEVEN
A GIN FACTORY, THE LOCAL BROTHEL AND US

In fact it was a delightful winter interlude in this bustling town. We managed to find ourselves a spot tied along the town promenade. It would eventually become part of the marina but so far no electricity was connected and would not be officially opened until the next summer. However there was water and so we tied alongside and for a very nominal monthly fee we settled there. There was mixture of visiting yachts, fishing and local boats and on the opposite side of the road were trees, walkways, a shortcut to town, the gin factory and the local brothel. I often thought that I would get high on the fumes while they were actually producing the gin. Everyone was invited to regular afternoon tasting. Unfortunately for my skipper they did not offer free samples at the brothel!! I only know that whatever time of day it was, these young ladies looked gorgeous and they all seemed to have such long legs. I discovered that several of them had come from their villages, were engaged and working here to earn money to enable them to get sufficient funds to marry, all with their boyfriends' permission of course. As we sat in our cockpit in the balmy evenings we would see cars park outside and clients enter, with no concern as to their being seen, we even saw one very elderly gentlemen with two sticks being helped in. Good luck to him. Coming from a country where we had no legal form of prostitution, it was fascinating. I think back to my formative years when such women were called twopenny ha'penny tarts by my Grandmother. Later as a teenager, I remember visiting Soho and watching with horrified fascination as the ladies of the night stood on their street corners. Now here I was finding out that they were just women like myself and were great fun to meet.

All good things come to an end and we decided that we needed to fly home for a short while as there had been financial problems in the UK and the bottom had fallen out of the Stock Market, resulting in our losing a great deal of our small investments. We placed 'Boon' in a regular Marina where she would be safer and flew back to the UK. There was no question of our returning to the UK with the boat. This was our life, we liked it and felt sure that we could sort something out and continue.

Our four-week 'holiday' in the UK was great and seeing the family again was wonderful. The same couldn't be said for the visit to our Broker. We could not afford to leave our dwindling funds where they were, although he advised us that they would regain their value in time. We had all the time in the world, but not without an income and we did not want to think of re-entering the world of work. After much head scratching we decided to put what remained of the money in a "safe" investment and try to live on the interest and draw as little as we had to from the capital. After all Trevor would be 63 this year and at the end of 1993 he was entitled to a small pension. There was only one detail that the Skipper was adamant about and that was we continued paying our annual boat insurance.

Once more we were back on board 'Boon, had her lifted out of the water and did the general maintenance ourselves including the anti-fouling. We had only brought one present for her from England and that was a spare self-steering unit. Our faithful Fred was still performing like the star he was, but I had a strong feeling that we needed a second. I could not explain the rationale behind it, but fortunately Trevor had faith in my very occasional strange premonitions and did not question it.

The time arrived for us to start sailing again, in fact we had quite enjoyed our time as landlubbers but were both ready to begin travelling once more. I must admit that I still did not enjoy the sailing as Trevor did, but I certainly loved the "arriving". Every new country or town brought with it a sense of excitement and wonder. So much to see and do. Before we set off we had some serious hours of planning our finances. We had enough experience now to "guess" how much we would need each month or in fact each year, to live. We allocated this amount under headings and would try to live within these boundaries. We would buy the local products, only eat out on special occasions, continue anchoring instead of ever thinking of using marinas or yacht clubs and for a while no more trips home. In fact these decisions shaped our cruising for this year of 1991. We realised that it was definitely a must to take a break in the winter months, not only because of the weather but using a boat full-time there needed to be a maintenance period. We had seen for ourselves this winter that this was not a time to sail in the Med. We had been aware via contacts and through the radio, that there were certain Wintering places that had proved attractive and although most were marinas they had a very inexpensive winter rate. Our summer cruise would be visiting some of these and checking them for ourselves; what nicer way to spend our days than cruising to find them and check them out? We provisioned with the local products, filled up our water and fuel tanks, got out our charts, said our good-byes and awaited the weather. Our first stop was to be Tunisia. It looked as if we would be sailing in the Eastern Med as although the West sounded beautiful we no longer could afford Italy, S of France, Monte Carlo and these richer playgrounds.

CHAPTER TWELVE
TROUBLE AT SEA

At last a weather window arrived and off we went. I seem to recall that the seas were bumpy and rolly and that I felt decidedly queasy but I put this down to the fact that I had not sailed for several months. We reported into our Net daily and listening to the forecast heard that there was a "disturbance" in the area. At that stage all looked well so we continued; we reckoned that if we turned back we might meet this disturbance. Actually the disturbance found us. We were about a day from the Tunisian Coast when enormous winds and seas caught up with us. Running with just a tiny scrap of genoa was just like being on a roller coaster. We were certainly going to reach Tunisia in a hurry but unfortunately not the area we were aiming for. We wanted to look at Monastire where there was a huge Marina which had been recommended for next winter, but we were being headed to a coast where there was a harbour called Bizerte. The problem was that we did not have a detailed chart of this area. The seas were getting even bigger and behind us they looked like a huge green wall. Up to this stage Fred was coping. We tuned into the morning ham net and gave our position and explained our situation. The calm voice of the Controller asked, "Does anyone on the net have details of the harbour in Bizerte?"

Silence.

Then a voice replied, "Yes, I do. Wait a minute while I get the pilot book"

More silence.

"Yes, I have found it but it is in French. My wife is out shopping but she could come up on tonight's net and translate. I don't speak French."

The Controller asked if anyone else could help. No one could. He checked that we were OK and that we would not arrive until after the evening net, and that we would come up then. There was nothing left to do. It felt such an anti-climax. Nine hours to wait. So we just sat and continued riding these awful waves. By now the winds had reached 50 knots and were gusting to 65. From time to time Fred could not cope and we had to hand steer. By the end of the afternoon we were exhausted but we could see the outline of the land. Then another enormous wave washed over the stern and dumped about a ton of water into the cockpit. We were wet through and so was Fred. He turned up his toes and appeared to be dead. By then we were really exhausted and the thought of hand steering did not appeal at all. We continued steering, each taking half an hour. We were thrown about and ringing wet. Finally Trevor struggled below and fixed up Fred number two and we were in business again.

By now it was dark and it was Net time again. We tuned in and made contact. We waited for the French translation with some guidelines on the entrance. Nothing. The Controller called them again. Nothing. I could have cried. Then came wonderful words from someone who had just tuned in and was in Bizerte. In no time flat we had some lights and landmarks to watch for and better still, we were told to tune into our VHF when closer and they would talk us through the Harbour entrance. We thanked everyone.

As we got closer in shore, the seas were subsiding a little and even closer still we had some shelter. But the wind was still howling and the seas wild. We called on the VHF and a friendly voice told us where to look and we would see flashing torches. We strained our eyes and for sometime could see nothing but the lights of a big town. We were to look for the Harbour red and green lights. We saw them. No they were traffic lights. We went closer in and still could not see them. Suddenly I saw the red and green harbour lights and then the flashing torches. We followed the hand held torches and they led us into a Fishing Harbour and again via the VHF, we were directed to another yacht tied up against the harbour wall and we rafted alongside. Once inside there was little sea or wind, but there were smiling faces and cups of minestrone soup.

There must be something special about this particular soup in times of stress. Anyway it was great.

The next day we could see exactly where we were and also clearly the faces of our lovely neighbours. We were actually inside the fishing harbour and lucky for us this friendly boat had opted for this spot rather than the expensive Marina on the other side. It being a Saturday we would not be able to use a Bank, but our newfound friends lent us money to buy some fresh food. It is amazing how quickly one forgets the bad parts and looks forward to the sights, sounds and smells of a new town. In the company of one of our new neighbours we headed for town, carrying four days worth of garbage.

"Show me where to leave the rubbish," said Trevor.

"Leave it by the roadside," was the reply.

We were shocked; we hadn't carried it this far just to dump it. We glanced at each other hanging on to our smelly bags.

Our new friend laughed, "Trust me please, leave it and walk on and when I tell you, turn around". We did, and seconds later when we looked back the four bags had completely disappeared. This was my first experience of real poverty where our rubbish was someone else's treasure. I felt humbled.

We arrived at the town and were absolutely fascinated by the people, produce and most of all the smells. The shops all seemed to be open-fronted and the markets seemed to stretch as far as we could see. None of the goods were pre-packaged, fruits and vegetables were piled high on sacking, thick hard naan bread stood in uneven piles and aromatic spices were everywhere. We wondered around stopping to taste and buy. Everyone was speaking in a mixture of French or Arabic and I suddenly realized that all the people actually doing the buying were the men. I wondered did they go with instructions as to what to buy, or did they choose and their women had to cook whatever turned up? So much to ask but so far no means of finding the answers. Never mind this was only day one.

It was amazing how quickly the horrible sail of the days before faded into the background. We wanted to buy a bottle of soft drink but found that without a bottle to return we could not have one. No wonder our rubbish was so precious. I had dressed carefully before leaving the boat. I was in long cotton trousers and a light blouse with sleeves and the local women were in ankle length skirts or trousers, long sleeves and scarves around their faces. Some were fully veiled and a few covered from head to toe, but in the main there appeared to be a fairly relaxed atmosphere regarding women's dress. Our shopping completed we stopped to have a coffee, but each coffeehouse was closed. Later we realized that it was a religious festival.

We took our papers to the officials and somehow managed to answer all the questions with the help of my limited schoolgirl French and a French/English dictionary. We had nothing to pay but we had to leave our passports and return in a few hours. There is always a bad feeling when one gets parted from one's precious papers. Nevertheless Trevor collected them and they showed him, that together with the returned passports, they had also stamped a piece of paper slipped in each with our arrival date. We never understood the reasoning behind this, but ours not to question why, especially when it concerned officialdom.

We spent a week in this fascinating town, there was plenty to see and it was exciting to find new vegetables and fruits and in the tiny little shops, the women were delighted to tell me how to prepare and cook them – mainly by sign language. Trevor decided that he wanted an Arabic/English dictionary. As Arabic has a different alphabet we needed one that was phonetic. This was going to stretch our sign language. In Tunisia the bookshops are run by the Imam (the religious leader) and sell mainly Korans and religious books. We found such a shop and on the wall we found an enormous poster of Sadam Hussein. The Gulf War was over, but we were left in no doubt as to where their loyalties lay and whom they thought had won! We were treated with great disdain, I guess we were infidels and needless to say he had no dictionary for us. Apart from this incident, everyone was very friendly, and were as interested in us, as we were in them.

We spent hours exploring the town, countryside and wandering through the narrow lanes in the Souk. Through the open doors of tiny houses we had glimpses of the private lives of these people. The women hurriedly covered their faces and disappeared from view while tiny children filled the doorways and solemnly stared back at us. One day in the market place we found men selling bags of grain with "for the people of Tunisia, a free gift from the USA" stencilled on the side. Further along we saw them splitting open sacks full of clothes and laying them on tables. These too were being sold although the sacks clearly stated "a free gift from Oxfam for the people of Tunisia." My heart went out to these poor people and also folk like my mother, who on a small pension tithed part of her tiny income for causes such as these.

Our lovely neighbours left and we met a few other yachties but decided that we would continue along the coast to eventually check out Monisterre after all that was our original plan.

CHAPTER THIRTEEN
TROUBLE ON LAND

This sail was slow, but uneventful, and as dusk began to descend we arrived at our next port, Kelibiah. From our pilot book we knew we had to enter a small area manned by the Police. Once again there was a free dock to tie alongside and the police helped us with our lines. By now it was quite dark, but they insisted that they check our passports. There should be no problem. I begin to fix supper while Trevor stood under the dockside light with our papers. I was quite shocked when I heard one of the officials say in broken English

"When did she arrive on your vessel Sir?"

Who was she? I stuck my head out and everyone looked accusingly at me.

Evidently at Bizerte only Trevor's passport had been stamped with the official stamp showing the arrival date and mine was blank, although they both sported the piece of paper with the same information. The anxious Legal Skipper/Husband drew their attention to this, but they felt this meant nothing. There must be a stamp in my passport. The more senior Officer said ominously, "BIG PROBLEMS, BIG, BIG PROBLEMS." Then they suggested that we turn around and sail back from whence we had come and get my passport stamped. My skipper firmly refused to do this, he would rather deal with the big problem here, after all we had the piece of paper that said it all. Finally they took our passports away and told us to retire for the night. Trevor felt that it would all be sorted out tomorrow with a phone call. Not a bit like it, they were in the middle of

Ramadan and the big Chiefs would not be at work for another week. There was no answer to that. I think that Trevor had a good night's sleep but I lay awake worrying about the situation.

The next morning with daylight we had a look around, and we appeared to be in a compound with two docks, a fuel station, no other yachts but some local motor and fishing boats. There was a guard on the only gate that led to the unknown world outside. Was I a prisoner? We had breakfast and ventured to the guardhouse. Big smiles all round and yes, we could go out and see the town, go to the Bank and shop.

Trevor explained that we needed the passports to use our credit card. No problem, he could have his, but mine must stay in the safe. Remember I was still a Big Problem. They would telephone Bizerte today, which looked more hopeful.

Off we went and found a much smaller town, a curious but friendly people and again an enormous range of fresh produce to buy. Our purchases cost very little, at least this would be a country where we could stretch our money. Local schoolchildren practiced their newly learned English on us and were delighted to lead the way to the Market. I watched as very arrogant Tunisian men paraded the streets with falcons on their arms; they were heading for a particular building and I guess this was their meetinghouse. Sure enough through the glassless windows we could seem them lounging on reclining chairs with the falcons on their wrists or perches.

In the market some women were around the stalls but they played a very low-key role in this society.

With difficulty we cashed some money as only one Bank here dealt with Visa. We always carried some emergency dollars with us as we had discovered that the greenback was acceptable everywhere but we only changed these when it was absolutely vital. We shopped and sauntered back to the compound to find that there was no-one senior enough at Bizerte to confirm that I had actually sailed there on 'Boon'. But this was accompanied with big smiles and I begin to relax, after all I guess there was a British Consul around, but after our last experience that did not give me too much confidence.

There followed days of delightful sightseeing and exploring, discovering more about the history, culture and nature of these people. We saw a funeral and heard firsthand the wailing and beating of breasts, their approach to loss was quite different from our very reserved British ways. Ramadan is a period of fasting during the hours of daylight, no smoking, eating or drinking until sunset, but children, the very old and pregnant women are exempt. I believe there should be no sex during the whole of this period. It seemed to us that tempers became very short and although the women had an easier time with little or no meals to prepare in the daylight hours they were often expected to get up in the middle of the night to prepare food for their men folk to eat just before sunrise. One is supposed to use this time in contemplation and renewing one's faith. It finally ended with celebrations; feasting and new clothes for the children and with it came the good word that I was to go to Tunis, the capital city. There, a decision would be made regarding my missing stamp in the dreaded passport. We actually telephoned the British Consul and explained the situation and were told that there was nothing that they could do at this stage. They felt sure it would be sorted out, but no way should we expect it to be done in one day, but we were advised not to lose our tempers. Great.

At the crack of dawn we caught the local bus and there began the tortuous ride to the capital city. The bus was full to capacity with locals going home to their villages after the festivities of Ramadan. Most of the women and girls had hennaed hands, wore lots of jewellery and carried beautiful babies who gazed at us with solemn black eyes. Everyone was very friendly and we hoped that this continued in Tunis. The journey seemed to take forever and I swear that the bus had square wheels.

We arrived and it looked like most capital cities, big, dirty, lots of traffic and everyone searching for taxis. We eventually found one and arrived at a dilapidated but imposing building, surrounded by armed guards who looked anything but friendly. We managed to find someone who could speak a little English and with a mixture of French and English explained the position. I was told to go inside but as the problem was mine, Trevor must wait outside. Certainly not what we expected. Nervously I went up two flights of stairs and at a desk yet again explained the position. Fortunately an official could speak English. First question was what was the date I was supposed to have entered Bizerte. With a flash of inspiration that astounded me, I said that I would have to fetch my husband as he had the date in his passport. Up he came. The question answered, we took a seat but at least we were together. The room was full of men and we were given a numbered ticket rather like a queue in a supermarket deli. There we sat. Officials kept coming and going but no one in the line moved. The hours passed. I was asked again to explain the situation. Once more I was told - Big Problem. Finally one young man leapt into the air, tore his tickets to shreds and ran away. Then we were all told to go away and have lunch and return at 2pm. And so we did.

We found a restaurant and I was relieved to find a few women at the tables. There we had an excellent meal, I used an indescribably filthy toilet and then we wended our way back to the office. There we sat once more. The office was run by the civilian who spoke very good English and he did smile once in awhile, assuring us that it would not be long, although it was a Big Problem. By now another young man had burst into tears and had been led away. I began to lose my nerve. Trevor spoke to the official and he implied they were contacting Bizerte right now. Another delay and we became concerned, we knew that the last bus would leave at 6pm and no way did we want the expense of a hotel room. Again Trevor went to the desk, this time quite firmly and actually banging the table he told them we needed to know how much longer this would take, we had been here all day and had to catch the last bus. In fact he got quite emphatic about this. There was a stunned silence, a flourish of activity and suddenly a door opened and a smiling face appeared waving my passport, duly stamped and we were free to leave. It happened so unexpectedly quickly.

Outside we found that time was running out, so we managed to grab a taxi and during the journey to the Bus Station we were asked where our ultimate destination was. We told the driver, Kelibia. Ah Libya, he could drive us there. No Kelibia. His English was poor, our French not adequate and he was convinced that we wanted to go to Libya. His veiled eyes lit up with money signs. We finally persuaded him to take us to the local Bus Station. Golly, think of the problems we would have had in Mr Gadaffi's country. Just in time we caught the bus and began the long trip back, wondering what had suddenly brought the big problem to such an abrupt close. Whether it was Trevor's loss of patience that had done the trick. Right at the beginning when we arrived in Kelibia, should we have bribed the officials or was this just the Arab way of doing things? We would never know.

Nearing our destination, the young couple sitting in front of us on the bus turned around and the wife started speaking in English. They were both schoolteachers and she taught English and he Sports. There followed a brief but absorbing conversation, which resulted in their inviting us for lunch that weekend. You must realize that with this life style the opportunity to delve into other people's way of life is fascinating. We left the bus and found our way back to the boat, the officials were delighted that our Big Problem had been solved and I at last began to enjoy Tunisia. By now Trevor had had enough, there was no way he was even going to consider Tunisia as our winter hideaway. We would not be coming back here for the winter months.

We had our Tunisian lunch with our new friends and learned so much about the country and culture. Although our hostess was by the far the better educated and spoke perfect English, she was very subservient to her husband. She cleaned the house, cooked food and coped with the laundry (no washing machine). She dealt with their fourteen month old son passing him to her mother-in-law while she worked fulltime at the Secondary School. Her husband had no lessons to prepare being a Sports teacher but did enjoy his spare time with his male companions. Eating cross-legged on the floor, we enjoyed lamb, vegetables and couscous, followed by juicy dates and figs. The drink was a thin sour yoghurt and I just couldn't get it down and during a diversion I swapped my full glass with Trevor's empty one. Thankfully he enjoyed it. During the course of the afternoon our hostess's mother-in-law arrived; she was a very formidable lady with brightly hennaed hair and personality to match. She asked us a million questions, translated by her daughter in law, and she wondered if my unmarried daughter would be suitable for one of her sons. After a while our hostess smiling shyly, told us that our visit was being invaluable to her, as her mother in law knew that she taught English, but she was now watching her actually speaking this strange language, doing the translations and linguistically jumping from one to the other. Mother-in-law was most impressed.

Two days later we returned the compliment and entertained them in our little home that they found fascinating. As we said our good-byes we promised that we would send English newspapers and magazines to help with the English classes. This we did.

Our Tunisian adventure was nearly over. On our last morning Trevor was busy filtering some fuel so I went to the office to get our papers stamped for departure. Not a sensible decision as two horrified policemen looked at me then at our passports. They looked at each other and finally asked me to leave them on the desk and where they would be dealt with soon. Back on the boat we quickly realized that they did not expect to perform such tasks with a mere woman. This was the responsibility of men. Trevor quickly changed into suitable clothes and went to the office and in minutes was back with the stamped passports. Needless to say I scrutinized mine to make sure that it had the correct stamp. Sometime later we heard of a young woman sailing single-handed, who had arrived at this port and the officials could not comprehend the situation and in the end a fellow yachtsman had to go to the office with her to enable her to get her paperwork cleared.

CHAPTER FOURTEEN
A COOK'S TOUR

We had studied our charts and decided to set sail for Malta to check out wintering facilities there. At least they spoke English. The sail to Malta was a delight and we arrived early one morning anchoring in a creek. There we dealt with the formalities and found ourselves a place to stay. There was nowhere to stay anchored around this little island but the Marina fees were reasonable. We checked our budget and decided to stay two weeks.

Once again we followed the pattern of exploring, visiting museums, trying out local foods and meeting the people. Trevor reckons that in all of his travels he has never tasted such good bread as in Malta. Very hard and crusty on the outside and moist inside. In fact this set a pattern and for Trevor, the quality of a country was governed by the taste and texture of its bread. During this time of course, we were constantly meeting fellow cruisers, old and new, and some of these friendships continue to this day.

Trevor is always fascinated by military history and we both learned a great deal about the role that Malta played in the Second World War. I never realized that the population had nearly starved, as it was so difficult to get supplies to this little island, the Germans being close by in nearby Sicily. Also the island of Malta had been awarded the George Cross, this is normally given to a person and not a whole country.

The island was mainly Roman Catholic and although there was a tremendous amount of poverty the Churches were most ornate and many gold statutes were in evidence. Children were constantly seen begging, carrying a piece of paper saying "yesterday we were eight, today there are nine of us". When I saw the wealth of the churches it sickened me and added to my already shrinking beliefs.

We had a tremendous surprise when we saw a boat that we recognized from our village of Turnchapel. Surely not? Upon investigation we found the owners, and yes Phillip and Arabella were here, running a sailing school. We had a great reunion. In fact during this first full year of sailing "Boon", we had seen two boats from our village and as there had been only 80 houses there at the time we left, this was a tremendous coincidence.

Too soon the two weeks were up and we decided to put Malta on a list of "winter possibles". Cyprus was next on our list and we were definitely getting through the Eastern Med. in record time. We stopped on the way to explore the Greek Island of Crete and loved this picturesque beauty spot. It had the most brilliant blue sea and the sun shone but Greek is a very difficult language. We managed however to get our tongues around a few basic words. Once again we were moored along a Harbour Wall together with a group of yachties. This was fun and we spent many delightful days and evenings in their company. One couple was working and living in Crete; another making their way to Mainland Greece and the last were travelling on board their boat and had decided to get married. Instead of flying home for the great day, they had invited close family members to join them in Crete for the occasion. By now we were waiting for a weather window to go to Greece en route to Cyprus.

Which would come first, the wedding or the window? Unfortunately it was the weather window, but in this windy area we had to leave or we could have got stuck for weeks. We were becoming seasoned sailors and had to have different priorities. Sadly we left.

Sailing was becoming fun, I was becoming more relaxed and the weather reports via the Net were invaluable. Not only the forecasts, but also the information from others who were actually out there experiencing it first hand. After a couple of stops in Greece we set off for Cyprus. This was really turning out to be a Cook's Tour. We arrived at this little divided island in late September and made for Larnaca Marina in Greek Cyprus. The marina was very large, with a travel lift and room for many boats to stay in the water or stand on the hard. We liked what we saw and more to the point we liked the price. There was a fantastic rate for the whole winter.

Being the sailing season there were not too many cruisers there at this time, just the local boats. The majority of yachties would be returning over the next month having cruised Turkey and the Greek Islands. We found the town pleasant and goods readily available. Sadly this island was divided and policed by a force of United Nations personnel. For a long time the Greeks and Turks had shared this idyllic island but now they were at cross-purposes and separated by a "green line". As visitors we could visit the Turkish side but only during the daytime. However this island seemed to be ideal for our winter maintenance and sailing break.

Now there was a quandary, we did not want to settle down for the winter just yet and felt that we had

104

a couple of month's good sailing in front of us. Where should we go? We had planned to cruise Turkey and Greece the following year so did not want to pre-empt that experience. Finally we decided that we could visit Israel. Out came the charts and notes, we tried to obtain more information from other cruisers, but found that very few had visited there. Because of the constant security situation in Israel we knew that we could not anchor but would have to report to, and stay in a Marina. We counted our money and made the decision that as we had such a good winter rate here in Cyprus, we could afford one month. We decided to make for Tel Aviv Marina after all they could only turn us away if full. The security problem was brought home to us when we were told that a few years previosly, an Israeli crew had been shot by Palestinians when they arrived on their boat in Larnaca Marina. The Cypriots were so shocked at this that they had placed a plaque in their memory, but had eventually removed it as it caused threats by the Fundamentalists who had been responsible. Nevertheless, Trevor being a Jew had a tremendous urge to visit Israel. He had been reared as an Orthodox Jew but now, no longer religious he felt the desire to explore his Jewish roots. We made our winter booking for Cyprus in advance, signed out of the island and set sail for Israel.

Once again we managed to get it right and had a pleasant sail. Tel Aviv was our destination and there was very little shipping en route. As usual we kept VHF 16 on and could hear traffic in the night and were surprised by the power of the Tel Aviv transmitter. Their call for ships fifty miles away could

105

be heard clearly. They began telling any ships thirty miles from the coast to please report in. We realized that we were in that category but our VHF would not transmit that far. However we did report in. No response. Ten miles further in we tried again. This time we heard a nearby ship relay our message for us. Finally we were able to make the contact ourselves. They fired a huge number of questions at us. Name of boat, size, last port of call, destination, how many were on board, nationality, our names, Trevor's mother's maiden name and so it continued. And then the wonderful words "Welcome to Israel".

We sailed on and by about four o'clock in the morning we were now wide-awake and could see the lights of the land in the far distance. There was no moon and we were surrounding by an intense blackness when suddenly a searchlight was beamed on us and we were momentarily blinded. A silent unlit boat had crept up on us and a voice boomed from the radio asking us show ourselves and then the boat circled us. It was Israel's Navy. The anonymous voice was checking the boat's name, the number on board and port of registration checking out all the answers we had given earlier. After a while the searchlight was doused and we were asked for our destination. Again we said that it was Tel Aviv Marina. Did they expect us? No. We were told to continue and they would inform them of our arrival. And then once again the welcoming words of "Welcome to Israel." We now appreciated that this little country took its security very seriously and it was for our safety as well as its own.

In the early morning we were bobbing around outside the Marina and we looked with horror at the surfing seas in front of us. The Marina was set in a long sandy beach, stretching as far as one could see on both sides. All the way along the beach were early morning surfers riding the waves. From our chart we could see that the Marina Entrance was not dead ahead but by a very sharp turn to starboard. With sails down and the engine on we took a deep breath and made the entrance, surfing ourselves as we went in, only to find that we had to make a sharp turn to port once inside. This move rapidly positioned us to come alongside the dock. Whow! We made it. Our lines were taken by very casually dressed young men, all sporting large guns. Very politely they repeated the same questions and came aboard to check us out. Then with big smiles, it was handshakes all round and guess what? "Welcome to Israel."

They found us a berth in the Marina, then we were shown around the facilities and quoted our price for the month including water and electricity. This time we did not have a stamp in our passport. The authorities realized that if we did, it would cause us Big Problems if we went to a neighbouring Arab country. We certainly knew about these Big Problems! The Israelis are realistic.

That afternoon we went ashore. Once outside the Marina we were in the centre of a thriving, noisy City. We just walked and walked and our eyes grew larger as they took in the colour, fashion and pace of this very modern city. We found the Tourist Office and were given a mountain of pamphlets and a map of Tel Aviv and from there we found a street café to catch our breath and read. There seemed so much to do and see but we noticed that prices everywhere were very high. Any conducted tours seemed to cost a fortune and when we paid for our two simple coffees we were in shock and even wondered if we could ever afford to eat again. Back on the boat we took time out to review the situation and plan our campaign. We would arrange our own tours and use public transport, we would shop at the markets in Jaffa which was a sea front walk from Tel Aviv. Oh how I wished that I had brought more provisions from Cyprus – never mind, next time.

A routine was established and we spent our days and nights discovering Israel. Friends were made in the Marina and we were given a lot of advice on where to shop and what to see. We borrowed books from the nearby British Council, they had the most fantastic library and also information on tours, concerts, films and exhibitions. From there and a local newspaper we discovered that some events were free and it was all systems go.

We filled our days and nights with the most wonderful variety of experiences. Some were sobering. I clearly remember the day that we were sitting at an outdoor café, sipping our soda water (the cheapest beverage on the menu). There was a string quartet playing nearby and artisans were selling the most beautiful craft objects from stalls under the trees. At the next table were three gregarious old ladies, all trying to speak at once. Their hands were frantic as they needed to emphasize a point, scarlet nails shining and large rings flashing and catching the sunlight. Then suddenly one leant forward to noisily contribute her opinion and her sleeve fell back, revealing a number tattooed on her arm. Her concentration camp number. I was stunned and when I looked at Trevor there were tears in his eyes, after all he had lost family members in the Holocaust. I sat silent, and saw beyond the old, lined face. When this had happened she had probably been a very young women or a teenager, before the word was even invented. She had survived, but at what cost to her youth?

Our month passed far too quickly, but we were determined to return in April at the start of our summer cruising. Sadly we left this vibrant country promising the friends that we had made that we would return.

CHAPTER FIFTEEN
ISRAEL AGAIN

The trip back to Cyprus was gentle and very quickly we seemed to be enveloped in a routine of maintenance and social activities. Once again the marina was in the centre of town and everything was in easy walking distance. We lived simply, buying fresh vegetables from the market, discovering local recipes and enjoying a very pleasant climate. The cruisers themselves arranged plenty of activities helped by the availability of a recreation room provided by the Marina. The beauty of it was that you could participate or not, however the fancy took you. There one could start the day with exercise and aerobics or just turn over in bed and listen for the energetic to return. There were bridge games, art sessions, classes for ham radio exams and French and German lessons. You name it and they seemed to provide it. All these were organized and run by the cruisers themselves. Upon reflection, one realized that there was a great deal of talent among this cruising community. It did not matter if you were rich or poor, if you had been a Doctor or plumber, you were a cruiser. You had been out there on the high seas, sometimes a very high sea and you had been scared. The sea is a great leveller.

Every Sunday we had a book exchange and Book Swap Bob had a starter of three hundred books. As bookworms this was a wonder to Trevor and myself. While we had been sailing we had constantly been looking for other English speaking, or rather reading cruisers, with books to swap. And here they were laid out in front of us. What largesse. Over cocktails and barbecues we discovered more about the Greek Islands and Turkey. We studied charts and pilot books and planned our summer cruising. But first of all we decided that we would start our sailing season by spending April in Israel. We never had any doubt that this was the life for us. We lived very simply and often had to forgo social events, eating out and organized tours but this in no way spoilt our enjoyment of the whole life style.

Spring arrived and once more we were in Tel Aviv. It felt like coming home and soon we were swept along with the bustle and pace of the country. As a race the people are on the whole, brash, outspoken and argumentative. They are extremely intelligent and love music and art. One of our joys was to walk along the promenade by the sea in the evenings. This stretched through the City to Jaffa and in the balmy evenings we could listen to the street musicians who performed with such skill under the stars. An interesting feature was that along this stretch on the walkways and on the sands were thousands and thousands of white plastic chairs. They were there for all to use. People sat on them, snoozed on them and often used a second chair for their feet. Babies were changed, fed or cuddled on them. Lovers shared them. Children used them for their games and there always seemed to be just enough.

Very late one evening we returned to the Marina and looking out to sea could hear the water lapping on the sands and at its edge saw two solitary chairs facing the darkness beyond. They were occupied by a middle-aged couple, holding hands, both were intent on gazing into the unknown. The water came nearer and nearer but they were lost in their dreams. During the night all the chairs were neatly piled up and the whole length of the beach cleaned ready for the dreams of tomorrow.

This time we visited a Kibbutz and spent a fascinating day among the people there, learning a little about the philosophy of this life style. Next time we would spend longer in a Kibbutz. During this visit many Russian Jews were arriving to live in Israel and one of our local friends was part of the welcoming committee. Everything was being done to help them make the transition from their world to this. Quite a culture shock I am sure.

We experienced the day when all Jews remembered those who lost their lives in wars and the Holocaust. There was to be a few minutes silence during the course of the morning. This is something that I can relate to as we have Remembrance Sunday in the UK for all those lost in our wars. We were actually walking along Disengorf when everything stopped. I mean everything. Every vehicle, every person, shops emptied, drivers left their cars, workmen stopped working and every single person stood, head bowed and there was so much silence that it actually hurt my ears. When it was over everyone quietly continued, but no one spoke. No way is my country's Remembrance Day like this. It was very moving.

On our last night we decided to visit a Folk Club. This was a first visit for us and checking our well thumbed map, we set off. Halfway there we were halted, as an unattended bag had been reported. The bomb disposal unit arrived and we all stood back as a controlled explosion took place. This time it was not a bomb, just a misplaced backpack. A sheepish student appeared; he had left it while he kicked a ball with his friends. It brought home to us that we were in a country where the enemy is often very close by.

Our folk evening was a wonderful finale. Plenty of music and poetry. Old songs and new. Many from around the world. Again a great deal of talent. We were made very welcome and were quite a novelty having sailed there from England. With promises that we would return in November hand in hand we walked the streets of Tel Aviv and found our boat.

CHAPTER SIXTEEN
HISTORY, WHICHEVER WAY WE TURNED

Turkey and the Greek Islands. What can I say? Idyllic sailing, magnificent scenery and a very friendly people. Turkey stole our hearts and we spent a wonderful summer season sailing in and out of tranquil anchorages and small harbours. The history and culture actually came down to greet us. One could anchor beneath rock tombs set in the cliffs and swim down to underwater cities. There were tiny shops, which only closed when the last customer finally left. Little glasses of chi (tea) always appeared whenever we stopped to make our purchases. Each village and town had its own market and once every week a visiting gypsy type market set up its stalls, an enormous affair. Shopping there was a delight; one had to taste a sample of everything before being allowed to buy. In fact we never needed any lunch on these mornings. Little stools were pulled up and different teas were tasted. Apple chi seemed to get the vote for the most refreshing.

In the area where we were cruising there was only one Marina, these being very few and far between in Turkey at that time, and I heard all the wonderful tales of how beautiful it was, with marble floors and Turkish carpets in the entrance to the shower block. I also heard how extremely expensive it was. This was very strange as our living costs in this lovely country were so low. We later discovered that the design for the Marina had been taken from Italy, and unfortunately they copied their fees as well!!

As my birthday approached, Trevor asked what I would like. I thought and made the decision; one night in this Marina. So it was to be. Early in the morning we motored in, early as I was determined to get my full money's worth. We tied up and as Trevor signed in I made a dive for the Showers. I was going to have at least three. There they were in all their resplendent glory just as I had been told. Marble floors and vanity units, fresh flowers everywhere, Turkish carpets and bowls of coloured cotton wool balls and so clean. As soon as one vacated a loo or shower a cleaner would dive in and wipe everything down.

During our second hour there the wind began to blow and by mid-day we were in the middle of a full-blown storm. It blew and blew and even blew some more. This went on for several days and there was no way that we were going to leave, go outside and anchor in this. So I had a wonderful birthday and as we seemed to be spending so much money we decided to be utterly decadent and visit the Turkish Baths. I will not spoil it for you but you must go and experience yourself. You will feel wonderful and your skin so soft and glowing, but don't be shocked when you see all the grey dead skin that falls away, the end result is certainly worth it.

So our wonderful time in Turkey sailing along this gorgeous coast, enjoying the tranquillity of peaceful anchorages, staying near vibrant towns and exploring all the history that we were offered was everything and more than we had expected. All the sites and museums were free and entertainment was levelled at a price that the man in the street could afford. We had planned to flit between the Turkish coasts and the Greek islands but found that Turkish officialdom ruled that one must sign out and in again every time one did this. Not a problem except that on the Turkish side it cost every time, so apart from visiting a couple of Greek Islands we had a Turkish season. The summer and autumn seemed to fly. Finally time came to decide on our winter arrangements. We really longed to spend this winter in Israel and checked the Marina fees for the whole of the winter. Sadly it was not to be, we couldn't afford that price. We looked at our bank balance and decided that a winter in Israel was not to be and so we signed out of this dramatic country to return to Cyprus, but we had already planned our summer cruise for next year it was to be a trip to the Black Sea and Istanbul.

Our winter in Cyprus was good and we decided to put the boat on the hard for this period. The reason being that (a) Trevor felt that it would be beneficial for the boat to dry out and (b) he wanted to do some extensive maintenance. During this time we talked about crossing the Atlantic in another year but I felt that this was currently beyond my grasp. I was definitely enjoying my sailing more and the lifestyle was wonderful, but I was daunted by a non-stop journey of over 3,000 miles. Trevor was quite happy to leave that decision to me; no way was he going to put on any pressure. After all we were both here to enjoy ourselves and we were definitely doing that.

There was a gliding club on our side of the island, which was run by NATO, this was opened at a very nominal fee to anyone joining them. Trevor signed up, not only did he learn to glide but became part of the safety team who helped get the gliders into the sky, put them to bed and generally did all the chores.

116

There was a lovely atmosphere at the Club and when I joined him I was giving the job of logging all flights, helping with the teas and generally being useful. I had no desire to learn to glide. There was a friendly bar, not opened until all the gliders were safely put away and flying finished for the day and I was quite prepared to enjoy that part of the game.

Trevor's eldest son, Max and grandson Jet, flew out to join us and for a short while we were able to share our lifestyle with them. We went day sailing and toured Cyprus and in fact played tourists for two weeks. Max took a trip in a glider and he and Jet did a tour around the island on a rented motorbike. Seven year-old Jet loved living on the boat and made himself a den in our sleeping cabin. He never seemed bored and while with us made a tremendous breakthrough with his reading skills. In fact he and I wrote a book together called, "Turbo Thompson, the Marina Cat." It was on the last evening that he made another momentous discovery. He suddenly noticed that we did not have a television set! He, the TV freak at home, had never even noticed. Another year later son Max bought his own little boat. Oh dear, what had we been responsible for?

CHAPTER SEVENTEEN
ISTANBUL

We were to leave Cyprus early to get well on our way to Istanbul before the summer winds began to blow. These usually didn't begin until May and blew from the direction that we would be sailing. We didn't relish a long sail with wind on the nose. So we started early and unfortunately so did the winds. In fact that year we were the first boat to venture out of the Marina and we had a fantastic send off.

We had our course planned; our lockers were well stocked with the easily obtainable goodies from Cyprus and the rest was up to 'Boon' and us. Our plan was to spend quite some time in Istanbul so our sail would be fairly speedy. Stopping at night and only visiting the more interesting places en route but we seemed to meet extremely windy weather all the way and were regularly held up in anchorages or harbours waiting for this evil weather to pass. Actually this meant that we stopped and explored far more places than we intended. This way we experienced camel racing, hot spring baths, explored ancient sites, bought local produce and got bitten by quite a few mosquitoes. We did find that other cruisers were constantly having tummy upsets or the Turkish Trots and this never seemed to happen to us. We finally worked out that we so seldom ate out but cooked our own food and that probably was the answer. As we travelled out of the traditional tourist areas the local produce became more and more inexpensive and although we did not eat out, we certainly had a range of delicious dishes.

Knowing that we would be travelling through areas where no English would be spoken, we had decided to build on our limited Turkish. I made flash cards and every day we would put some new words together with phrases on the walls, testing each other as we sailed along. These would be changed daily and every Sunday we would check each other's new week's vocabulary.

One day we had to again seek shelter and seeing a little harbour wall decided to anchor behind it. The local fishermen saw us and indicated that we should enter and tie up by their boats. This we did and instantly became somewhat of an attraction. Remember we were seriously off the tourist track. We had a constant stream of visitors, all men of course. This certainly stretched our Turkish. By now I had the local chi and tea glasses. I was going to do this entertaining in Turkish style. Very quickly they indicated that they would prefer a beer, so much for the Moslem nondrinking rules. At last the final one departed and I felt drained, trying to talk and understand, even with the dictionary, had been quite a strain for both of us. All this time one solitary man and his son had been mending their nets nearby and as I began to enjoy our solitude, he came over and introduced himself. Trevor invited him on board and our guest sent his son off with some rapid instructions. Out came the last beer and away we went again. As it became obvious that he spoke no English I was able to say to Trevor that I had had enough. I was fully 'turked-out' and wanted my boat to myself. So after a decent interval Trevor held out his hand and implied that it was goodbye time, but the man kept glancing anxiously along the road to where his son had disappeared. More conversation and by now I was really fed up. Then his boy galloped along the track clutching a parcel. With a big grin it was handed to father who graciously gave me a bowl of home produced honey and a freshly baked loaf of bread. WITH an invitation to go with him as he and his wife would like us to join them for Supper. How petty and small I felt. There followed the most wonderful evening, they spoke no English but we were surprised at how much Turkish we had managed to learn. The little English/Turkish dictionary was rapidly passed from hand to hand and we even managed a couple of jokes between us. They had a small plot of land and a cow and some hens. They grew most of the things that they needed but the thing that made them different was that they had saved and borrowed to buy a tractor. This they used and rented to the other farmers thus enabling them to expand and eventually build an extension to their small house. When we visited, the house was now on two levels. On the ground floor where they lived, it was a very conventional Turkish house with a basic kitchen and hole in the floor toilet but above, a very western house with all mod cons including a bathroom with shower and flushing toilet. Who this was for I never quite worked out.

They had married when she was fifteen and had two children very quickly. We managed to ask them who was the one with ideas and the decision maker. She explained that to the outside world he made the decisions but not before they had discussed and agreed everything together.

We continued wending our way towards Istanbul and the strong winds came too. We tacked up the Dardanelle's weaving our way amongst the huge ships there. At last we were in the Sea of Marmarus and at last the strong winds died but a fog arrived. So near and yet so far. We found a little harbour and tied to the wall with stern anchor out and went ashore to explore his interesting looking town. We found that it was where marble was quarried. We watched fascinated as huge chunks of wonderfully patterned marble were lowered into flat bottomed boats to be transported to who knows where. As we watched there was a sudden exodus of all the local boats from the harbour. Before our very eyes they all began to frantically leave almost like Dunkirk. As we rushed back we saw a huge barge pulling dredging equipment entering the harbour. We soon found out that the harbour was to be dredged. It could take a week. No-one had been warned it just happened. We jumped aboard and were the last boat to leave the harbour. Whew. Once outside we soon found a little cove to anchor.

The next morning we decided to leave and head for our final destination. Off we went and within half an hour were surrounded by a thick dense fog. With radar we continued, listening to the whistles around us as the fishermen warned us of their proximity then the solemn sound of the big foghorns. It is very eerie to move in fog, noise seems to be deadened and vessels seem to silently appear from out of nowhere. We were making for a small fishing village about twenty miles from Istanbul and by lunchtime we arrived. At least we thought we had arrived; we could see a harbour entrance on the radar and we crept in. Through the swirling mist we could just make out the row of fishing boats and gently squeezed into a space, dropping our stern anchor as we entered. No doubt they would tell us if we were in the wrong place. All was well; we negotiated a price with the fisherman who seemed to be in charge, linked up to electricity and felt good. We could now relax and tomorrow we would visit Istanbul and play at being tourists.

There followed a wonderful month. We would catch a train to the big city and that was an experience in itself. It costs us literally pennies and we would be entertained between stops by a variety of salesmen. One would board, give a demonstration of his wares, plastic pegs, a needle threading device or whatever, make some sales and jump off at each stop diving into the next compartment and start all over again. From time to time a particularly zealous Moslem would produce his prayer mat and call to Allah and quite often fellow travellers would try to find out who we were and where we had come from. Young boys made the hazardous trip by hanging outside the carriages.   The journey always flew.

We visited all the sights and I particularly fell in love with the Topkapi Palace. This was in perfect condition and one would have no problem actually reliving life there. Everything was intact just as it had been left. We explored the Harem where the tiles and friezes were as bright as if new. We were told how the King's mother would choose which wife her son would sleep with but we also saw the little spy holes where he could watch the women pass. In fact his slippers were designed in such a way that as he walked through the passages and halls, their distinctive sound announced his arrival and all the women disappeared, so he needed his little spy holes. He also had a hidden view of the tiny pool which would be filled with milk and the girls would bath in this creamy liquid.

The Blue Mosque was incredible and one wondered how it had been built with the limited equipment of the time. I will not spoil your visit there, as I hope you will put it high on your itinerary. There was so much to see and do, and again everything was deliberately low priced so that even the poorest of people could visit and appreciate these wonders.

I must however mention the 'Pera Palace' Hotel. This hotel was built to accommodate the passengers from the Orient Express. When the Express first made its journeys it was decided that they needed to build a suitable hotel in Istanbul for these visitors. The 'Pera Palace' Hotel is still there and has not changed at all. Everything is as originally designed, built and furnished. There is a beautiful, delicate birdcage lift, pure silken lamp shades, very heavy furniture, lots of brass and when Trevor and I stopped there and had a cup of tea, we sat at little round tables, in old fashioned arm chairs and behind Trevor's head were some bell pulls. One was marked waiter, one footman and the last one, groom. We visited Agatha Christie's bedroom where she wrote her thriller called, of course, 'Murder on the Orient Express'.

Life, for us, was very easy here. We could eat out extremely cheaply, find so much to do and thoroughly enjoyed this part of Turkey. There were a few other yachts around but mainly we were with the Turkish people so our vocabulary grew daily. Not everything was good. I did not like the performing bears and would certainly not recommend a visit to a zoo, and if you could find them, any toilets were terrible. I also did not like the salesman's ploy of having a very young animal tied to the entrance of his shop. Puppy, kitten, rabbit, what you will; with huge eyes all very attention catching. Then as they grew they would disappear and another baby would appear. I never dared ask where they went. Actually throughout all our travels, animals were treated very casually and usually cruelly. You will find that many cruisers have a cat or dog on board with a horror history. I think that the worst was the kitten that was rescued just before he was cut up (alive) to become fishing bait. He is now a large fat Tom living the life of luxury on board his boat, and very much HIS boat.

Children however, were wanted and much loved. Most seemed to regularly attend school and parents were very interested in their progress. Once home again they helped their parents in any family business. It was a form of apprenticeship and the small boys and girls helping in shops or restaurants seemed incredibly proud of their roles. They all seemed to have time to play but toys were always in short supply. I'm sure that there were many sights that we did not see. We heard of young girls, often as young as eight, who worked incredibly long hours weaving the fine silk carpets. Their little fingers were needed to work with the very fine threads. Although school had become compulsory in the country such things were not seen or checked as in the town. My son-in-law will not visit Turkey as he feels that their human rights record is so bad. I do not know. Wherever we travel in the third world life is cheap. I'm sure that prisoners are treated badly, there is tremendous violence to woman and drugs abound. In many, particularly Moslem countries, women are rated as second-class citizens but if we don't visit and let them see another way of life how can it change? Over the sailing years I've seen many cruisers pay for a youngster to go to school, have medical treatment and many of us regularly give blood at local hospitals. Of course our money helps their economy.

We met other cruisers and shared experiences. Some were continuing to the Black Sea and Russia. They had done their research and found out what was most needed. They seemed to be taking mainly canvas shoes, clothes, aspirins and packets of plasters. Before we had a chance to consider such grandiose ideas we had a slight disaster. I remember that it was a Sunday and we were still tied to the harbour wall when Trevor decided to check the rig. We'd had a very hard sail, sailing hard on the wind and eventually tacking through the Dardanelle's and the forestay seemed slack. I winched him up the mast and once at the top he shouted for me to bring him down, but very slowly. This was done. He quickly explained that at the top of the forestay all the outer wires had snapped and the forestay was hanging on a very thin inner wire and the mast was at risk. First of all the sail must be taken off. We gently unrolled it, then before our eyes the forestay came away from the top of the mast. It could have fallen on us, it could have damaged either boat next to us, but it just slipped gently down and landed in the sea in the six-inch space between boats. Of course it could have happened as we were sailing and then we probably would have lost the mast.

A passing Dutch man said, "If there is a God up there, he smiled on you today." We agreed.

There followed a frantic tour of the whole of Istanbul and surrounding area trying to get stainless steel wire of the correct size, to make another forestay. There were plenty of boats built in the area but not yachts and the sort of stainless that we wanted was not available. During this time we certainly saw areas of Istanbul that were not on our schedule.

Now a mast is supported by stays – back, front and some at the sides. All of these are vital. We knew we could get what we wanted in Marmarus so a friend lent us a stay and another supplied us with a hank on sail. In this lifestyle friends are incredibly helpful and generous. We said goodbye to Istanbul and slowly sailed back to Marmarus, in gentle weather this time, stopping at some favourite spots. We called in at our fishing harbour and handed out all the photos that we had taken, especially the ones of the memorable supper with our fisherman friend and his wife. I keep my photograph of their gift of honey and the large loaf; this is to remind me that things aren't always as they first seem and I must not be so quick to form my arrogant opinions.

We fixed our forestay and spent the rest of the summer in this incredible country and I began to say to Trevor how lucky we were to be here at this time, on our own boat and enjoying such a wonderful life.

His reaction was and still is, that one makes one's own luck, most people could do what we are doing. It just takes the first step, and then with careful money management and the will, anything is possible.

CHAPTER EIGHTEEN
WILL WE EVER CROSS THE ATLANTIC?

It was time to return to Cyprus and again we couldn't afford a whole winter in Israel, so once more we would take up the special rates for a full winter in Cyprus; nowhere was it any cheaper. During our stay I broke my arm, but apart from that it was a good time. For the record, private medical treatment was excellent and extremely inexpensive but if necessary, there was a free hospital. We had a friend, Pat, who while in Turkey thought that she'd broken her arm at the elbow. She found the free public hospital and joined the queue. She was seen by a doctor and x-rayed and yes her diagnosis was confirmed, but although the treatment thus far was free, she had to provide her own plaster to set it. Off trotted husband Eric with money and a dictionary and bought the necessary stuff. Back in hospital the doctor and nurse looked a little surprised but none of them had the necessary words to investigate further. The plaster was mixed and applied to Pat's now extremely painful arm. The plaster was piled on and on and on, until it was all used up. It dried and Pat left weighted down with this enormous burden. As they climbed into their dinghy she suggested that they go carefully because if she fell in no way was she ever coming to the surface. Later they found out that they had bought far too much plaster but as they'd paid for it, the Turkish Doctor felt duty bound to use it.

I still did not feel ready to cross the Atlantic so we decided that the next summer we would revisit Israel, Turkey and spend more time in Greece and the Greek Islands. No sooner said than done. The whole summer sailing season was again magic. We went to Israel first and found it as vibrant as ever. Again it was too expensive to spend more than four weeks but we packed our time with many fascinating events. We walked everywhere, joined all the free walks on offer and spent hours at the museums. We took gallery walks at the Art Galleries and learned so much from our guides. We even revisited our Folk Club and were amazed when the same man at the door announced "You're late, you were going to spend the winter with us, two years ago, what happened?"

We left this vibrant country wondering if we would ever return, there was no time for regrets as we had a glorious sail to Turkey and Greece. There, we went to wherever the fancy took us, finding many places that we had never seen before. By now we were meeting more and more old friends, both Turkish and cruisers. It was an idyllic summer and once more we went back to Cyprus.

Again we lifted the boat onto the hard and fairly quickly I had a telephone call to say that my mother was ill and that I was needed at home. Within two days I was on the plane to Athens and then on the London. Once back in Canterbury I found that my mother had collapsed with nervous exhaustion, she was nursing my uncle who was quite ill and my aunt was beginning to show signs of short time memory loss which had gone un-noticed by her Doctor and poor Mum had been at the receiving end of all this confusion. I was home for some time and during this visit my uncle was hospitalised and then died. There was a funeral to organize, paperwork to deal with, wills and a ton of other stuff, not to mention helping Mum on the road to recovery and dealing with my Aunt's problem. One thing at a time and slowly we began to sort things out. Mum bounced back and now everything was calm again Aunt Phyllis' seemed much improved. I left to spend a week with my daughter where I watched to see if Mum could cope. She could. What a fantastic week that was. It was very late in November and my daughter, Jane arranged an early Christmas party for all our friends and local family. We had the traditional food, silly presents even more foolish games and it was wonderful. I met my son's new girlfriend, ate and drank too much. Someone videoed it and I arrived back in Cyprus to share the film with Trevor. He had been having a good time of his own, as it had been his birthday while I was away. I think that everyone had felt sorry for this lonely husband and he actually had three birthday parties. I think that he disgraced himself badly when he didn't turn up for the last one, as he'd subsequently received an invite to go sailing on a huge boat with sails that slipped into the mast. He'd been dying to try this out and the earlier invitation had gone straight out of his mind. Oops.

Once back I had some personal serious thinking. I could not stay in this part of the world forever. I had two choices; we either went out of the Med. And possibly back to Europe and England after all we hadn't visited Ireland, Germany or the Scandinavian countries or we crossed the Atlantic. By now several friends had made the 'jump' and we were receiving news of these beautiful Caribbean islands. Why was I hesitating? I told Trevor that I would be prepared to 'cross the pond' and suddenly it was all systems go. It appeared that several boats in the Marina were of the same mind, so there began a few meetings. First we all studied the charts and pilot books and shared this information, then we had a talk from a couple who had just returned and so all the information was 'red hot' and last of all the women had a great day. We used the Yacht Club Kitchen and made bread using a variety of different techniques some traditional, one using a pressure cooker, beer bread and variations on the theme. Looking back I realise it was only the women who were expected to learn how to bake bread. Evidently our men folk had much more masculine tasks to do. Actually once I did cross the Atlantic the situation changed dramatically. There I was rubbing shoulders with many more of my American sisters, blimey, if it was suggested there, that only the woman did the baking, there would have been a riot. Anyway, whoever did this practice baking in Cyprus, there lingered the smell of hot, homemade bread and everyone's mouth watered. Let's hope it would be as good in the Atlantic.

Serious maintenance was done this winter and by April 'Boon' was ready and I guess so were we. Of course first of all, we had the serious business of sailing out of the Med to the Canaries and that was a marathon task it itself. We decided that we would have a farewell trip to Israel and again we were the first boat away. This time the farewells were more emotional. Seasoned sailors that we now thought we were, the sail was a piece of cake!

This was to be a very special occasion as we were due to arrive on the day of the Jewish Passover (Seder

Night.) We duly arrived and before we had time to draw breath, we were given an invitation to the Supper by friends. We spent a memorable evening surrounded by a Jewish family celebrating this wonderful occasion. Across the candlelit table I looked at Trevor wearing his Yamulka, surrounded by this Jewish family from Iraq; the two younger sons of the family were serving in the Israel Army, another was in business and there were beautiful dark eyed daughters. The Father, the head of the family had his small grandson on his lap teaching him the Traditions of Passover. The gentle mother smiled serenely and when the meal was over her huge sons insisted on clearing the table while she sat centre stage. Remember that the mother is the heart of every Jewish family. This is an occasion I know will live forever in Trevor's memory.

Then everything happened in a rush, as we did not want to miss anything as who knew if we would ever have an opportunity to return. We spent a week in a Kibbutz where we both worked in a factory. We were not expected to work, but both felt that we wanted to put something back into this generous community. As I sat at the assembly line folding cardboard boxes, I knew that finally I had found the job I had always wanted. No effort, no particular skills, time to think and certainly a job to drop the minute the lunch bell rang. Not a bit like it. No sooner had I got into the rhythm than the Supervisor came across with a box of beautifully produced labels. These needed to be placed on each box in a precise place, with exact measurements on all sides and owing to the sticky back, one had only one shot at getting it right. He felt

132

that I would be most suitable for this task. So off I went with another job to worry about.

We were given our own little flat. Food was provided either ready cooked and eaten in the restaurant or with the free food that we collected from a store and could prepare in our own kitchen. There was a swimming pool, theatre and schools. Cars were available and one signed up when wanted one, and fuel was provided free. The atmosphere was friendly and relaxed. Doctors and Dentists were available. There was a bar open at weekends and vouchers for free beer were available. Whether this would be the life for me I do not know. My concern was for the young people. They were so unworldly that I wondered how they would fit into the outside world. All young people, boys and girls, had to do three years conscription. I guess this must have been a culture shock to them. Also they were so trusting, they never needed to lock their doors or protect their possessions, they did not have to budget for food or clothes. Somehow they managed, and those born in a Kibbutz always seemed at some time, to have the need to return to live this life style. We made many friends. The old idea that the Kibbutz is mainly agricultural is long gone. They started that way but now they have moved with the times, they have to make a profit and whether it is a plastic or electronic factory or fish farming they go for it. Our week flew and then began a frantic time doing all those things that we had promised ourselves on earlier visits. We visited our Folk Club and were greeted at the door, by the same guy who immediately said, "Nice to see you again." We felt as if we had come home.

The Russians had also now made their mark on this little country. Everywhere we went there was an even higher standard of classical music being played. Whether it was at the street corners or in the little orchestras, the Russians had brought their skill and love of music with them.

On our last full day we had decided to visit the Diamond Museum. We had read about a free trip in the newspaper. The day before we were telling the dignified looking man who owned the boat next to ours in the Marina. He looked very serious and then asked if we really wanted to go on the free tour. We were puzzled until he explained. He was a Director of the Museum and actually owned a diamond business in the Diamond Centre and he would love to give us a personal tour. What an offer. The next day found us in the museum, which was fascinating and then we were taken inside the Diamond Exchange itself and we watched the trading. Finally we went to his office where we sat with a cup of coffee while his son poured bags of diamonds both cut and uncut onto the table. The buildings that housed all this were fascinating; they were linked by underground tunnels and everything was housed there. Banks, shops, hairdressers, you name it and it was to be found. Employees had no excuse to leave the premises until the end of the working day and therefore better security was assured.

Time to move on and out of the Med. We had no definite plan only to be in Gibraltar around September and in the Canary Islands about October, and there to wait for the Trade Winds around November or early December and then go. If you say it quickly enough it sounds easy. Of course there is always a downside, the conditions are such that it is easier to enter the Med. than to leave it. Anyway we managed it going via Crete, Malta, Sardinia, Sicily, S France, Balearics and S Spain. This time we had extra crew as some cockroaches had jumped on board. Try as we could, they were never persuaded to depart. Needless to say they always put on a command performance when we had visitors. It was a blustery sail mostly with the wind on the nose but we managed some nostalgic revisits to Malta and Mahon. We had friends and relations in the South of France so felt that we must pay them a visit. It was a grand reunion and although they did not know one another we had one day altogether which was great fun and they became friends. We visited many places missed on the original sail into the Med. and were really enjoying ourselves. We were almost tempted to stay in the Western Med and make the Atlantic trip the following year; these thoughts did not linger for very long as we were really geared up for our big Atlantic adventure. Looking back I'm amazed that I never once did a mental backtrack and had concerns over our safety, after all who better than me knew that anything could happen especially those things that go bump in the night?

One lovely sunny day we slipped into Gibraltar, which sadly had not improved since our previous visit. I think that Trevor had read somewhere that it was the armpit of the Mediterranean but they did have wonderful facilities to stock up for an Atlantic crossing. There we were advised to mix a cocktail of boric acid and condensed milk and leave it in strategic places for our rapidly multiplying crew. It worked. I had made lists, more lists and lists of lists. I think every woman is the same; she is convinced that food will run out in mid Atlantic. I have never heard of this happening and in fact most of us were eating our Atlantic stores for years afterwards. Anyway we left Gibraltar to go direct to the Canaries and for once we did this with no problems. In the Straits we saw a lot of traffic but this thinned out and off the Moroccan coast we did see some dilapidated fishing boats. In fact the crews looked fairly ferocious and were shouting at us, which was quite nerve racking. By their hand signals we realized that they were indicating that they wanted beer and cigarettes. Having none, we shook our heads sailing on and they left us alone. Later we found out that others hadn't been so lucky. The fishing men had indicated by actions that they should follow a certain route and when they did this they became caught in fishing nets. Of course this was a scam and the men wanted money to cut them free.

We kept our regular three-hour night watches keeping to our own boat rules. On night watch one does not go on deck without waking the other, whatever the weather and safety harnesses are worn at night at all times. Our landfall was Puerto Nous where of course we arrived in the middle of the night. We finally found an empty jetty and tied along side. At first light we found the area designated for yachts and moved. We had completed our first step. We found several boats that we had seen in our travels and it seemed that all were preparing for the Atlantic crossing. But first things first, we must get some local money, and the Canaries being Spanish we needed to obtain some pesetas. We discovered a busy modern town and finding a Bank, put our credit card in the cash point machine. Pressing the magic button for English we carefully read the instructions and requested a certain amount of cash. Various lights blinked and a hum told us that things were happening, when we read on the screen 'WE CANNOT ACTIVATE THIS AMOUNT OWING TO LACK OF FUNDS. PLEASE CONTACT YOUR OWN BANK'.

We looked at each other in shocked horror. Of course there was money in the account and we did not understand what was happening. It must be a terrible mistake let's try again. We did and had the same message. Let's try an over the counter transaction. We did this and the counter clerk had the same message. What to do now? He suggested that we should phone our Bank. We explained that we couldn't, as we had no money. Could we make an international phone call to the UK from the Bank? The answer was of course, sorry, and no.

We decided to return to the boat, get phone numbers and see exactly what cash money we had. Once there we found that we had a five-pound note and a little Spanish, French and Italian money. We had stupidly let us ourselves run out of US dollars. Back to town and our assortment of cash was all turned into Spanish pesetas. We found the Telefonica and with the UK Bank phone number, made the call. After a short conversation it appeared that the Bank was at fault, money had not been transferred from another account and to compound the error, our never used emergency Bank overdraft facilities had not come into play. Many apologies from the Bank and it would be rectified. When? At midnight tonight when any such alterations took place, and not before. That was that.

The next day, the hole in the Bank wall spat out lovely crisp notes and we were in business again. Being still somewhat miffed by the whole mess, I wrote a very haughty letter to the Bank, and to my amazement I had a letter back apologizing and informing me that thirty-five pounds had been credited to my account for phone calls made and any inconvenience caused. So there, Banks do have hearts and I walked around all day with a smug look on my face. Trevor had thought me stupid to write to the Bank in the first place. But there was a lesson to be relearned; in future we would never let ourselves run out of those green back dollars.

We had lots of fun in Puerto Nous, finding a very international crowd of cruisers all preparing for the big jump across the Atlantic. Of course lots were old friends and many we had not met before. There was one Italian who had quite a small boat but entertained everyone to spaghetti and wine. We crowded into, onto and around his boat until I thought that we'd sink her. Americans surprisingly were more formal in their entertaining and always called drinks provided in the early evening 'cocktails'. I never actually saw a cocktail but it was fun. Australians, New Zealanders and S Africans always had sundowners and we Brits had 'drinks'. Truthfully most of us were just providing beer or local plonk. The Spanish plonk was in one pint cardboard cartons which were ideal for travelling and of course there was no risk of bottles breaking but tasted very rough. We had some pontoon parties and generally were very light hearted. On one boat we were fed a gorgeous homemade pizza and each guest was given his own cardboard 'brick' of wine. Others decanted it into carafes and others served in crystal glasses. Sadly whichever way it was served it tasted pretty awful. (Once we arrived in the Caribbean we never saw cartons of wine again and I remember a couple of years later someone producing it and after the first sip I wondered how we ever all drank it and survived). But here we were in the Canaries and it seemed that now we had all made up our minds to cross the Atlantic, we were very laid back about the whole affair perhaps helped by all this cheap wine. Time would tell.

For some reason, and I can't remember why, we were all going to move to Los Palmas for the jump off across the Atlantic. We had to wait until the "Arc" had left. This was a huge group of boats that were travelling across together under an organized scheme; starting on an agreed date, with several safety rules and radio contact daily. No single handers were allowed. Not so ourselves, we were all going independently, leaving whenever we each felt that the weather was right or we were ready. We had many single handers and several of the boats were really tiny. One thing everyone did have in common was that we were all making sure that their boats were up to scratch.

The day that the ARC left we sailed across to Las Palmas and as we arrived we saw over a hundred little boats underway. Unfortunately there was no wind so most were motoring but they did leave lots of room in the Marina for us. Daily more and more boats arrived and there began to be an air of excitement. Over the radio we heard reports from the ARC that the wind was still slight and sailors were making little headway. Remember with a voyage of over 3,000 miles one can't use too much fuel. A sailing boat can only carry so much, certainly not enough to motor the whole way. All fuel needs to be carefully used and some reserved in case of any problems.

Trevor had done a lot of maintenance in Cyprus, had a recheck in Gibraltar and now was to do the fine-tuning. We could be up to or even over 30 days at sea and he wanted to be as ready as we could be. This made my provisioning seem quite small fry in comparison. Just before we left we would lift out and anti foul. We had a great time here and again had one of our home village coincidences. We were in the boat yard when a young man stood some distance away, watching us. He eventually came over and we could see it was a friend from the old days, in fact one of the group who helped to plaster our original boat. This world of ours was certainly shrinking. He was here with his latest boat. We certainly used a lot of midnight oil catching up on news. I think that when travelling, meeting old friends in new places is one of the nicest things.

Eventually the great day came when Trevor said that he had been listening to all the forecasts and he felt that the trade winds were established and we should be off. Course planned, charts ready and this time we were the proud owners of a GPS (Global

Positioning System). This told us where we were, how far to our destination, our speed over the ground, the day, the time, our course and much more besides. (We still had our faithful sextant tucked away for emergencies. Who better than we two knew about Murphy)? We had also acquired a wind steering vane. This meant that we had wind steering as well as our faithful electronic Fred who had not died in Tunisia but had temporarily gone into a coma. Don't forget we had his twin brother for emergencies. Our emergency container was carefully prepared and this time I put in some click (or zip lock) bags, no fear of throwing human waste into the sea!!!!! We had taken heed of the warning from last time. Actually although we were making all these emergency preparations I still don't remember being overly concerned regarding our safety

CHAPTER NINETEEN
WHAT WAS ALL THE FUSS ABOUT?

At last with a clean bottom, store lockers overloaded, brimful of water and fuel and our obligatory hand of green bananas swinging from the cockpit awning, we were ready to go. Without much more ado, we did just that. We seemed to quietly slip out of the Marina (we HAD paid our bill) and were on our way. As we reached the open sea we found a lively following wind and we turned off the motor. 'Boon' seemed to adjust her skirts, settle in the sea, and the lady that she was, began her magical sail to Barbados. In fact we did not need the motor again until we were in sight of Barbados. Except for the occasional time for battery charging our wind generator kept us topped up with power.

What can I say about the trip? Perhaps we were very lucky or I guess Trevor got the timing and the course right. It was just perfect. We settled swiftly into a routine. We kept the same three-hour watch keeping system. Every morning we tuned into the Atlantic Net to report our position and hear where everyone else was. The radio was manned by a lady from Barbados called Trudy. It was a joy to daily hear her voice and I always held my breath when she gave the weather forecast. It was fun to check how far the other boats had travelled in the 24-hour period and to know that we were holding our own. We heard of one or two problems but nothing that could not be sorted out by good advice on this net and a little help from friends. These magical days passed gently; we both had one rest period during the day to make up for broken sleep at night. I baked bread every other day and made a variety of cakes. Strangely on this trip we never managed to catch a fish. We did though, get very interested in our food and would together discuss the day's menus. As I've mentioned earlier (sorry American sisters) ours is a very traditional arrangement, I do all the cooking, washing up, etc. And on this trip there was no laundry and only a little cleaning up. This leaves my man to do all the navigation, deck work and any maintenance. I would watch Trevor every morning walk the deck and looking aloft to check all the fittings, rigging and sails to see that all was well. He would sit at the chart table and enter our position on the chart, check the weather and our daily mileage. The rest of it was all very casual and in the daytime we wore no clothes and usually only a tee shirt at night. It was seawater showers, for this read a bucket of seawater chucked over each other, followed by the tiniest sprinkle of fresh water to hopefully remove all the salt crystals. Conversely I had plenty of time to feed moisture cream into my skin, pluck my eyebrows and write letters already to post when we hit Barbados, not literarily I hope. We read, listened to music and chatted a lot. While on watch at night enjoyed all the talking books my daughter had sent to us. On many a starlit night I would sit in the cockpit and laugh out loud at Tom Sharpe and Sue Townsend and I particularly loved Libby Purves' 'One summer's Grace'. I wished that I could write as they did. Since my article in the Practical Boat Owner I had not tried my hand at any more but it was something that might come later, but don't all cruisers say that?

The trip was very peaceful and quite a time for reflection. There were moments when I would watch Trevor as he plotted our course or tweaked the sails. He looked fit, tanned and his whole body language and smiles told me that he was having the time of his life. I was so glad that I'd gone sailing with him and more so that we were making this particular journey together. I was approaching my sixtieth birthday and hadn't started sailing until well into my forties and here I was in the middle of the Atlantic. There were many times particularly at night, when I was filled with wonder, blanketed with a million stars feeling the gentle movement of the sea beneath me and with Trevor asleep I was almost alone in the world. We had a few squalls, but these were always visible in the distance and one could take action long before they arrived. For me the incredible thing was that we never saw any of the other yachts and in fact once past the Canary Islands only saw one boat and that was an American freighter. It was on Christmas morning and we called him on the VHF to say "Happy Christmas". At first he couldn't see us, and then when he did he was shocked to see such a small sailboat. He thought we were crazy to be out there. So much for our Christmas greetings.

On December 27th we pulled into the docks at Bridgetown, Barbados, twenty-three days after we had left the Canaries. I climbed ashore and felt that, Pope like, I should kiss the ground. I had done it. I had sailed across the Atlantic. I felt so delighted with myself and looking at Trevor and seeing his corresponding huge grin, knew that he felt the same.

Smartly dressed we went into the appropriate offices and were welcomed into the Caribbean.

Paperwork completed we sailed back to the anchorage spotting friends on the way. We passed our Japanese friend, who had sailed alone, and when he saw us he performed a war dance on deck to celebrate. It's certainly a great life.

Barbados is a beautiful island, very lush and hot with wonderful flowers, and the people friendly, well dressed and with a certain air of dignity. We were invited to meet our ham operator Trudy, and together with our Japanese friend had a gorgeous day in her home. A low bungalow surrounded with beautiful gardens, a swimming pool and a wonderful distant view of the sea. There we drank rum and coconut water, ate cristophines for the first time and found out that Trudy, although sporting a beautiful British accent was actually German.

We spent three weeks on this island; sightseeing, taking organized walks, discovering some of the history and attending lunchtime concerts. I loved going ashore on a Sunday and watching the Barbadians attending their local Churches. How fantastically they were dressed; best brightly coloured dresses, colourful hats, crisp shirts and ties with children decked out in ribbons and bows. On the anchorage we spent many hours entertaining or being entertained in various cockpits. All talking of the crossing of course and fairly soon where we were going next. It appeared that nearly everyone had a different destination; of course there are so many islands to choose from.

From our anchorage we daily had a mini adventure just getting ashore. In our dinghies we had to head for the beach, fortunately it was golden sand, but there the sea broke with a vengeance and often unceremoniously tipped us all in the water.. I guess that one out of three trips ended in a soaking. The order of the day became to go ashore in bathing suits with clothes sealed in plastic bags. On this empty beach the problem was where to get dressed when one arrived. It was all good fun.

While here we visited the American Embassy and obtained our American Visas. Cruising non-Americans cannot visit the USA without an up to date visa. This has to be obtained before arrival there. Time came to move on and we decided to sail to the islands of St Lucia and Martinique.

The sailing was fine if a little boisterous and again we had a regular radio net and made contact with friends. St Lucia was beautiful and Martinique was delightful. Very, very French and so chic. Everyone seemed to have an air of Paris about them. We greedily ate baguettes, pate, lots of French cheeses and of course drank delicious French wine in bottles of course. Can you imagine any self respecting Frenchman putting even vin ordinaire in a carton. The officials were very laid back and signing in was a delight. Sailing around this island, finding one pretty anchorage after another, was exactly as I had imagined the Caribbean to be.

Unfortunately reality was beginning to catch up with us, we were finding that it was expensive to live in these islands. In the past most of the islands were agricultural but once tourism landed, farmers turned

146

over to being taxi drivers, tour operators, waiters and whatever. The land changed faces and became sites for hotels, hotel complexes, etc. so food was imported and of course the costs rocketed. We had spent a lot of money preparing for the crossing and we also needed to make a few renewals. Our dinghy and outboard were getting very ancient and as we now were anchoring again these were a vital part of the equipment.

The last thing we wanted to do was to delve even further into our shrinking capital. Again it was discussion time. We had kept in touch with friends on the Caribbean island of Sint Maartens and they had been working there for the last year. They felt that we could easily find work for a few months and that way top up the kitty. So off we sailed.

Another good sail between the islands and that night on watch, I seemed to follow a silver path caused by a brilliant full moon, it was truly miraculous. By dawn we were in the bay outside the lagoon in Sint Maartens. This is on the Dutch side of this divided island, the other side being French. Once again more history to discover. We anchored but knew that we had to wait for a bridge to open but did not know what time this would happen. Then yet again we had one of our incredible co-incidences. Anchored the other side of this bay was a large boat. Trevor commented that it looked like the classic wooden boat that had once moored in Turnchapel. Out came the binoculars and lo and behold it was the same one. Curiosity got the better of him and he dinghied over to check it out. When he eventually returned, it was to tell me that is was the same boat and surprise, surprise the skipper was in fact one of our friends who had helped plaster 'Sea Mandala'. Would it never end? Anyway he'd found out that the bridge opened in half an hour.

CHAPTER TWENTY
HURRICANES, WHAT ARE THEY?

The bridge duly opened and we entered this land locked lagoon where there appeared to be hundreds of boats. We found ourselves a spot, dropped the hook and promptly went to sleep.

During the next few days Trevor found himself a job and left me with the dinghy to start my own job search. This did not turn out to be too easy, as although this was a 'tourist' island and there were lots of boutiques, bars and day trips, all needing to employ some of the cruisers, I did not exactly fill the bill. I was not young, or sexy with it. This appeared to be the criteria for the American Tourist trade. I did an awful lot of pounding the pavements at this time, but with no success. I felt despondent and felt that I was not pulling my weight but also so very bored.

Eventually I got a job acting as childminder to an American family on holiday. Often I had to sleep over but at least I was helping with the family exchequer. From there I was 'spotted' by a Boutique in the same complex, the owner decided to open on a Sunday and needed a reliable person to run the store on her own. I guess age equalled reliability and was useful on this occasion. Then the shop next door needed someone to run the shop every afternoon and all day Sunday and so I was home and dry. The dollars began to grow and we began to buy goodies for 'Boon'. In fact we ended up with quite a long wish list that we were steadily working our way through. We still managed to have some fun. With so many friends I celebrated my 60th birthday and people began to talk of the hurricane season. Hurricanes, what were they?

To find out we attended a Hurricane Awareness Talk. It sounded pretty terrifying but as everyone said, Sint Maartens had never had a serious problem, Hurricanes always veered before they reached the island. Our immediate neighbours were sensibly moving out before the Hurricane season started, so we bought their hurricane mooring and decided to stay put. After all we still had a cooker, computer and printer on our list to buy. We did take heed of the talk and when June 1st (Day one of the Hurricane Season) arrived we were fixed to this new mooring, had taken off the sails and sheets and were, or thought we were, ready for anything. Life continued a pace and several hurricanes were reported in various places but so far not near us. The local Supermarkets issued Hurricane charts with your groceries and they were used to enter the Hurricanes movements as they approached or hopefully disappeared from Sint Maartens. Then Hurricane Iris appeared and she came very close, so close in fact that she only missed us by a few miles. We heard of the damage in other places by this ugly quirk of nature but still thought that it wouldn't happen here and to us.

So what are hurricanes? They are giant whirlwinds in which air moves in a large tightening spiral around an extreme low pressure. They reach maximum velocity in a circular band extending outward 20 or 30 miles from the rim of the eye. The circulation of these storms is always counter clockwise. They build in four stages. First is a Tropical Disturbance and once it reaches speeds of 38 miles per hour (33 knots) it is then a Tropical Depression. As this continues to move westerly across the warm Tropical Ocean, it has a high possibility of gaining in strength and size. This determines the wind speeds and turns it into a Tropical Storm between a mere 39 miles per hour and 74 miles per hour. Once it sustains speeds of 74 miles it becomes a hurricane. Take it from me you don't want to meet one of these babies.

Denise, my boss decided to visit New York and left me in charge of the store for a month and Trevor began to work for himself. It was a very active and happy time. A lovesick friend returned to the UK and we were suddenly the custodians of his pretty cat called Charisma.

Then Hurricane Luis appeared on the scene. It was well monitored and we were well aware of it as it developed through the various stages and in fact, with modern weather forecasting, no one can be taken by surprise. The problem with these little charmers is that there is no guarantee as to which way they will turn. If one tries to go out to sea and outrun one, you must have a boat that can reach excellent speeds and duck and dive as it changes direction. Not us unfortunately.

So it was a waiting, worrying and watching time. By now everyone had their own personal hurricane chart for plotting the progress, or lack thereof. It took several days but Luis never changed route just progressed straight for this little island. We all began to prepare. Those ashore began planning in case they had to leave their houses. The cruisers topped up with food and water putting out second and even third anchors or moving to more sheltered locations. It still came closer and increased in speed.

Decision time for us. We decided that if the winds were to be in excess of 100 miles per hour we would leave our 'Boon' and go ashore, after all this is what we had insurance for. We had already received an invitation to stay in a friend's apartment nearby. We would take the cat, a change of clothes, our handheld VHF, some food and water and a small camping gas stove in case the electricity failed. We never felt the need to remove any of our treasures; we were sure that we would be coming back.

Finally the day came when Louis was nearly upon us. We removed the dodgers, spray hood, the boom, and the deck containers and put everything below – what a jumbled mess. We climbed into the dinghy with our limited possession and the cat of course, her litter tray, her basket, her food and bowl and to the tune of her howls, motored away.

Trevor dropped me at the Boutique where I had to stow the stock and securely close up the shop. He went on to our temporary abode with a still complaining cat and then returned to 'Boon' for last minute adjustments. By 1 pm we were all back at the apartment. The Government had announced that every place of business must be closed by mid-day and by 1 pm everyone should be at home and aware of their nearest Shelter.

There were five of us in the apartment. Joanne, the American owner, two South African cruisers, Trevor and myself and let us not forget the cat. She was stretched out thoroughly enjoying the attention and space. Our windows were boarded and we knew that once it started we would not be able to open the doors for fear of them not shutting again. We turned on the TV and saw that there had been no change in Luis' direction but the winds were rapidly gaining in speed. We filled the baths with water, as St Maartens has no fresh water supply, everything coming from a desalination plant on the sea's edge and this was pretty certain to be damaged. Between us we had plenty of torches, candles, two VHF radios, food and a good supply of rum. By the evening it was no worse and we ate our supper but it tasted like sawdust. We saw from TV that Luis was nearly upon us.

At about one o'clock, in the early hours of the morning of 4th September 1995, he struck. We heard the leaves begin to rustle, and then get louder. The doors and windows began to rattle and then an orchestra of noises surrounded us. Then it began to roar like an express train. UNINVITED, LUIS HAD ARRIVED. There was very little that we could do.

We checked all our windows and doors and soon saw trickles of water appearing from every nook and cranny. Up came the rugs and up jumped the cat, finding safety on the back of the sofa. Back to sleep for her. Not so for us. We tuned into the VHF knowing that those few who had chosen to remain on their boats were monitoring an agreed channel. Their voices came over the air, loud and clear against the background of the mayhem around them. All of us seemed to hold our breath. We knew almost everyone that was out there. The hair stood up on the back of my neck as I listened and for a moment I felt ashamed that I had deserted them but again, glad that

I was on terra firma and hopefully safe in the apartment.

I could write a dramatic account of everything that happened in that thirty-six hours but so much has already been written. However, I feel that some of the conversations overheard on the radio during that time would probably give you a different angle.

* * *

"Look out there's a boat dragging down on you, st'board side."

"Missed."

"Man this is something else."

"My God the barometer is still dropping."

"We are keeping our engines running."

From a VHF ashore
"How are you darling? Just take care. We are thinking of you."
The reply from on board
"I am OK and I love you. Look after the kids."

"Look out everyone, three more of the Sun Sail boats have broken lose."

A few hours later and we in the apartment were frantically trying to keep the water level to below our ankles. We were working with the drumbeat of the tiles crashing from the roof. But this was nothing to the drama in the lagoon.

The faceless voices continued.

"I wish I knew where I was. Visibility is about 10 metres."

"Christ, I've got two boats caught in my anchor chain."

"I've lost all my anchors and I'm going to drive the boat onto the rocks by the Sambuca Restaurant. Wish me luck."

There came a laconic British reply, "Book me a table."

By now the winds were registering 150 and gusting to 180 knots. Trevor always remembers the scream of the wind, which never seemed to pause for breath.

Visibility had gone and everyone in their cockpits was wearing a snorkel mask to stop ingesting water.

Our friend John had another boat T-boned onto his bow and he crawled along the deck to cut it off. Liz remained in the cockpit with the engine running. Later she told us that hours seemed to pass. At last, thinking that he had fallen overboard, she also crawled on her hands and knees and found him on the

155

bow, still sawing through the chain, but now with two broken fingers.

The voices relentlessly stayed with us.

"My God I've a concrete boat one side of me, a steel boat on the other and mine is in the middle, so small and made of wood."
The reply, "Have you any ideas?"
"It's too late for ideas."

Reports kept coming of boats dragging, hitting each other and getting tangled or untangled.

More voices.
"I'm holding on to three boats here, but would you believe after that collision I'm still alright."

"Dad's cutting us free from another boat, I'm at the wheel now. Mum is lying down, she can't stop being sick. Apart from that we're fine." South African Natasha was fifteen years old.

Advice to someone in distress. Such a calming woman's voice.
"Get your papers together. Put on a life jacket. Do you have a Dan buoy so we can see your light."

More advice from a man this time.
"Wedge everything you have in the hole – sails, bags, clothes, anything."

Then came the voice of Sandy.

156

"Our boat held up after a wild broach, the engine was full on and we've made it to the Fuel Dock. Right now it's like a walk in the Park"
(One hour later, pounding against that dock, her boat sank).

Then followed a lot of voices all on top of each other.

"We've got a lot of noise – Christ the wood's cracking up."

"We're going to hit the rocks shortly. Have a good evening. See you soon."

"Man, There's carnage ashore."
"We've lost our boat, but Zoë and I are OK" (Zoë was aged ten).

"May Day, May Day. I've lost my husband." (We never heard of them again).

"Man, I'm fucked"

* * * *

At the height of the hurricane, the Air Port instruments measured gusts of 208 miles an hour.

When we all surfaced we found that of the approximate 1,300 boats at anchor, only 100 were still floating. The rest were sunk or mainly stacked in piles ashore, all the way around the circumference of the lagoon. Some were wedged under the Bridge and later aeroplanes reported having seen mastless vessels out at   sea.

When the winds were down to about 60 miles, we ventured out. There were no leaves left on the trees, many trees of course were down, roofs off and debris everywhere. No electricity, no water. It was indescribable.

Of course 'Boon' was no longer on her mooring, and nowhere to be seen. We stumbled our way through debris around the lagoon. Eventually we saw our own very distinctive buoy floating over a flattened mast. Underneath the water was our boat. Buried at sea. We stood in each other's arms, weeping and not able to speak as we paid the last homage to our lady who had cared for us for so long.

So much followed. There was looting and we had at dusk to dawn curfew. One evening people were shot. No one was allowed into the Dutch side of the island. Planes and ships were standing by to help us but the officials would not let them enter. Everything went crazy. Boats with ham radios got messages out, and a local Company allowed cruisers to make a quick phone call home. This continued until their batteries ran down.

A Holiday Complex, which was closing down for a major refit, opened its doors to the homeless cruisers and many even had a small apartment. As there was no electricity they provided two meals a day using all the food in the melting freezers. In fact on the first night everyone had lobster followed by steak. On the other side of the lagoon, the Church was providing beds and three meals a day. We heard stories of survivors who escaped from their sinking boats or climbed out of their vessels as they were blown ashore. Because of the high winds they had to crawl on their hands and knees often hanging onto trees and lampposts as the gusts came. Eventually they all managed to find shelter somewhere.

A couple of weeks later Hurricane Marilyn arrived and went and we barely noticed her, perhaps we were all numb or maybe her winds of about 80 miles were child's play. We moved into a vacant boat that Trevor had earlier worked on. Everyone was stunned. Many people were in a Catch 22 situation. They were on this island because they needed to work. Because of the disaster they had no work. Now they needed money to repair their boats. Many had saved no money. We began to realize that we were one of the lucky ones. After our previous disaster, Trevor had insisted that we could not afford to go sailing without insurance.

The cruisers, Boat Yards and Chandlers in Trinidad were wonderful, in no time at all they had organized clothes, and had provided fibre glass, resin, wood and general building materials, some tools, and a boat was soon on its way to help us. It slipped into the French side and at night crept across the lagoon to join us. The Dutch side would still not let anyone enter. You cannot imagine the delight when I sorted through the clothes and found shorts and a tee shirt that fitted together with shoes.

Unfortunately no one thought of panties for women. So my only pair was always hanging out to dry and on alternate days I wore a royal blue pair of Y fronts.

You must realize that if the shops hadn't been blown away, they had been looted and so there was nothing to buy.

Once again we were all humbled by the generosity of others. The Cruisers' Church was able to help with water making equipment. Water was made and the Minister took a bowser into the hills and slowly people appeared from hiding to get the precious liquid. These were frightened; mainly Haitian illegal immigrants and rumour had it that they had buried their own dead in these hills. The Government was still denying any figures of the death toll. In fact when we finally left Sint Maartens, the Government resigned. It seemed to us that the officials thought that Sint Maartens was such a popular island with tourists, in fact it was their only form of income, that if everything was kept quiet life would continue and the tourists would still come. How they would explain no sand, no palm trees, broken down hotels and damaged boats everywhere, hadn't yet been worked out.

Things slowly began to return to normal, our Pantaenious Insurance Assessor arrived and 'Boon' was confirmed as a write off and there was no doubt that we would soon have our insurance money. The owner of the boat that we were squatting on asked us to deliver it to the USA at the end of the Hurricane Season. Perhaps we would find our new boat there. There never seemed any question that we would take our insurance money and run back to a life on land again, it was still a life on the ocean wave for us. You must think that we are gluttons for punishment. One woman looking at her damaged boat said to me,

"When I heard that you were staying for the hurricane season I decided to do the same. After all, I thought that as you had lost one boat already, it couldn't happen twice and we would all be OK. I feel so sorry for you, at least I still have my boat."

Trevor dived onto "Boon", but once inside he was so entangled in the ropes, boom and general mess that he had to retreat before he became another casualty. Everything looked as if it had been mangled in a giant crazy washing machine. I guess it had.

An era had ended, but we were well and had the opportunity to pick ourselves up and start again. With our insurance money in our pocket, we would take up the offer of delivering the boat to the USA and hopefully find our next boat there.

PART THREE
CHAPTER TWENTY-ONE
YET ANOTHER 'BOON'

The Hurricane season nearly over and we were enveloped in the preparation of 'Carpathia' for her return to the USA. We were safely tucked up in an attractive marina. Well nearly attractive, just a little rough around the edges from the hostilities of Luis.

Life was still difficult as looting was prevalent and now it was from the seaward side so the Dutch sent their Navy to protect us. We still lived under evening and night-time curfews. The whole island looked stark and even though it was still brilliantly blue and sunny, there was an air of desolation everywhere. The local people bounced back quite quickly but the cruisers took much longer. Maybe the locals had so little to lose to begin with or maybe they were just more resilient, but I like to think that their normal attitude of tomorrow will look after itself, helped them. Most of the islanders had this approach of living for today; they don't seem to have the need to plan for tomorrow or even the next hour. This often used to infuriate us when they didn't turn up for work when promised, just swanning along several hours late and amazed at our annoyance. Anyway whatever it was, it helped them cope with this dreadful situation.

But back to 'Carpathia', she was truly a beautiful yacht, fifty-five feet long, fibreglass, a cutter (that is one mast but two foresails) and with attractive lines. She was built in Taiwan and fitted out to her owners' specifications. Below she had gorgeous burgundy coloured curtains and upholstery, together with matt finished varnish. When we finally met the owner he told us that when he visited Taiwan to discuss the final details, he found that the workmen were completing the varnishing, stark naked. Reason – no fluff or cotton from their clothes should stick to the pristine finish. No cost had been spared and it certainly showed in the final product.

We now get to the fun part, after the simplicity of 'Boon'; I could not believe it when I wandered from the fridge/freezer, microwave, and icemaker to the full sized washing machine and tumbler drier. Needless to say there was a built in generator to support these goodies. The galley was large but well laid out and the main saloon seemed enormous. The master bedroom was complete with a king-sized bed adorned with richly coloured bed linen and it boasted a bathroom – yes a shower, toilet and a BATH. Of course there was even a water maker to help fill this bath and would you believe, to flush the toilet as well. Unheard of in cruising circles, wasting precious water down the loo when there is an ocean outside to do just that. Further forward there was another cabin, which had two single bunks, and a hidden bed, which cleverly became single or double at will and again a second shower room with toilet. A more mundane toilet with flushing sea water, perhaps this basic one should be called a lavatory.

The grand plan was to bring her to standard for the sail to Fort Lauderdale and from there begin the search for our boat number three. Trevor kept busy checking all the systems and making good any repairs. I became cleaning woman as this lovely lady had been left unattended for two years and certainl needed some tender loving care.

The other cruisers were slowly beginning to come to terms with their own personal problems. Some of which were horrendous. In many cases boats lay three or four deep on the rocks and with Sod's Law, the ones on the bottom had the money to pay to be pulled out but those on top, hadn't. Just another catch twenty-two situation.

Our owners flew in from the USA to check their boat and I guess check us as well. After all they were putting her in the hands of complete strangers. Plans were made for the delivery once the Hurricane season was well and truly over and the repairs completed. The intention was to make the trip direct with no stops en route and Trevor and I felt that we did not need any extra crew. Finances were discussed and a contract drawn up. We were about to head for a new adventure while earning a little money on the way.

Once more we were left on our own and in such an ideal situation, we were able to entertain friends in style. Never having possessed one before, I had a love affair with the microwave oven. This meant all suppers on board were accompanied by a large jacket potato and accompanied by whatever delicacies could be popped behind the magic oven door.

Joanne, our American hostess during the Hurricane, was a regular visitor and began to get involved with our preparations. She was at a loose end, as the Keep Fit Centre where she'd worked before Luis, had not reopened. She would help with some minor repairs, join Trevor in planning the course and in fact she was fascinated with the GPS.

She drove one of the dinghies, in fact we had three, ours miraculously salvaged and two of theirs. Joanne helped in a multitude of ways. She had never sailed on a boat but certainly asked some very astute questions.

Out of the blue we received a fax from the owners and while they had been finalizing their insurance cover, they were told that it would be a requirement that there should be a Captain and a crew of three. Oh well, we were not too bothered, after all this meant that we would have more sleep on passage. Via the morning net on VHF, we put out a request for crew – a trip to the USA with a return air flight to St. Maartens or money in lieu, and all food provided. The only proviso was that the applicants needed to have American visas. Not as easy as it sounded. Most people on the island were either frantically working on their own boats or still shell shocked and not ready to make any decisions.

Anyway Sam finally appeared at the dock. She was South African, lively, had crewed from her own country to the Caribbean, was between boyfriends and needing a change of scene. And she had an American visa. Trevor felt that she would fit the bill. Crewmember number one was chosen. No one else appeared.

One afternoon while Joanne was busying herself on the boat, Trevor remarked that she should come with us, visit her folks and have a paid flight home again. After all Roger, her husband was in England at the time. We all laughed and had yet another cup of tea. The next morning she appeared and astounded us, by saying that she had spoken to Roger on the 'phone and he had approved and yes, she would come with us. I don't know who was more surprised, Trevor or Joanne. From them on it was fantastic to watch her. She wanted to learn everything and immediately. One evening Trevor gave her a book on knots and highlighted three she should learn. Next day she returned and could tie the whole damn lot! I was still struggling with the bowline. I don't know if I've already explained that I appear to have two left hands, seem to forget anything mechanical and as for tying knots, well forget it. It was a good thing that I liked Joanne so much or I would have hated her.

The departure date was fixed; all the paperwork was OK, when another fax arrived. Problems, in fact I could say Big Problems and you'd remember that we have had some of those. For some reason the owner's wife had been talking with the Coast Guard and had been told that an American must skipper the boat. The reasoning behind this was that a delivery was classed as a commercial enterprise. We were stunned. How would this affect our plans to get to USA, earn some money and buy our new boat there? Trevor made a rapid decision; he would ask American Joanne to be captain for paperwork purposes. But how would she feel about it? She was after all, very correct.

We soon found out - not at all happy. After much discussion with her sister-in-law a lawyer and yet another conversation with her husband, it was agreed that she would be Captain and Trevor would have to be Sailing Master. Needless to say no one expected me to be anything but cook/crew/and chief bottle washer. In fact I was quite happy in this role. The irony of the whole thing was that the authorities wanted an American Skipper but did mention the need to see any qualifications.

By now Trevor and I thought that we should untie the lines and disappear over the horizon before any more faxes arrived. So on a lovely sunny morning we signed out and sailed away. Sam christened us, we were to be the Bimbo Crew and Trevor was the Bimbos' Boss.

This trip was wonderful. It was a completely different experience sailing on a large yacht. We seemed so high out of the water and we certainly covered more miles each day. The crew was a delight and I think that the captain revelled in it. One day 'Boon' fell off a large wave causing Trevor to fall off the toilet seat appearing with blood pouring down his face. A male crew would have fallen about with laughter, but the Bimbo crew anxiously surrounded him, sitting him down, mopping his face and generally showing great concern.

Sam was efficient and anxious to gain more sailing miles to put in her log. Joanne continued as before and soaked up everything like a sponge. Sam had a slight bout of seasickness but that never stopped her. Joanne seemed surprised when Trevor asked her if she felt OK. She was a natural born sailor but there was only one problem, her Barbadian husband could not swim and disliked the sea. It was obvious that she intended to enjoy every minute of this trip, as it probably wouldn't be repeated. In fact the time flew. There was never a cross word and the watch keeping seemed so easy. We sailed outside the Bahama Islands and saw little traffic. The owner had brought us a chart of the canals around his house in Fort Lauderdale and as this boat drew seven feet, we had just a limited time at high tide when we could safely arrive at his dock.

As we got nearer to the Florida Straits a Northerly was forecast and the winds were promised to be quite high. Now with a Northerly in the Straits it is wise to wait for a change, so Trevor decided to put into a small Marina in Grand Bahama Island. We made our approach and through an incredibly narrow inlet, we inched our way. Thankfully this opened up into the Marina and seeing an empty slip, the Skipper together with his eager crew, had Carpathia alongside and tied up as if we'd been doing this for years. We all sat back beaming and our neighbour confirmed that the space was not reserved. Of course this is sailing and nothing is ever as easy as it looks. Within five minutes officials told us that we had to move across the water to another dock and there present the papers. Never mind we could handle anything. We did just that and when the same official eventually came back Joanne took the papers from Trevor's hand and smiling sweetly at him, conducted the whole thing as if she had been doing it all her life. After all she was the Captain. No problems and then back to the slip, but of course the wind had come up by then and the whole exercise was much more difficult. We certainly didn't look as slick as before.

We all took a walk and while buying fresh fruit Sam spotted a flyer announcing a disco that evening. She found out that it was in the nearby town but there were no buses to get her there. Never mind she would safely walk there and back. We had supper and Sam went to shower and change, coming back looking like a million dollars. We didn't know that she had that little black dress in her backpack. In fact even in her bikini we hadn't seen quite so much exposure. Whow! Trevor began to worry. How was she to get there, let alone back again? Would she be safe? Joanne and I hastily frowned at him; after all she was in her mid-twenties and had been travelling around the world for the last three years. We watched her leave the boat, stooping to pick up a small rock that she held up for us to see and then put it in her pocket. The rest of us pretended to spend the evening sedately sipping wine and reading, really we were all worrying about our youngest crewmember. We finally retired for the night but heard nothing and when we arose next morning there was Sam blissfully asleep with her earphones still around her ears.

That day the forecast was good and trying to get our arrival time to coincide with the high tide in Fort Lauderdale (of course an impossible task), it was decided to leave at about 5pm. This we did and eventually arrived at the Florida Straits with no problems. We kept to our normal watch-keeping schedule and there was enough wind to sail. In the middle of the night Trevor was on watch with a decreasing wind so decided to turn the engine on and motor sail. He did this, only to find that the gear lever would not go ahead or astern. So he turned the engine off and let the light winds slowly take us. I came to take over my watch but there was no rest period for Trevor as he tried to sort out the problem. First of all he had to get to the gearbox but as it was so difficult, he decided to try the top end first. This entailed removing the compass. By now Joanne had woken up and needless to say had to get into the act, as this was something new to learn. Trevor found nothing wrong at that end so we had to excavate further. To do this he found that he had to remove the full sized washing machine. Remember all this was in the middle of the Straits and at night. Once underneath the gearbox he found that the gear change cable had snapped. As we had no spare it was decision time. We certainly would need to change gear as we approached the entrance to Fort Lauderdale, negotiate the bridge and navigate the little waterways.

Trevor needed to think and also pay a visit to the heads; squeezing past the washing machine which now stood in a gangway and moving the piece of wood that it had rested on, he disappeared into the master bathroom. Joanne and I sat together in the cockpit sailing very slowly towards the land. I think that this was the first time that I saw Joanne concerned. I reassured her that Trevor always came up with a solution. From the look on her face I don't think that she had my faith.

Time passed but Trevor did not return. More time passed, so I went to see if he was OK. As I got nearer the bedroom I could hear frantic banging. Immediately I could see the problem. The piece of wood from the washing machine had fallen in front of the cabin door and wedged under the handle. No way was he going to get out. He must have been trapped there for a very long time. Much disgruntled he hurtled out amazed that none of us had heard him. Anyway a decision had been reached. When we needed to change gear one of us would go below, squeeze into the space and manually operate the gears. When we were in the waterways the lucky one would stay there and Trevor would have a stamping code. One for ahead, two for astern and three for neutral. The engine was turned on and the gear manually put ahead and off we went to finish the crossing.

At daylight we were near the Florida coast; this area is well buoyed, as it is very shallow in places. Over breakfast there was a smug air of achievement as we were nearly there. We in turn smartened ourselves up and made sure the boat was tidy, after all we were about to turn her over to her rightful owners.

Approaching the entrance we could see what looked like hundreds of boats; of course we had forgotten that it was a Sunday! Lottery time, who should go below to become a human gear change lever? Joanne lost.

Down she went, muttering to herself. "One ahead, two astern, three is neutral."

With VHF on, we approached the cluster of waiting boats, we joined them and could see the bridge, and unfortunately it was one that had to be manually opened. Never mind it was nearly opening time, sounds like a pub! With so many boats surrounding us Trevor had to manoeuvre, so it was stamping time. At last we could see the bridge begin to open but the rule is outgoing craft first. So more stamps. In fact it sounded as if we were moving to the sound of drumbeats. Last boat through, great, then the radio voice announced that everyone should wait for a towed barge to depart. More juggling for position and now a regular drum beat. At last we were off and through.

We motored on and called the owners on the VHF. Wonderfully there was an immediate reply. Trevor explained the position, and was told that if he preferred there was a space in a nearby marina. Trevor looked at the time and decided that we would continue. We could just make the high tide and the gear changing seemed to be working. Off we went. We followed the little waterways, passing the most beautiful houses, and the time seemed to be slipping away too quickly. Would we make it? At last the final turning. We slowly continued, looking for a sign to indicate which was our dock. We saw it by the smiling faces of our owners and the boat made the dock. Later Trevor admitted that we actually slid across the mud for the last few meters. Joanne came up from below, cool and efficient. We introduced the Captain to the Owners and there were smiles and handshakes all round. WE HAD ARRIVED.

We all visited the Customs and Immigration Offices in town and became official, returned, had a celebratory drink and made plans. Joanne 'phoned her sister-in-law and was whisked away. Sam decided to try and get another crewing position and we were delighted when Michael suggested that we stay on 'Carpathia' while operation boat search was conducted.

This was the beginning of our discovery as to how generous and hospitable Americans are. Trevor accepted on our behalf but insisted that he repaired the gear change lever and a few other tasks, so honour was satisfied. In no time at all Sam had found her next crewing job and we actually met the skipper, Trevor, not only gave Sam a good reference but he was relieved to find that he liked the Bimbo's new Boss. As they all disappeared into the distance we suddenly realized that we were once more on our own.

I fell in love with America. As a child growing up in the Second World War, I had been fed on a diet of American movies. In the absence of our fathers, like many others I had fallen in love with the American servicemen. And do not let us forget the wonders of chewing gum. We all used to chorus, "Have you got any gum chum?" as we followed these sweet smelling, generous men. I loved shopping in Fort Lauderdale and was amazed at the size of the Super Markets never believing that they opened twenty-four hours a day. The range of checkout packers was startling. During the day they were senior citizens and in the evenings they were students, then again at night they were often mums and dads taking a second job.

I was surprised at the concept of breakfasting in a restaurant. At that time in my country everyone ate the first meal of the day at home. The bread was too sweet and the fruit, although beautifully clean and wholesome, was far too hard. It never seemed to ripen. But who am I to complain, this was a shopper's dream.

Trevor was not at all amused when visiting a Men's Boutique, to be leapt on by a very gay young man, who waxed lyrical about the cleverly faded look of Trev's shorts. As he clutched Trevor's leg, my man fled in horror and I chuckled to myself as these were a very handed down, washed out pair, from the hurricane gifts. Could we start a fashion? Enough of this, we had more serious shopping to do. Buying a boat. Acting on advice we collected the free boating newspapers and under the 'for sales' marked the boats in our price range. With a bag full of quarters we headed for the public 'phones. The first two were broken, the next was covered with something unmentionable sticky but the fourth seemed OK. We dialled. No reply. We tried another number, the answer was in Spanish and we made no progress. The next had a recorded message telling us that the cell phone was out of range. This continued for what seemed an eternity. The prospective boat buyer/type husband got so frustrated he nearly tore the 'phone from the wall. Any American listening would have known that the image of a Brit, as a perfect gentleman, was completely false and my husband was nearly starting a new fashion in 'phone rage.

We decided to visit Yacht Brokers where we would explain our situation. We were serious buyers not tyre kickers, we had limited funds and did not want to exceed $35,000 US. We wanted a sailboat suitable for ocean sailing. The size thirty-six to forty feet. Reasonable condition and age not important. Over the next few days, in between working on "Carpathia", we were shown a variety of boats. Most of them were never meant to go to sea. We appreciated by the very flimsy rigging that a lot were intended for Inter-Coastal cruising only. Some were downright dangerous. Many broke our hearts as the owners were selling because a crisis had arisen; partners with cancer, someone dying or dreams gone awry. We tried several different local Brokers and were beginning to feel very despondent.

In the meantime our hosts were delightful. Occasionally they wined and dined us. They would put on a video for our delight and one weekend we all went sailing together. But it all came back to one thing; we could not find a boat.

One Sunday we visited a SSCA Meeting (Seven Seas Cruising Association). It was a very enjoyable morning and we met some old friends and made many new ones. This left us with a free Sunday afternoon. As we were actually in a Marina we decided to check out the Yacht Brokers. Sadly they all seemed to be closed. We never actually worked this out as we felt that the working population would be free on Sundays and an ideal time for business, anyway we did finally find one open. Looking at the window display I realized that this was for luxury motorboats and motor sailing boats, nothing seeming to be less than sixty feet in length. But too late, the enthusiastic soon to be/Captain again, was inside. Remember that we still had not replaced our wardrobe.

Once inside it was opulent with a deep pile carpet, luxurious armchairs and a wide mouthed, smiling, Californian type receptionist. Once again Trevor listed his requirements and I waited for the sky to fall. But no, she buzzed for the Broker and soon we were in his even bigger office sipping coffee. No paper cups here but bone china. I sunk further into my chair with embarrassment. Very seriously he listened to Trevor and then gently said, "We do not usually have boats of that type or price, we cater for a different market." There was a terrible silence, and I did not know what to say. Then he jumped up saying, "Wait you guys, I might just have something." After searching through his files he explained that they were in the process of selling a large motor yacht to a client who had a small sailing yacht to sell as part of the deal. He did not actually have the details of the yacht but would 'phone the owner. No sooner said than done. He gave us the specifications. Hughes 38', fibreglass, designed by Olin Stephens in 1969, professionally built in Canada and priced at $38,000. The Broker checked this price in his guidebook and told us it was within the correct price range, although high, but if in good condition, a fair price. It was not on his list but he would phone the owner again if we wished to see it. We did, and he did.

In no time at all we were driving to Coral Gables. I will not prolong this but we saw the boat, in immaculate condition, well built and suitable for serious sailing and told the owner we would phone him the next day and if interested, could we have a trial sail? The answer was yes. We decided to have the sail and everything went well. The owner was American but his absent wife was English and in fact an airline pilot.

There followed a great sail, the weather was perfect and we all had a good time. When we got back to his apartment we made an offer, subject to a survey. A week later we were back on the boat together with a Surveyor, the owner and this time the Airline Pilot Wife. We meandered along waterways to the Boat Yard where the boat was lifted out and the Surveyor did his stuff and generally a good time was had by all.

We sailed back; the Surveyor departed telling us that he would fax his report the next day but he felt that all was well and to quote him "he would sleep well at night if we bought the boat." The next day the survey arrived, was OK and only showed a few small defects. A deposit was paid and arrangements made for the electronic transfer of our money.

A week later we moved on board the new 'Boon' and slipped away from the dock towards an anchorage in Miami. We owned a boat once more. We had thought long and hard about her name. She had been called 'Lowdown' but the owner who was called Jim Lowe wanted to keep the name for himself! We were not sorry – apologies Jim. We thought about 'Boon Again' or 'Boon Too'. Then common sense prevailed; sadly the first 'Boon' was no more, so why not use the same name? So sailing into Sunset Harbour off Miami Beach, the two of us raised cans of beer and drank to her baptism. While Trevor steered his way I disappeared below and there discovered a fund of goodies left for us. Having heard our hurricane tale, they had provided towels, sheets, sweaters; in fact they seemed to have provided two of everything, including lots of Air Line packs of earplugs, tooth brushes, tooth paste, soap, eye-shades, etc. It was just like an early Christmas.

CHAPTER TWENTY-THREE
AM I REALLY LIVING IN DOWNTOWN MIAMI?

We soon packed all these goodies away and began to make this boat our new home. Trevor was anxious to check everything thoroughly and I guess I was as keen to personalize our new lady. This 'Boon' had a very old fashioned layout below. Remember she was designed in 1969 and was originally a racing boat, so although the longest boat we had ever owned she was very narrow. Converted to a cruiser she had an enormous icebox beneath the companionway steps. Both sides and going back underneath the large cockpit were two berths. These are called pilot berths. Going forward again on the left of the steps, was the chart table and seat and to the right a stowage for such things as lifejackets, safety lines and wet weather clothes. A seat and a small fitting with two drawers and a top, then a half bulkhead and the galley ran beyond that the length of the main salon.

On the other side, was the seating area with table. This could fold down at night and provide a double berth. You continued and on the right were the heads with wash basin and shower and opposite a hanging wardrobe and six deep drawers. Then through a door to the double sleeping berth with a king sized bed, which filled the whole area. Needless to say there were numerous lockers, shelves, etc. and I guess these would soon be full. The engine was in the middle of the main salon and as it was higher than the floor, it had a well-varnished cover. Needless to say we constantly fell over this during our early weeks.
Actually it was not the best layout but the strength and lovely lines of a Hughes 38, over rode this.

First came a great shopping spree, and what better place to play shops, than in this wonderful retail paradise. We visited Home Depot and could not believe our eyes, as we looked open-mouthed at stack upon stack of tools. Trevor bought very wisely and replaced tools, amazed at their range and prices. I was puzzled to see both cash desks and the return desks almost equal in number. We visited more enormous stores and were tempted to shop till we dropped but I am glad to say that we didn't go mad. Next Trevor ordered a wind generator and we bought a Ham/Single Side Band Radio and so it continued. As usual everything we bought seemed to be for 'Boon'.

Anchored in the Bay overlooking Miami, Trevor began the job of checking our new home. Fairly soon he was up the mast inspecting fittings and rigging. Then out came his knife and I saw him investigating the spreaders. These protrude either side of the mast, nearly at the top. When he came down he announced that they were made of wood and not aluminium as he had thought, AND they were rotten, his knife had gone right through. I am sure that the previous owner had not known this but it was something that we wanted to rectify pretty quickly.

So now began a period of hard work. Buying wood and sawing and planing, this was all done in the cockpit so I am sure you can imagine what a mess it was. We checked the boat systems and followed which wire went where and also where all the pipes ran. At the same time I decided to use the oven and not just the gas rings on top of my cooker. I found that the oven would not light. Apart from that everything else seemed OK.

We installed our brand new wind generator and after two weeks this overheated and I awoke to the strong smell of electrical smouldering. After many frustrating 'phone calls this was replaced by the Manufacturers. For the next two weeks we held our breath but everything else seemed to be OK. Of course we still had not found the parts for the oven, and I was still cooking on the two gas rings. I always seem to draw the short straw.

Of course it was not all hard work as we had lots of fun times as well. We discovered Lincoln Road, which was a pedestrian stretch, lined with the most fabulous shops. There were art galleries, cafes, boutiques, a theatre and a dance studio where one could stand and watch the rehearsals through the huge windows. There was a Departmental Store, which shall be nameless, but it provided a discount for senior citizens one day a week. We found a Dollar Store and more besides. The street itself was fun and we watched the rollerbladers in amazement, such skill and dexterity. I even saw Grannies roller-blading with their shopping and once I followed a young mother pushing her baby in the buggy while flashing along on roller blades, hardly changing pace as she bent down and retrieved the discarded toys.

Most of the women here looked very elegant or crazily dressed, it was great fun. I needed to change my image. Of course I found the answer; there was a Charity Shop on another street and this one was run by gays. It was like entering an Aladdin's cave of glitz and glamour. I had some wonderful times there and completely renewed my tiny wardrobe and even managed to get Trevor into a very chic pair of pink shorts. The customers were fun too, lots of very camp people and one or two cross dressers. They loved helping me choose my new clothes and I'm sure that some of my more adventurous buys came from them but I didn't regret any. There were no children's clothes here and of course this was not surprising, as it was before the time when it was the norm for gays to have kids. I did however, find one very lost looking teddy bear at the back of the shop, his cross eyes watching me and seeming to cry out for love. How could I resist? He joined us on 'Boon' and as I write this in England, he is sitting in state on top of my wardrobe, loftily viewing us in our new land based lifestyle. Now he is accompanied by Rupert Bear, Winnie the Pooh, Sooty and Paddington and even more, in fact a most motley collection of bears, all purchased of course from Charity Shops. But he is King, after all he is a much travelled, sailing bear with many a salty tale to tell.

But back to then; time went on and we had Christmas in Miami, eating our Christmas dinner with a friend at the 11th Street Diner. We registered our boat with her new name, made a lot of new friends and continued discovering what an incredibly friendly place America is. I felt like Maria and wanted to sing, "I want to be in America." We took 'Boon' sailing and found that the autopilot was failing so with a deep financial sigh, bought a new one. What a king among autopilots. But being the boring people that we are, we christened it, guess what? Yes, Fred.

Reading my diary I discovered that on our Wedding Anniversary, 28th December, we'd been invited to an evening party. That morning we shopped, for "Boon" of course, and returned to the boat for lunch. Far too many bagels, cheese and muffins. So we both turned up our toes and went to bed. No, not to sexually celebrate nineteen years of marriage but to escape from the drizzle and the cold and to sleep. This city living is tiring. That evening we had a wonderful time partying with our newfound friends and as she was originally from Liverpool, the menu included such British delicacies as Pork Pies and Penguin bars. What a treat.

The New Year arrived and with it some incredibly cold weather and we awoke one morning to a very cold and frosty deck.. The sort of day to remind me why we'd left the UK in the first place. This was not what I expected of Florida. We went into town to try to replace the secret inner workings of my cooker. We nearly made it, but $33 poorer and with still one more fitting to get, we ran all the way home to keep warm. On January 1st 1996 we decided that we would change some of our old habits. We would try and imitate 'Boon's' previous owner and behave like Neat Freaks and we would also take more care of our aging bodies. Over the sailing years we had gradually changed our eating habits. We had enjoyed more and more vegetarian type meals, eaten mountains of fresh fruit and now in this land of plenty we could make sure that we were taking enough vitamins, herbs and minerals.

We continued working on the boat, shopping for charts, grease guns, funnels, and a load of boring things. We went for short sails testing our new equipment and so it continued until we almost forgot that we should be seriously sailing. So with 'Boon' proudly boasting her new goodies and we both, feeling hype with all this magical mixture cursing through our blood, decided that we should start 'proper' sailing again. Of course there were still a million and one things to do and see, so we allowed ourselves just one more week to play. We certainly packed a lot into those seven days. From an Art exhibition in the Miami Convention Centre, to an Art Deco Street Parade like no other that I had seen. More shopping, cockpit cocktail hours and lots of good-byes and 'please come back again'.

Finally we visited Immigration to sign out of our favourite country. We were greeted by the Officer who within seconds told us he was a Psychic Healer. Paperwork was completed in minutes and we eventually managed to get away, not only with our stamped papers, but with a lucky snowflake stone each. This would surely give us power, energy and luck, and also information on Super Blue Green Algae. According to Frank this is cell technology and is the world's richest natural whole food product. Dazed, we left deciding to stick to our own diet and a few vitamins.

The next day, 14th February, was St. Valentine's Day and we planned to sail to the Bahamas. So that evening, as we had been too occupied with preparations and talk of green algae, to buy each other a card, we wrote secret St Valentine letters to be read while we sailed. We'd been through so much together in this sailing life; a shop bought card certainly did not do it justice.

14th February 1996

My darling Trevor,

It should be a dozen red roses, an intimate dinner for two or even heart-covered underpants. Lordy, lordy that would not be us!

As I write this we have been round and round in circles trying to get everything done. At last we seem to have got it all completed or near enough. So I guess ' near enough' sums us up. Never quite enough money and never quite made it to the top, but to quote your favourite phrase "but near enough". So happy St Valentine's Day. Many more of them – all in the sun and on 'Boon', I hope.

For me, you are quite the best, so let's keep having adventures and chase the fun and the sun. May we never grow old, dull, inactive or boring? Sex rules OK and I love you very much.

I like the way that you do my sort of thing, appreciate my cooking and my boat keeping and yes, darling, I do want to be your valentine. I like the way Joyce on "Mood Indigo" at concert, introduces her husband. I will steal some of her words and add some of my own. This is Trevor, he sails the boat, he repairs the boat, he's fun, he's sexy and HE'S MINE.

I LOVE YOU. Ley

Trevor's letter to me is still a secret!

CHAPTER TWENTY-FOUR
HERE WE GO, SAILING AGAIN

It was a beautiful clear morning as we sailed into the open sea and began to discover the joy of sailing this 'Boon'. She would move in very light winds and with her longer water line she travelled quickly and lo and behold she would perform beautifully when going to windward. Once more we crossed the Florida Straits and gently made our way to Grand Bahama Island, where we visited the Marina we had used on "Capathia". We really wanted to show off our new toy especially to the couple we had earlier met there.

As we gently rocked to sleep, safely tied to the dock, I prayed that we would have no more adventures and that this boat would outlive both of us. I thought back to when we first saw her and how beautifully she had been maintained. Could we live up to this standard? I chuckled when I remembered how after washing the decks, the owner had laid two mop heads on the deck, and while we stepped on each, he'd made a path with them for us to walk on, without dirtying this pristine surface. No way could we live like that but we would do our best to give her lots of tender love and care and in return hoped that she would look after us.

We spent our day in the Marina and then sailed away knowing that there would be no more Marinas for us in future, we'd spent far too much and our funds were shrinking fast. We were heading for a reunion in Nassau where we had Canadian friends from the old Turkish days. We anchored in the Bay and soon became entrapped in the delights of this town. We met up with our friends and of course never stopped talking; we explored by car and visited the most fantastic aquarium linked to the sea by a transparent tunnel. This was attached to a palatial Hotel and for a morning we saw how the other sort of tourist lives. How grand and extravagant and from then, if I wanted to emphasise that sort of lifestyle, I always called them the "beautiful people". I am sure that most women will know what I mean. These people have matching luggage, but never seemed bowed down under its weight. They arrive in just the right outfit that is never crumpled and of course their hair always looks freshly cut and shampooed. People seem to make way for them and of course the taxi always pulls up on cue. Needless to say I'm always waiting for a bus. My secret dream (don't tell Trevor) is to join the 'beautiful people'.

In the evening in contrast, we'd sit in our cockpit and watch the Haitian work boats passing on their way back to Haiti. These were wooden with very little, if any accommodation. Their gaff sails were often patched with old sugar sacks and each has an enormous tiller for steerage. We were told that they had neither engines nor instruments and must have relied on years of experience in these seas. They plied their goods between the Bahamas and Haiti, skimming the sandbanks and passing through the reefs. One evening we watched one leaving Nassau with no lights and tacking into a strong head wind. They needed to pass under the narrow arches of the Bridge and the helmsman swung onto the gigantic tiller as he eased his craft into the right position to make his passage through the very small entrance. Of course he made it and we felt privileged to watch such seamanship.

We made lots of new friends and for me it is always difficult to pull away from a happy anchorage and start sailing again. This time I had very little choice as a very strong storm was forecast and this anchorage did not have the best holding. Also we did not fancy being in such close quarters with so many other boats. Where should we go? After discussion with knowledgeable neighbours it was decided to make for Royal Island. This was a tiny, deserted island that almost curled around a well-protected bay. Once safely through the narrow entrance one could pick up a buoy and wait for trouble to pass. Sounded good and the next morning four of us left to do just that.

In fact we were the last of the four to leave and we had a magical sail, in fact catching up and overtaking our friends. Let us hope that they were still talking to us when we arrived. Being the worrying kind I hoped that there would still be empty buoys upon arrival. There were plenty and we each chose one and were soon tied on. One of our newly found friends invited us all over for tea and showed us that he had used his video during part of the sail, and there in glorious technicolour we saw 'Boon' doing her stuff. You have to remember that when you own a boat you never see her sailing performance. We sat back like proud parents at the school concert.

The storm was still heading our way but did not seem in a hurry, so we went ashore. We explored and found that at one time the island had been occupied as there were a few shells of houses and what looked

188

like the remains of a large plantation without buildings, also some paved streets. We followed a track to the other side of the island and looked out to sea. We tried to guess as to the life style of those who had lived here. Upon our return we found that our path was blocked by a seriously angry snake. This was his walkway and no way were we allowed to use it. Trevor tried every persuasion, sticks, stones, shouting and stamping. He would not budge. We stood there looking like idiots, this was worse than the threat of a storm. We couldn't run either side of him, as his speedy reactions had been fierce and ferocious. What to do? We weren't familiar with the behaviour of snakes. Then unexpectedly, having made his stand, he slithered, silently into the undergrowth and was gone. So were we, at the rate of knots.

The next day the buoys were full and boats were also anchored. A local fishing boat arrived and took our money for the use of the buoys, giving us each a freshly baked loaf. We had the choice of regular bread or johnnycake. Johnnycake was the locally preferred bread and of course we had to try it. It seemed to me to be more like Madeira cake and was definitely not to my taste. In all these islands the locals seem to have a desire for sweetness and this is reflected in all their dishes. No wonder the rate of diabetes is high.

Eventually the storm arrived and we violently swung on our buoy, regularly checking our ropes for chaffing. After about twelve hours it departed but quite a strong wind remained for the remainder of the week. We heard from the VHF that during the height of the storm, one man had been blown off a bridge and died and everywhere damage had been done. There also followed a period when the entrances to many Bays and Harbours were unusable. Once everything settled down, we ventured outside again and began exploring these beautiful islands. Our new lady drew six and a half feet so we had to be very careful while we sailed over the sandbanks and through the reefs. A pattern began so that in these conditions one would steer while the other would lean over the bow, closely checking for any obstacles, and hand signals would indicate any rapid change of direction.

I think that I was surprised with the Bahamas. I always imagined these islands to be very grand and sophisticated. In fact they were truly beautiful but extremely primitive. The swimming and underwater sports were perfect but if this was not your forte, it left little else. Anyway I enjoyed it and as the purpose was to test 'Boon', it was going very well. We made a few stops and finally decided to do a night sail to George Town on Great Exuma Island. Reading our pilot book it appeared to be very popular with cruisers. It was a perfect night and we had the right amount of wind and in the right direction. Things were improving; perhaps we had had our share of things going wrong.

In the middle of the night while Trevor was on watch, the engine overheated. He woke me up and while I sat in the cockpit on watch, we sailed along while down below he began the investigation. What had happened was that the overheating alarm had sounded and being a little deaf, and the alarm having a very high tone, he had not heard it over the noise of the engine. He delved into the depths of the beast and ended up taking it apart at sea and found the problem could only solved on land with a new exhaust manifold. No more motoring for us.

Of course as we continued, Murphy arrived and the wind began to drop and drop and as we approached George Town what little wind there was, was right on the nose. So began long laborious tacking. We checked into the morning net and were advised by David Jones the Caribbean Weather Forecaster, not to attempt the George Town entrance under sail. Of course all this happened on a Sunday morning and as we reached the entrance, we called George Town on the VHF. We were offered a tow and questioning the price were told that it would be very reasonable. What else could we do but accept? Eventually we were towed in and would certainly agree that the entrance was very tricky. Finally the towboat ran us aground so were left on our own and there we had to sit until the tide lifted us again. Then like magic the pilot arrived and placed us in our final resting-place. Smiling he told us the fee. $350 US. We were aghast and Trevor began the long process of haggling. Our rescuer did not budge. It was Sunday, double time, he'd used fuel; he'd come back at high tide to finish the job. No mention of the fact that he'd ran us aground in the first place. We got nowhere, so we paid up and looked big. Oh boy, sailing is like a game of snakes and ladders. Up the ladders and down the snakes. This was definitely a snake and a sizeable one too.

CHAPTER TWENTY-FIVE
MURPHY GETS IN ON THE ACT

So life began in George Town. Trevor was absorbed in the engine repair, so I explored the town. All one street of it. Once again it was really a very primitive small village but the difference being that hundreds of boats were anchored in this gorgeous bay. This, of course, influenced the situation ashore. It enabled it to have a Tourist Office, a Library (courtesy of the Cruisers themselves) a large well-stocked expensive supermarket and a few bars and tiny shops and a tremendous number of social activities, including afternoon volley ball. And let us not forget the regular Scrape and Rake, or was it Rake and Scrape music sessions? (You will have to visit the Bahamas to find the answer to this one.)

Endeavouring to save money Trevor spent three days trying to fix the fault himself and then decided that we had to bite the bullet and order a new exhaust manifold from the States. So as we awaited the arrival of this, we got heavily involved in all the activities. With so many cruisers here there was plenty to do and we had a great time. Eventually the spare part arrived and we discovered that we had been charged for freight twice and because of the supplier's error, we had to pay excess duty. There were many more expensive 'phone calls before this was sorted out. Now with the advent of e-mail, these problems can cheaply and easily be put right. Not so then. After the long wait the weather was quite wrong to leave, so we continued to enjoy being proper cruisers; we swam, explored sights, entertained and were entertained, got involved with regattas and concerts and read, read and read using the wonderful library. It was a joy to watch the Saturday session when the local children all arrived for story time. The cruisers had provided a fully stocked section just for them. Most of these cruisers were American and many of them spent six months of their lives anchored in George Town and only left when the hurricane season approached. One American cruiser had watched with pleasure as the local kids chose their library books. Her parting gift was a beautifully hand painted bookmark for each child. Not only that, she'd obtained a list of their names and each was personally labelled. She left some blank ones just in case new readers arrived. I must admit that Americans en masse are often overpowering and noisy but I can forgive them everything, as they are the most generous people that I have ever met.

At last the weather was right to move on and as we motored across the bay, the oil silently dropped out of our compass and we were left with a little card flapping around with no nice big bold numbers to tell us where we were. Was there no end to it? Trevor's attitude was one of 'OK, we have a GPS', mine was 'did we really want to rely on a piece of electronic equipment especially with our current record of failures'? So anchoring once again we faxed a supplier and watched our Bank balance drop even lower. As I wrote the fax I noticed that it was April 1st – April fool's Day. Oh well let's choose another library book and start playing volleyball again.

We waited, the weather was good, we waited even longer but no compass arrived. We waited some more. Another expensive phone call only to discover that I, yes folks it was my fault, had given them the wrong visa number. The weather was perfect as we waited again for the compass. It arrived and within seconds installed, and then we had to wait for some very high winds to pass. Finally everything seemed OK and we made the very tricky exit through the rocks. Thank goodness for the waypoints on the GPS. At last we were on our way to Rhum Cay.

Rhum Cay was not to be, as once outside we found high winds and a very strong current coming from the direction we wanted to make. We tried and Trevor being rather determined, tried some more. I think that the fact that I'd won on the matter of a new compass meant that he was going to win this one. In fact with the strong current we ended up going back rather than forward. So finally he decided to abort that trip and make for Conception Island. The minute we turned around and changed course the whole sailing world changed in our favour. We could sail and soon seemed to be skimming over flat seas where before we were bouncing up and down and getting nowhere. It was truly a delightful sail. You must realize that we do in fact have a lot of these, but they do not make such interesting reading. It is as they say, and I apologize for repeating it, 'good news is not news, but bad news is headlines'. I do not know who said that, but I wish that I had thought of it.

We arrived at Conception Island and found a beautiful but deserted paradise. This island is a nature reserve and uninhabited. We edged our way through the coral heads and anchored. There was one other boat anchored and during the day several others arrived. In fact we numbered six. We spent an idyllic period here, exploring, swimming, snorkelling and of course socializing. We could join up with the others or just wander across the island on our own, with or without clothes. We were all heading for Trinidad to get below the hurricane belt. By now it was the beginning of May and the Hurricane Season begins on June 1st. The wind was not in our favour but as the Pundits calculated, in this part of the world, 70% of the time the wind blows from the East, so as soon as the weather window arrives sailors must grab it. On day six the window opened and we all climbed out of it and set sail for San Salvador. Another beautiful sail and thirty-seven miles later we dropped our hooks.

San Salvador was a tiny town but fun and while there I used it as an opportunity to get my blood pressure checked and stock up with the appropriate pills. In the Doctor's waiting room I studied all the posters. How entertaining they were and designed to read like a comic strip. Very user friendly and in fact, on the Doctor's door was a sign which read, 'smile 'cos the Doctor loves you.' My turn, and through the door I went, smiling of course. He smiled back. He was wearing a bright tropical shirt, shorts and a Club Med cap. Blood pressure taken and pills provided I was on my way again AND it had hardly dented my pocket. Days passed and still no change in the weather. You must realize that the problem is the tremendous current here and with this prevailing easterly wind, anything above 15 – 18 knots makes progress, on our boat anyway, very difficult. Boats with big engines just plod through it. Of course we could tack but it was a long way to Trinidad and after all we were there to enjoy ourselves.

CHAPTER TWENTY-SIX
I LOVE TO BE IN AMERICA

Trevor set a cut off date of 14th May and if there was no change, we would turn around and spend the next six months in the USA. We would much rather take our chance with a hurricane in a first world country than the third world. The 14th came and went, and so did we, towards our friendly US of A. We had wind on the quarter but a big bumpy sea, but we made one-hundred and thirty miles in the first twenty-four hours and were well pleased. We left behind some good friends and I calculated that at San Salvador we were a group of boats from S Africa, Australia, Canada, Britain, Switzerland, Texas and Virginia. Quite an international gathering.

The seas went down and we had good sailing, and then we were motor sailing and finally there was no wind at all. Motoring in the middle of the Florida Straits we had the most tremendous thunderstorm. Lightening seemed to strike down on either side of the boat and the crack of the lightening hitting the sea was unbelievable. We seemed to be the only boat out there and we wondered if there was something that we did not know. The thunder roared, the lightning flashed and it stayed with us for a couple of hours. Later we discovered that America has dramatic thunderstorms but nobody had told us about them.

This time we made for Palm Beach and finding a good anchorage fell fast asleep. When we awoke it was late afternoon and too late to sign in. Next day we did just that, with our American Visa we had nothing to pay, we filled up with water and moved on to another anchorage on Lake Worth. There we found several boats and a dinghy ride away, a huge supermarket and a shopping mall with all those American delights that we had learned to love.

We planned to explore the States via the Intracoastal Waterway and at some point stop and once again, replace a few of "Boon's" bits and pieces and it was agreed that we would have a new cooker. Would you believe that I was still cooking on just two rings?

So we did just that. We had bought charts as far as New York and a book showing the various anchorages along the way and soon were covering thirty to forty miles a day. One can only travel during the hours of daylight and unfortunately because of the narrow, winding trail, it has to be done by engine and not sail. The waterway winds between very well marked buoys and as long as you keep well inside, you should not go aground. Not quite as easy as it sounds as winds, tides and current sometimes change things. Anyway the bottom seems to be soft mud or sand and little damage is done. Towboats roam up and down these waterways and seem to make a very good living, so it is no shame to get stuck. We usually managed to find an anchorage for the night, but of course this must be outside the buoys.

It wasn't all travelling; we stopped when and where the fancy took us. We explored little towns, shopped and once again were made very welcome. The Americans seemed to love our English accents but they were often aghast that we had actually walked a short distance to a supermarket and even carried our own shopping. In fact trying to cross some

197

of the busy roads, I was sure that we were the only people on foot.

We had a wonderful visit to the Kennedy Space Centre and were open-mouthed in amazement at all the technology, films, and exhibits. Everyone who worked there was so knowledgeable and it was the waitress at the café who told us to look out that evening, as a TV satellite was to be launched. We did just that and from the bow of our boat with rum and cokes in hand, saw the incredible sight. Trevor decided there and then that when he grew up he would be an astronaut. From there, anchoring en route, we travelled to St Augustine. We were beginning to find a 6ft 6in draught something of a liability in this waterway.

At St Augustine we lifted out and did the following –
Checked all skin fittings and replaced two seacocks'
Installed new log and depth sounder
Fitted zincs (anodes)
Removed all varnish from toe rail and repainted
Made a mahogany board for the new instruments
Made and varnished two new hand holds
Anti fouled and cleaned and polished the hull
And removed the damaged trim tab, damage done
before we bought 'Boon'. Trevor cleverly filled the
gap and rebuilt the shape, watched by the
professionals who had wondered how he would cope
with the repair.
Brownie points for Trevor.
We did all this in just under four weeks and felt very
pleased with ourselves.

We also visited Pot Bellies Movie Theatre, which was a picture house unlike any other I have ever visited. It was small and intimate, with a tiny museum at the entrance; there were comfortable chairs with tables to hold your drinks and to top it all we saw 'The Bird Cage' with Robin Williams. Our reward to ourselves for all the hard work. Oh yes, I forgot to say that it cost so very little.

We continued, exploring as we went. We saw Jeckyl Island that was the playground of the rich and famous, circa 1903. This was absolutely gorgeous and we certainly saw how the beautiful people used to live in those days. But there is always a down side. Tropical Storm Arthur passed us by, but a little close for comfort and after over three hundred miles of this type of motoring, Trevor was not a happy sailor. 'Sailing' being the operative word. He wanted to turn the engine off and experience once again, the beautiful silence when the sails fill and the boat glides through the water. So we went outside into the real sea and had a glorious three hundred and forty mile sail. Surprisingly we saw very little traffic and quickly slid into our watch routine.

We came back inside again at Beaufort and had an unexpected but wonderful reunion with old friends last seen in Gibraltar. As I'm constantly saying, one of the joys of this life is turning the corner, anchoring, and then finding that a nearby boat belongs to old friends.

We continued, still exploring as we went, until we came to Great Bridge, which is nearby Norfolk. By now it was extremely hot and we both began to feel that we needed a break. We had been through a category four hurricane, lost everything that we possessed, delivered a boat and had worked extremely hard on the new one. After much thought and discussion we decided to throw financial caution to the wind, leave the boat in this secure place and fly home for a break. Our limited capital was certainly taking another dive. But everything was arranged, family informed and tickets booked when Hurricane Bertha struck. At Great Bridge we were OK but not so far away tremendous damage was done. Waiting for Bertha we watched the staff hard at work, actually working non-stop for thirty-six hours. They made sure that every boat left in their care was secure. Everything was removed or tied down, extra fenders were in place, dinghies deflated and only then they were satisfied.

Our visit home was a delight and the time flew. We saw all of our eight children and of course, the grandchildren. One had been a leggy, skinny little girl wearing glasses and sporting two pigtails three years before, but now before our eyes stood a beautiful blonde, confident in her new contact lenses and smiling broadly. There was to be a new arrival in the family and we felt him secure in his mother's nest and then out came the photo of him. Yes, these days with a scan, babies can be ooh'd over before they have seen the light of day. I found my mother in her new modern flat, safe under the watchful eye of a warden but still maintaining her own independence. She looked ten years younger. The visit did the trick; we came back refreshed and ready to continue.

We decided to complete 'Boon's' refit and presented her with the much-promised new cooker, a holding tank, radar and a wind direction finder. We did all this and for a while we lived high on the hog, while we ate all those things that can be cooked inside the oven - cakes, pies, crumbles, banana bread and, well you name it and I seemed to bake it.

Still at Great Bridge the owners of the boat nearby made the horrendous discovery that we did not possess a TV. An unbelievable fact to their American taste, so one morning they arrived, he carrying their spare TV and she walking behind holding an aerial aloft. This was to be on loan while we were there. That night we tuned in discovering that American TV was not to our liking. The adverts appear far too often and certainly far too long. There is built in artificial laughter with every situation comedy and altogether it was not our scene. Playing with the buttons Trevor suddenly found Public TV and soon we were engrossed in some extremely good programmes and our favourite was a drama/documentary on the West, from the days of wagon trains, to the railroads and the gold diggers. This was run over several evenings and we certainly learned a lot more about this interesting country. Americans, generally, seem humbled by the fact that they have no ancient history; watching this programme I feel that they have a recent history to be truly proud of.

Time to leave for the Chesapeake and return the TV of course. We said our good-byes and entered our first lock in the whole of the waterway. Safely through we began a very slow journey enjoying the motion of the boat again. I think Norfolk, Reedville, Annapolis and of course Washington were the highlights.

The Hurricane season was well and truly over, we were now out of the Intracoastal Waterway and managing to do some sailing. We spent some quality time in Annapolis, which I consider a cruisers' paradise. Sublime anchorages; with nearby street providing us with little dinghy docks, garbage containers and fresh water taps. We were astounded by the colours of their fall; our own autumn colours are very pretty but nothing as dramatic as these. We paid many visits to Washington appreciating the variety of the museums there. So much to see and to do. We had left it too late to visit New York and were shocked to find how cold it was getting. Most of the other boats were well on their way South. Once again we needed to chase the sun and began to plan our next cruise.

We decided to sail direct from Norfolk to Sint Maartens and then go South to Trinidad for the Carnival in February 1997. We stocked up with food, as we knew from experience that Caribbean prices were very high and of course in this shoppers' wonderland we could buy anything. We also laid up some bottles of Californian wine and champagne. We really wanted to spend Christmas in Sint Maartens, making sure that our friends were all OK and up and sailing again. The weather turned even colder and we had to buy gloves, hats, socks and warm sailing jackets and trousers. This seemed ridiculous, as once nearer the Caribbean, they would never see the light of day again. We probably would only wear them for a few days.

We began regularly to listen to Herb from Canada, giving his SSB radio weather information. This was daily, on a set frequency and time, and he would answer individual weather questions and give information on conditions and routes. Most sailing people in this area when travelling some distance, use Herb as their own personal weather guru. We checked in with our position and planned voyage to be told that conditions were not yet right. We knew that this was not the ideal time of year to make this trip, so needed to be well prepared when Herb said to "GO." In fact our American neighbours regularly told us that we shouldn't attempt this journey at this time of year. We checked our pilot books and it seemed OK and Herb seemed happy for us to make the trip. After all we had just been through the six months of the Hurricane season when the journey would have been impossible, and now there were local rumblings of concern. Finally we decided that it was the caution of the American cruisers with us at that time; after all they really only travelled the waterways and venturing as far as the Bahamas was a great adventure for them.

My time in the States had been wonderful and I do not think that I have done justice to the wonderfully changing scenery as we travelled. The dramatic thunder storms, the variety of bird life and the surprise of seeing a deer peeping at us through nearby foliage. The shock of our first alligator and snakes, then little turtles popping up in the water. The untidy osprey nests with young protruding from the marker buoys all along our route. Also our own personal blue heron at Great Bridge. I mustn't forget the huge manatees wallowing in the muddy waters, but it was time to move on.

CHAPTER TWENTY-SEVEN
A VERY BRITISH BERMUDA

The next afternoon Herb told us that the weather was right and to go for it, so we did just that. Of course deep down inside I felt the usual stirrings of concern, after all these years I still had anxieties over a long passage. So we left the safety of the waterways and ventured out into the open sea and were soon on our way. For a long time we had never felt so cold and listening on the VHF radio to our American friend Garry, who originated from Alaska, we realized that he knew the answer. Under his sailing jacket he had a hot water bottle tied to his back! He was making for Puerto Rico but we would be together out there for sometime before he made his turn.

About two hours out into the open sea, these two hardy cruisers got sick. Not heaving, spewing type sick, but queasy sick with terrible indigestion. We found that we could not eat and worse of all, we could not drink. It was a very uncomfortable situation and we'd never experienced anything like it before. Trevor managed to swallow a couple of sips of water and then his throat closed up and he could manage no more. I found that I could take a couple of sips of beer and then the same thing happened. In fact my can lasted twenty-four hours. Now 'Boon' just loved it and crashed along through big seas, sailing beautifully. So we just lay back, literally popping our heads up every ten minutes or so. We spoke daily to Herb and saw very little else. We spoke to Garry but although close, we never saw each other. Two days out we reported in once more to be told, as I remember it – 'A gale, no storm system, was coming, caused through a convergence of bad weather from Canada and Mexico and we should make for Bermuda. If we continued at the speeds we were reporting we should be alright.'

We spoke to Gary and he decided to make his turn earlier and hopefully miss the bad weather. We said our goodbyes; we had known Gary from our early days in the Med. He'd become a good friend. He was a single-handed sailor in more ways than one. He had lost half of his right hand in an earlier accident. He could do everything on a boat, including the elusive knots, as well as any two-handed sailor.

I think that 'Boon' felt that she was not getting enough attention from her sickly captain and crew, as the next morning she kicked off her boom. We could not believe our eyes, the main sail seemed to be holding the boom in place but we could see at the gooseneck that it had come unattached from the mast. We managed to remove the main sail and fold it into its sail bag, and lash the boom to the side of the deck. So much for keeping up the good speed. Never fear, with just the genoa 'Boon' continued to roar along averaging one-hundred and thirty miles each day. Of course we were still experiencing our weird symptoms, and by now were aghast at the colour of our pee. It was a case of mine is darker than yours, but we still couldn't manage to drink more than a few mouthfuls of water at a time.

Anyway we made Bermuda, just three hours before the storm struck. Bermuda is surrounded by a reef and we had to keep well off as we approached. So near and yet so far. Eventually, through a buoyed channel, we made the entrance and could see the tranquil water inside with the welcoming sight of the Customs Dock. We were greeted by immaculately uniformed Bermudans, very black, but with perfect Oxford accents. We signed in and were directed to a dock right in the town centre where we could repair our boom.

Some of the boats that came after us were in a very sorry state. Portholes stove in, hatches broken, one dismasted and one boat had had a man overboard. Fortunately he had been retrieved. We heard via the SSB radio that Gary had also suffered some damage, nearly losing his life raft but had eventually made a safe landfall.

Once in this tranquil harbour we discovered that we could drink once more and finding our appetites, we made for the nearby super market. We thought we would like some fresh fruit but as we entered we could smell roasting chickens. We traced this delicious odour and bought one, red hot from the spit. We raced back to the boat and without knives or forks began to tear it to pieces, savouring each mouthful.

Bermuda was a delight. Very clean and very pretty. We repaired the gooseneck, and once again the boom was secure. The other boats took longer as their damage was far greater. The bad weather continued outside, and we enjoyed the pleasures of this delightful little island. Just think if it had not been for the storm we would have sailed straight by. Actually we played tourists once again and watched the re-enactment of the nagging wife being ducked in the ducking stool. I believe it was not for actually nagging, but talking too much. Sobering thoughts for me, as according to Trevor, I'm 'verbally hyperactive'. As a South African friend has recently said, "At least Trevor is polite and doesn't call you motor mouth." No comment from me.

We visited the fort and beautiful gardens and then had a lovely surprise, as we met up with an old friend last seen in Cyprus but who now lived on this idyllic island. We met at his Drama Club and wined and dined with lots of "Do you every hear from, and where is so and so, and did you know that.....?"

Back on board we regularly listened to the weather reports and after ten days we had the OK to set sail again. We held our breath as we continued our trip to Saint Maartens, but the strange sickness did not return and we had a fantastically fast and comfortable sail, averaging one-hundred and fifty miles every day. We seemed to fly and fairly quickly we were anchored outside the lagoon. We discovered that to go inside the lagoon one now had to sign a Waiver, to the effect that we would not make any damage claims, if we hit any of the sunken boats inside. We decided to stay outside and dinghy in to visit friends. When we did we were shocked to see so many boats still up on the rocks, most of them deserted. They did not seem to discourage the tourists, maybe they had now become one the of the tourist attractions?

It was nearly Christmas and the two of us had a very quiet Christmas Day at a beautifully, intimate restaurant. Over our after dinner brandy we 'phoned Trevor's Number Two son to see if the new baby had arrived, after all we had a vested interest in this one don't forget we had seen his photo before he was born. Yes, he was there and was christened Matthew. We drank his health with the remains of our brandy and went home glad that his birth had given us such warm feelings. Up until then we had still felt raw in this sad island, so many boats sunk or damaged or even deserted with their owners having returned home with their lost dreams. But it was time for us to move on, this was history and we had new places and even adventures to find.

There followed some wonderful sailing and exploring of new islands. No big problems, not even little ones. We found idyllic anchorages, beautiful scenery, good friends old and new, and discovered some of the history of these islands. Quite often we felt ashamed of the historical British influence, especially with regard to the slave trade. Trevor told me that a lot of Liverpool as well as London was built on the proceeds from this dreadful trade. Time flew and while in the quaint island of Bequia we realized that if we did not get a move on we would miss Carnival in Trinidad.

Deciding to bypass Granada, Trevor planned to sail direct to Trinidad. Saying our goodbyes we left in the morning and had a pleasant sail. By late afternoon we were passing Granada where we could see the buoyed entrance to the capital of St Georges. On we went until we could see the island disappearing behind us. Trinidad here we come. Suddenly, out of nowhere we had a forty-knot wind on our nose. The whole boat shook and we felt our bimini would take off. Enough of this, we would turn around and go back. We did just that and were flying along with the wind on our tail, when it stopped as suddenly as it had started. It seemed to have settled, so we turned around again and off we went. Half an hour later the same thing happened but this time it stayed. Enough of this, we were not meant to go on, so back to Granada we would go.

By about midnight we were near Prickly Bay but Trevor remembered someone telling him that it was a tricky entrance and having never entered this anchorage we were loath to do it in the dark. We decided to make for St Georges as we had earlier seen that it was clearly marked. Off we went and by about two in the early hours, we arrived. But oh dear, it looked so different in the pitch black. We crept in between some buoys but it got more and more shallow. About turn. We tried again, but every way we went, we seemed to lose the depth. Once again I must remind you how everything looks so different in the dark. In the end we made for the Commercial Harbour that was deserted with just a few fishing and tourist boats lining the docks. Yachts were not allowed to anchor here. The exhausted skipper decided to drop the hook right in the middle of this harbour, we would soon be moved if we were a problem.

Early next morning at about 6am we were obviously a real problem, as two irate harbour officials were banging on our hull, shouting that we had to move, we must not anchor here. We assured them we would move, so they went away and we hastily began to lift the anchor. We do not have an electric anchor winch, ours is the manual variety so Trevor began the hard work. The anchor started to come up and then suddenly it stopped. More hard labour, but nothing happened. It was well and truly stuck. We tried using one of the primary winches. Nothing. What on earth was at the end of our anchor? I looked up and suddenly saw the reason why the harbour officials were so anxious for us to move. An enormous cruise liner was slowly entering the harbour. Yes, it was coming our way.

More sweated labour, with me on the winch and Trevor in the dinghy. We begin to drift away, as at last we had lifted the anchor, but it appeared that we had half a concrete wall still attached to the end. Trevor managed to remove it just as the liner made its turn and we saw that it would have missed us anyway. Whew!

We left the Harbour and decided to recover from our early morning labours in Prickly Bay. As we entered we saw that it was an open and easily anchored bay, so much for our previous warnings. When would we learn not to listen to such advice? Safely anchored we looked around and liked what we saw, so we signed in for a few days. Granada is called the Spice Islands and there is plenty to see, do and smell. We found that is was a very pretty island with friendly people, there was the scent of nutmeg around the whole of the tiny harbour. We discovered the reason, when we spotted that all the soil was covered with crushed nutmeg shells acting as a kind of mulch. We returned to St.George's Harbour, by bus this time and explored the little town. Whichever way we went we had to climb up or down steep hills, but it was worth it as we found an open-air market, fascinating shops and lots of colourfully dressed people.

One morning going ashore in the dinghy, we passed a boat. Now we must have passed this boat every time we made that journey. This time we both did a double take. It was "Holona Nani" owned by Bill and Zahala, last seen in Israel and actually it was Zahala's parents who had entertained us on Passover Night. It couldn't be. She and her American partner

Bill should be safely tucked up in Tel Aviv Marina. We pulled closer and could see her seating in the cockpit. She casually looked up and this time she did the double take and covering her face with her hands, cried out "Oh my God." We were quickly on board, Bill appeared and it was hugs and kisses all around and nonstop conversation. We were all talking at the same time. As I keep repeating this is one of the wonders of this life style, old friends discovered in the most unexpected places. We had a wonderful few days together. This year they had left Israel to cross the Atlantic and then go to the States where Zahala was to meet Bill's family and they were to be married. Their landfall had been Granada but not from choice, they had lost their self-steering at the very beginning of the crossing and had hand steered nearly the whole 3,000 miles. So we joined them in their well-deserved rest.

Eventually it was time for us all to move on. We to Trinidad, and Zahala to her exciting new life in the States with soon to be her husband, Bill. This time our trip was uneventful. Our GPS interfaced with faithful Fred kept us well on course. We had no unexpected winds just a pleasant sail. As morning approached the clouds deepened and everything went black, and then it began to rain. It was intense rain that seems to be a specialty of Trinidad. One minute we were looking at the coastline and the next it was completely wiped out. We knew that we were approaching the entrance called the Boca de Monas, the mouth of the Monkey. There are three entrances to Trinidad and in total they are called the Mouths of the Dragon, so you can guess that at times it is a pretty violent entrance. With this incredible rain we couldn't see our way in. We turned on the radar, and yes there it was, but we still could not see it by eye. It all looked very eerie, then suddenly the rain stopped, the mists cleared and we once more had eyes that could see and we were sailing straight through the narrow entrance. Inside we gasped as it was just like entering a jungle. On either side were rock like walls covered with luxuriant foliage, so green and steaming with the result of the rain. We could hear birds calling, parrots squawking and the howler monkeys making their early morning calls. We had never seen anything quite like this. To our amazement we were guided in by a group of dolphins. It seemed as if everyone was celebrating our arrival. We had arrived in Trinidad. Land of the calypso, pan drums and carnival. We could not wait to see more.

CHAPTER TWENTY-NINE
CARNIVAL AND TREVOR LEARNS TO GRIND

Mundane things first, we had to sign in. We motored into Chaguaramas Bay, anchored and made our way to Immigration and Customs. Quite painlessly we completed the usual forms and this time had nothing to pay. One paid as one left. We could stay for three months and if necessary this could be extended. Passports stamped, and you can guess I still checked mine and then we were on our way. Here the choice is to anchor in one of the few anchorage or stay in one of the many Marinas. We were going to the anchorage of the Trinidad and Tobago Yachting Association (TTYA) but knew that everywhere was very full as Carnival was ten days away. We arrived and dropped the hook among a large number of boats. Already we could see many familiar names. After our night passage it was heads down and toes up time.

Later, revived, we blew up the dinghy and ventured ashore. As we made our way in, we realized that a large number of boats were on moorings. In the main these were the local boats. Great, there would be a chance to meet these people. What nicer way to discover a new island than with the local sailing community. We found the dinghy dock, tied up and immediately began to find out what a yacht friendly island this is. At Reception we were greeted and given a welcome pack, which included among other things, two small bottles of rum. We paid for a month's stay. At this time it was roughly £1 per day and this covered the use of the dinghy dock, water, office services, showers and toilets, a workshop, a bar and restaurant on site, washing machines and beautiful gardens to sit in, plus security guards for twenty-four hours each day. There were electrical points ashore for plugging in laptops and sewing machines. What more could we want?

Needless to say we found the bar and some old friends. We soon discovered that we were very late for Carnival, as believe it or not, it had all started two months previously. Everyone had been encouraged to join in all the preparations from band practices, to costume design, the heats for everything from Miss Carnival, Kings and Queens, to every form of music that you could imagine, providing it was loud of course. Never mind we could still participate in the actual parades.

Trinidad unlike a lot of the other islands, appreciates the effect that cruisers have on its economy. In the Marinas and anchorages we are well served by local traders. The green grocer and the Roti man call on us. We start the day with a daily net run by the cruisers themselves and this covers security, weather, social and general information, help wanted and any treasures of the bilge. These items that are of no use to you but may be exactly what Joe Cruiser needs. We soon found out that we could watch a video on a Thursday evening, BBQ was on Monday and Trivial Pursuits on Tuesday and that was without even leaving our situation. We could travel cheaply to town in maxi taxis, providing that we were not of a nervous disposition and did not mind the loud music. The whole of the Chaguaramas area was geared for cruising boats. The boat yards, Chandleries and skills were available, at a price of course. I never stopped realizing how lucky I was that Trevor could do most of our maintenance and repairs himself.

There was so much to experience, but first of all we had to find out more about carnival. We immediately regretted our late arrival as we had not experienced the build up and had missed the Cruisers' seminars. These were fun afternoons where we novices found out what carnival was all about. Why there were moko jumbies, blue devils, why sailors are an important part of the whole thing, and all the rest of its fascinating history. Never mind another year.

Trinidad Carnival is an experience like no other. It's far more than the two days of masquerading. It is a whole explosive season in itself lasting nearly two months. Songs are pouring from recording studios and performed nightly in Calypso Tents. Costumes by the thousand are being stitched. More than a hundred pannists (drummers) are becoming a giant unit and there are many of these units. Visitors are welcome to see these rehearsals and can sit and lime (chat), sip a beer straight from the bottle or just soak up the music. We mustn't forget the statutory free bowl of corn soup.

The carnival is not a spectator event; the full excitement is to join in yourself. You can visit the "mas" camps (mas as in masquerade), see the costumes being made, meet the people and choose one to join. Over the whole period the calypso songs are being judged, as are the pan bands. The Kings and Queens are being chosen – not for their good looks but for the incredible costumes they wear. These are usually supported on a wheeled frame and made out of bamboo, plastic tubing, wire, etc., and it hardly

216

seems possible that there is an ordinary man or woman at its centre. Of course there is a separate carnival for the children.

Each year at the conclusion of all this preparation at 2am on the Carnival Monday, yes 2am, the greatest show on earth is born. The revellers hit the streets. Jumping, dancing and shouting, helped I must admit by the local rum. This early Mas is called J'ouvert and means day begun. No pretty clothes are worn, just simple fancy dress or old clothes with face and body paint. There are lots of devils called jab-jabs, midnight robbers and much more of the black side of life. People pour into the streets, bands play and mud and water are thrown. Everyone dances madly and I believe the whole experience is to get rid of any inhibitions. As Trinidadians do not seem to have any of these, it is very confusing. The fact that the children are kept at home must tell you something!

After the Dirty Mas, as this is called, comes the sea bathing. We cruisers, who came by maxi taxi, had to wear a giant rubbish bag for the return trip home, for fear of trashing the maxi. We weren't even allowed to use the Club showers, we had to hose each other down with the boat cleaning hoses. Then Pretty Mas begins. Off we go again. The processions take all day and evening to pass and the dancing gets sexier. Trevor was grabbed by a beautiful black girl and introduced to the Grind – her butt into his stomach with a lot of circular movement performed with gay abandon her end. They do seem to be bum people. It is just a continuous explosion of noise, music, lights, laughter, sex and incredibly colourful clothes. Towering over everyone are the Moko Jumbies, those giants on stilts.

We experienced the whole day and evening, our senses numb. For us it was time to go back to the boat. There was a lot of carnival culture that we did not understand, it was over for this year but we would have to come back earlier next year to begin to appreciate it completely. Eventually with some difficulty, we found our maxi and once back, boarded our dinghy and as we slowly rowed to 'Boon' we could see the night sky over Port of Spain, brightly lit and we could hear the pounding drums as the revellers continued. Once on board we soon fell asleep to their rhythm and would you believe when we woke up they were still there. The people of Trinidad certainly know how to party.

CHAPTER THIRTY
TRINIDAD, A TRUE MELTING POT

Carnival is followed by the flu. Yes, you read it correctly, influenza. Whether it is caused by all the dust and exhaust fumes inhaled following that mammoth parade, or whether it is truly a flu virus attacking the revellers' weakened systems, no one knows. Either way half of Trinidad seemed to be laid low with the horrible virus. We managed to escape and began to discover what a fun place this scruffy island is.

It is an island of different races. There are Africans, Indians, Chinese, Europeans and many more, a true melting pot. Desmond Tutu called Trinidad the Rainbow Island. Upon our arrival we were surprised by the strong Welsh accent and only recently was it suggested that it came from the Welsh Regiment that had historically been stationed here. In the main the talk is 'Trini' English. Trevor is slightly deaf and the first time he sat next to the Maxi Taxi driver he couldn't understand a single word. He asked the driver what language he was speaking. The shocked driver in disgust replied, "English of course!" With all these differing nationalities come the diverse cultures and religions. In the main Trinidadians are a very religious race. Their religions stretch from Roman Catholic through the other Christian beliefs to the Shouting Baptists, then we have the Rastas, Indian beliefs, the Jewish faith, Moslems and a little voodoo to give it spice. We had a lot to learn. We also had plenty of time in which to do it. There was no plan to go anywhere immediately just to enjoy what the island had to offer.

We visited bird sanctuaries, saw the leatherback turtles lay their eggs and in the evenings watched the scarlet ibis flying back to roost. Once settled, they looked like a mass of red blossoms hanging from the branches over the waters. Every morning from our anchorage, parrots would fly across the water, flapping their wings at an alarming rate. In the evenings they would perform the return trip, squawking during the whole flight. We have never discovered why they made this daily journey. The early morning rumblings of howler monkeys echoed around us sounding just like distant lions roaring. While under our keels a variety of fish feed. Many a ship's cat could be seen watching this performance with glinting eyes but they are too wise to dive in. Of course they usually get a breakfast of the flying fish that land on the deck. Around the circumference of our anchorage march the vultures like dignified lawyers in full dress. In the main, the average Trinidadian has not yet discovered garbage bags or the need to take his rubbish home with him; they just drop it where they stand. So by this water edge where they swim and play is a dumping ground. Fortunately the vultures arrive in the early hours of morning and clean most of it up ready for the next day's load. One afternoon we watched a massive manta ray feeding in the water between the anchored boats. With rhythmic movements it scooped up its lunch hardly causing a ripple. A friend on board was so enchanted she dived into the water and together they swam side by side.

One day we visited the local zoo and were amazed to find out that the howler monkey is only about twelve inches high but his mouth and throat are shaped like a trombone. Now we knew how he made his noisy wakeup call in the early hours of the morning.

There are many spin offs from the Carnival (Carnival in Trinidad deserves to have a capital C). It seems to have provided the local people with an outlet for artistic talents, whether it is music, dance, playacting, dressmaking, art or the spoken word. Part of the Carnival is Expo where two performers will take a given topic and challenge each other to keep it going with the rhyming. Everyone has heard of Calypso; news or gossip to music, this is where it was born and performed. Of course the Pan drum was first made in Trinidad and is the national instrument. To listen to classic panning is a wonderful experience. We discovered all this and more and for a few months became tied to the land rather than the sea.

One morning Trevor announced that with all this good living he did not feel fit. He felt that we needed more exercise than our little early morning workout on board. How to achieve it? What we needed was a gym but where? We soon found another of Trinidad's treasure; The Body Works in a nearby Mall. For just £15 per month each we could exercise as often as we wanted to and for me joy of joys, end with a hot shower. We joined. I decided to write an article about it and this was printed in a Trinidadian Sailing Newspaper so not only did I feel fitter but also I got paid for my efforts. This became a pattern and if something interested me I would put pen to paper and scribble my thoughts and from time to time some kindly Editor would publish my efforts. Do not get excited these were all local papers and I was not likely to become another Libby Purves although it was still my dream.

During this time I had a very special appointment every Thursday morning. At 8am, along with several cruisers, I would have a maxi taxi ride to a Children's Home. Driving through the huge gates we were instantly overwhelmed by clamouring voices, all shouting, "Miss, Miss, look at me. Look what I can do. Come over here. Stand by me. Miss, Miss." We were hugged, touched and clung to. Every child wanted our attention. These were some of the children from this orphanage who were to have special reading and arithmetic sessions. With a variety of backgrounds some had missed out on regular schooling, and now in the local school had been identified as needing extra tuition. There were no spare teachers to do this so we had volunteered to do just that. Of course they got some of our tender loving care as well and it was very obvious that they all wanted physical contact in the form of a hug or just holding hands. This was generally in short supply in the Home. This schoolroom was not my destination though and with great difficulty I left them enjoying the attention of the other volunteers.

I ran the gauntlet of all these kids and made my way up the hill, which got steeper with every step. Breathlessly, (what happened to all this fitness), I reached the top. I passed a series of bleak grey buildings; they looked just like deserted barracks after an attack. These were the houses where the children lived. The only splashes of colour were the flowers surrounding the beautifully painted Nuns' Quarters! At last I arrived at the top and the very last grim building housed the Nursery. I entered through a rusty metal door and there were my toddlers. Every one of them shouted "Mummy," as soon as they saw me. Bright little black faces with demanding hands and soon I was surrounded. There were fifteen of them, all under four years of age. The four and five year olds had already left for Nursery School. We had a room to play in with a stable door but there was only an empty Wendy house, a plastic slide and one ball.

Usually there were two of us entertaining the youngsters for the morning enabling the staff to do something else. The toddlers were extremely clean and well dressed and they had enough to eat, just enough. In fact it was wonderful to see the way that they ate. Each mouthful was savoured, nothing was rushed and we certainly didn't have any picky eaters here. They were just short on attention and the normal things that our first world kids take for granted. A box of toys, sitting on a lap, being read to, someone listening, identifying colours and just talking with them. When we started this project we asked if there were more toys to play with but were told that the children seemed to break them. So they stayed locked in a cupboard.

We needed to gently change the system. So we took our own toys and books but by the next week they had disappeared and all we got was a shrug from the House Mother and "Man, I tink dey broke." Plan B and we took more toys and sadly took them back with us at the end of the morning. This was accompanied by the loudest of wails and buckets of tears of course.

One week I collected fifteen large cardboard boxes and two of us taxied these to the top of the hill and that Thursday the children discovered all the ways they could fit in, under, and on top of a box. They pushed them, pulled them, sat in them singly or in twos. Of course they fought over them. Angel, who was a tiny moppet with the most wicked grin, of course wanted two. If ever there was an outburst of anger or distress from one of them, we only had to look at Angel to see her innocent face turn into a grin of triumph. I always felt that somehow Angel would succeed in life. The backgrounds of these children were often horrifying, and when I sadly looked at their surroundings I had to constantly remind myself that the life that they had left behind was much, much worse than this.

But our stationery life continued and reality struck. Sitting at anchor in this climate and in this particular stretch of water, had its problems or rather one particular problem. Barnacles. They just loved it and what better place to live than on the bottom of boats. Especially ours that didn't seem to be going anywhere. Trevor regularly dived and scraped them off but they finally won the race; they came quicker than he could scrape. Lift out time again.

A date was booked; seven days seemed sufficient and certainly a little easier on our bank balance. We managed to motor around the corner with our barnacle encrusted propeller barely turning. We arrived at the lift out slip and with slings in position; 'Boon' was gently lifted from the water. She was certainly covered with the little fiends and some were even surrounded with weed in glorious technicolour.

224

In no time at all these were scraped off and the boat pressure washed. She looked better already.

Trevor anxiously examined the hull, no little blisters, no dents, BUT what was this? Where the keel is fixed to the hull was a decided gap, where no gap had any right to be. Did we have a problem, a big problem? Life on the hard is just that, hard. One climbs up and down the ladder numerous times a day. Why did we spend our money at the Gym where here, fitness comes free? One could no longer use the boat toilet or wash basins, after all there isn't a friendly sea and fish anxious to dispose of all our waste and usually the boat is planted on mud and however careful, this gets trodden everywhere. Immediately life begins on the hard, my bladder seems to change routine. Usually sleeping all night I now need to visit the toilet at least once. So it is either down the ladder or in the bucket. During this time I discovered that nowhere on this island could I buy a bucket with a lid. Even in Trinidad, the modern world had caught up with us. Buckets with lids were designed for soaking dirty nappies and in today's world there is no such thing. Disposable nappies just get thrown away. Oh well a bucket with an old tray on top will have to do.

On closer inspection Trevor and some knowledgeable friends agreed that over the years the keel bolts holding the keel to the hull might have loosened a little. This resulted in the slight gap. As our engine is in the centre of the boat, and sits on these massive bolts, it would mean removing the engine to check them. It was decided to just refill the gap. The most suitable filler was discussed with the experts and after cleaning and much grinding, the new mixture went in. After that it was the normal maintenance that we do ourselves. A case of checking the skin fittings (those holes with fittings in the hull that live under the water), sanding and repainting the bottom and cleaning and polishing the topsides.

All squeaky clean again and hopefully the problem solved, 'Boon' was ready for re- launching. It was weekend and we were to be the first splashed on Monday morning. During the Saturday afternoon a large but old fishing boat glided into the slip for a twenty-four hour lift out, scrub and antifoul. No way could the owner lose more than one day's fishing. I watched as the diver dived into the water to position the straps, noticing what a tight fit it all was. Then the travel hoist began the lift. Half way out of the water there was an enormous bang as the straps broke and the boat fell back into the slip, splashing the dock, nearby boats and the people standing by. Two people were even knocked into the water. But where was the diver? I held my breath, was he hurt? But all was well; he had climbed out before the lifting had commenced. Apart from a few scratches no damage seemed to have been done. Nevertheless I approached Monday and our lift out with my heart in my mouth. Monday arrived and all was well and we were back at anchor once more.

We were now ready to move on. It had to be west, as it was hurricane time again and going north would bring us into the hurricane belt once more. Venezuela sounded delightful so we decided to leave all the pleasures of Trinidad behind and we set sail.

CHAPTER THIRTY-ONE
DISCOVERING VENEZUELA

It was six o'clock in the morning when we up anchored and made out way to the Boca, this time the Dragon's Mouth was flat and calm and we exited through Boca Grande. There was a gentle wind behind us and a strong current to push us on our way. We were to take the coastal route stopping en route and then over to the Island of Margarita. The boat looked good, performed beautifully and we both felt the joy of sailing once more. Yes, even I was enjoying this type of sailing. Ahead of us was our first stop, a small fishing village, truly small, about eighteen houses. We read up our pilot book, dropped the sails and anchored in this little bay. To one side were the houses with small fishing boats pulled up onto the sandy beach. Behind the beach was a fantastic backdrop of mountains covered with luxuriant growth. We viewed all this from our cockpit while we ate lunch, hardly curbing our impatience to get ashore.

Dinghy blown up, oars out and we were off. We were greeted by a small group of children with shy smiles. We had come prepared with two packets of biscuits; we knew from our pilot book that these people had very little. They could only travel via the sea, as there was no access behind their houses. They fished from tiny boats and relied on the large fishing boat, which came with its refrigerated hold to stand by and receive the fish as they caught it. I guess he delivered any goods they needed as well.

We found one of the mothers and gave her the biscuits, which were swiftly divided into outstretched hands. The kids then gave us a conducted tour. They were very proud of the swiftly running stream behind the houses and by sign language suggested that we bathe or do our laundry. We could see that the houses had no doors and earth floors. The rubbish dump fascinated us; this was a mass of thick glutinous mud where refuse was deposited. Remember that probably all their waste rubbish was perishable. In the centre of this cocktail were two handsome black pigs, eating, snorting, wallowing and thoroughly enjoying their own particular life style. Chickens roamed and a couple of dogs lay in the mid-day sun and Trevor practiced his almost forgotten Spanish with the children. It is always good to speak to the kids, especially the young ones. They speak slowly and use the simplest of words. Obviously they all understood him and we were joined by a few of the mothers. Most fathers were fishing or sleeping in hammocks under the trees. I guess these were the night shift or just being typical men. One mother gave some rapid instructions to two children and off they rushed, soon to return with mangos and avocados for our supper. This was in return for the biscuits. Nice to know that they did not want to encourage them to beg. Clutching our goodies we returned to 'Boon'.

As we rowed back we saw a Customs Boat enter the Bay and once we were on board it headed in our direction. What was this? When alongside an officer came on board and his boat stood by with two crewmembers holding rifles. Speaking only in Spanish our papers were checked, and with a quick look around he asked if the villagers had given us any trouble. We quickly replied that they had been extremely friendly. There seemed nothing else and as he left, he only then began to speak in English. We understand that the drug route from Columbia comes along this coast and would imagine that this is a regular check.

Later in the afternoon we were visited by a couple of fishing boats. The first one asked if we had any of the plasters that they had seen on Trevor's leg. They showed us that one of their group had a very nasty ulcer. We gave him a tube of antibiotic cream and half a dozen plasters. We were rewarded with a nice fish for supper. Shortly afterwards a boat full of giggling teenagers arrived and asked if we had any biscuits. Obviously the word was out. Another packet handed over and they motored away shouting, "Gracias."

What a delightful community. We ate our free supper, slept extremely well and before first light sailed away as we had a seventy-two mile trip. With the wind, current and a little bit of luck we could make it before dark. Remember dark comes very early here and entering an unknown harbour at night is quite daunting.

Our sail was great, a following sea, and fifteen to twenty knots of wind; everyone's dream. We just cruised along the coastline impressed with the dramatic views and general magnificence of this country. There was very little traffic only the fishermen working hard to maintain their meagre living. We caught a fish and decided once again, that this was a wonderful life.

We made it just before sunset and rounding the point, rather like a hammerhead, we found ourselves in a large Bay with no other yachts but a variety of fishing boats. This was a much larger fishing community with a fish factory and several little shops. Fuel and water were available at the dock and the sea here was covered with a slight film of oil. In fact our Pilot Book warned not to teach Granny how to swim in this water. All we wanted was to cook and eat our fish. As we ate we became aware of an aroma of dried fish in the air. As time went on this got more obtrusive. Evidently the fish factory was in operation. This did not stop us having a good night's sleep. Morning came early with what seemed like an armada of fishing boats roaring past us.

After breakfast we went ashore and found a very friendly but scruffy little town. There was very little to buy and the few shops seem to stock rice, bread, eggs, numerous plantains and bananas. Every shop seems to have bleach, washing powder and a type of washing up paste, (I never worked out how to use it,) but Trevor found it was excellent for getting oil, grime and unmentionable stuff off his hands.

One bonus was that we could buy a block of ice for 80p at the local fish factory. This by the way was a 50lb monster. Having had two boats with no refrigeration this one boasts an enormous icebox. Up until now we have used multiple bags of cubed ice and found it very successful. This seemed even better. The iceman helped Trevor carry it to the dinghy and then we triumphantly went back to the boat. You will realize by now that it still does not take much to delight us. Now the fun started, trying to get a giant block of slippery ice from the dinghy to the boat is quite an intelligence test, as well as a test of strength.

No problem, we are now super fit and an old blanket around the block eased matters somewhat. We spent a peaceful day only interrupted occasionally by requests for cigarettes or cans of beer!

Next morning we set sail for Isla de Margarita, no longer sailing along the coast but it was another pleasant sail; calm sea and gentle wind and we were there in record time. Anchoring among a large number of boats we very quickly began to rock and roll. In fact preparing supper became quite a feat. Tomatoes and eggs rolled every which way and although there was no wind, a swell seemed to sweep into this anchorage. We noticed that many boats had anchored to a bridle so this must be quite common occurrence. A bridle is a way of fixing your anchor so that you no longer lay across the swell and it's more comfortable.

We were advised to sign in with an Agent and there began our first experience of Venezuelan officialdom. Let me explain, one set out for this beautiful country with an entry visa, acquired in Trinidad or wherever (paid for of course). Once there one had to sign in Internationally, signing out nationally every time one left for another State. Upon arrival at the next Port one signed in again and then out when leaving and so it continued, until once finally departing the country one could sign out internationally this time. Wait for it, every three months one has to renew a personal visa, and every six months get a new visa for the boat. Are you still with me? One may keep the boat in this country for up to eighteen months. To cruise Los Roques there has to be a special permit. All these pieces of paper cost a lot of money and if you are still following me, you are much more intelligent than we were; we got lost early on in the equation hence the need for an Agent.

We spent a short while in rock and rolly Margarita and then began a period of most beautiful sailing. We explored little islands, bigger islands, minute anchorages, investigated the Gulfs and found more hidden bays. Anchored by tiny villages with enough room for a couple of visiting yachts. Met delightful people and swam in clear turquoise seas where a variety of fish teased us and glorious coral and plants were in abundance. Puerto la Cruz supplied us with our city needs of Banks, laundries, supermarkets and chandleries. There were a few Marinas but not for us. At that time there were some security problems; mainly solved by lifting dinghies at night and securing them to the boat with steel cables; never leaving any goodies on the deck or in the dinghy and definitely chaining the dinghy to a tree every time we ventured ashore. Again our dictionary was much in use and Trevor's Spanish began to reappear and I began to learn a little. The cost of living was low, caused often by the fact that certain goods were not available and we could live simply on local produce. We loved this country.

One day while swimming, Trevor decided to dive to check for barnacles and found to his horror that the gap between the keel and hull had reappeared. Lots of discussion and we decided to return to Trinidad, lift out and remove the engine this time and check the keel bolts and tighten them. We had only been in Venezuela for three months but had seen enough to know that we wanted to come back. This was when the fun started. All that beautiful sailing that brought us here with following winds and current in our favour, was now going to be against us. Weather watching time once more.

We found a window and literally fought our way back. It is amazing how the sea changes. In one direction it is a benign friend, gentle and kind, then turnaround and it is the enemy, violent and rough.

Anyway we made it, arriving in Trinidad on a beautiful calm day. We signed in and truly appreciated the simple procedure for signing in. We anchored again at the TTYA anchorage and were greeted with a "Welcome Home."

CHAPTER THIRTY-TWO
THE EARTH MOVED FOR US

We decided that we would like to have Christmas in Trinidad and then stay and see the whole of carnival. So we would put off our lift out until after this time. As we did not plan to do any sailing there would be no strain on the keel and why not wait until we were ready to leave again and then of course, put on another coat of the bottom paint as well.

About this time some Jewish/American friends arrived and they planned to sail to Tobago for Passover. There some family and friends would join them and then they'd all go sailing together. Tobago is the Sister Island to Trinidad. Two quite contrasting sisters. Trinidad busy, noisy, scruffy, and full of life, commerce and people. Tobago; quiet, rural, gentle, quite beautiful and with few people. These friends invited us to join them. We did not need asking twice. Trevor being anxious over the state of the keel, did not want to take our boat so we decided that we would go by the Ferry. Something quite different for us. We did not book any accommodation in advance as local friends assured us that in Tobago there was an abundance of houses with bed and breakfast on offer at ridiculously low prices. That sounded fine.

Our friends, Sid and Rebecca departed and a few days later we were boarding the Ferry. It was due to depart at 2 pm and arrive at 8 pm. We settled in our seats and there followed our usual pattern. Me "people watching" and Trevor with his nose in a book. I was intrigued, why were people carrying jackets, blankets and some even sleeping bags? I mentioned this to Trevor and all I got was a grunt.

One man put his bag on the floor and climbed in it, even though it was 32 degrees C, strange. The engines started. From the window I could see that there was an enormous line of lorries and cars still to join us. The time passed 3 and then 4 o'clock and all the while the temperature dropped and dropped. Finally the boat began to move and we were off. The Bar opened and everyone seemed to be drinking bottles of ice cold beer and the air conditioning system seemed to be working overtime. On went the jackets; over went the blankets, and bodies climbed into sleeping bags. The temperature dropped even more. We froze. This Company was certainly proud of its air conditioning system.

Eventually we arrived three hours late. It was 11 pm and very dark. We searched for the multitude of rooms to let. We asked about them and no one seemed to know of any. We asked at the Bars and cafes - nothing. We stopped a taxi and the driver thought for a while and then said that perhaps Musti might have a room to let. Who and where was Musti? "Top of the hill man, and on de corner to de right. You can't miss it." Up we went and the area got seedier and seedier. We came to an almost derelict house. There was nothing here so we went down again. The taxi was still there so we explained the position. The driver hailed someone and told him to take us to Musti's. He did, and it was the derelict house.

By now it was midnight. Our guide went in and swiftly came out, with we guessed, a half dressed Musti. Introductions and before I could back off, we were shown his best room. This was above street level and had an open hole for a window with a rough brick ledge beneath, a double bed balanced on four tyres, one pillow and an ill fitting under sheet, a chair with three legs and a length of cable strung along a wall boasting two wire coat hangers. This was obviously the wardrobe. The walls were in fact sheets of uneven lengths of plywood with gaps where they should have reached the corrugated sheets of the roof. Up there hung a wire with a bare light bulb. Trevor looked at me and said, "What do you think?" I looked out of the window and under the streetlight I could see a motley selection of passers-by. One of whom was decidedly drunk or drugged. Musti anxiously told us that the bed was clean and producing an enormous padlock and key assured us that we would be quite secure. Three pounds for the night. I nodded not trusting myself to speak. Money changed hands and we became the proud custodians of the room and the padlock. I needed the toilet and was taken outside to a shack with no door. The deed done I flushed the loo with a piece of wire and washed my hands in the very basic kitchen sink.

Back alone, in the room we looked at each other and began to giggle. You have to realize that whenever the going gets tough, we always remember, "It beats sitting in a life raft." There was no discussion as to who had the pillow, I just grabbed it. Attired in tee shirts and panties we lay down, sticky, from the ferry ride but not wanting to leave the security of the room to wash. The room was lit by the streetlight and suddenly the handle began to turn, then it rattled. My protector type husband shouted, "Go away!" It sounded like our guide who I guess had expected a tip. He was checking if everything was OK. I was now entirely wide-awake and lay rigid wondering how we ever got into these situations.

I could hear footsteps around the house and from the gap above the wall could hear female voices. Perhaps they were on the game? This would be interesting; perhaps I'd learn a few tricks of the trade. Suddenly there was another noise, but closer. What on earth was it? I lay absolutely still; then I realized it was Trevor snoring. How could he sleep? I lay rigid, sleep never coming. I did know one thing however and that was tomorrow we were going to find the finest hotel in Charlottesville and for at least forty-eight hours, join the beautiful people. Still awake at 4 am I needed the loo. Trevor was lost in the depths of tranquil sleep. How could he? My problem became more pressing. I had no intention of leaving the room and not wanting to wake the sleeping beauty; I crept out of my bed and searched my handbag. Yes, there was a small click (zip lock) bag that housed our passports and ferry tickets. I emptied it and with great difficulty, used it. I stood holding it, not certain what to do next. I clicked it shut and carefully balanced it on the brick ledge beneath the window. It stood there looking just like the bags they give you at Fairs when you win a goldfish. All I wanted now was the actual fish swimming around. I climbed back into bed and mercifully fell asleep.

When it came, the bang was enormous, it echoed around the room, along the street and everything vibrated as the house shook violently. The vibrations lasted for a very long time. We clung onto our bed and each other, confused and very frightened. There were loud voices in the street outside and we heard someone say that it was an earthquake. We both lay rigid on the bed; it was dawn and just getting light. As soon as possible we would leave and catch the first maxi taxi to Charlottesville. We giggled as we said that we could now say that the earth had moved for us! Then came the second bang, much worse than the first. It was the aftershock. Voices shouted for everyone to run to the streets. We needed no second invitation. Gradually everything calmed down and outside we became acquainted with our neighbours. Musti was there and our guide from the night before and the rest of the household. They were sad men, who having no homes sometimes managed to raise a little money by selling fruit or finding enough empty bottles to pay for a room for a night. We had spent the hours of darkness in what we call a Doss House. With extreme courtesy they insisted that I used the toilet first, and all turned away so I could have some privacy. We got dressed, caught a maxi and found a beautiful hotel in Charlottesville.

We arrived just in time for breakfast. Then we showered and sat on our own personal veranda enjoying the fantastic view. We could see a fabulous bay with our friend's boat swinging to anchor and suddenly all was right with our world. We enjoyed the Passover Supper with good friends, the traditional food and a superb environment. The time passed far too quickly and far too swiftly our friends were setting sail and we were back in Scarborough waiting for the Ferry. To send us on our way nature provided us with yet one more earthquake. Of course, by now we were far more blasé.

Christmas came and we were invited to spend it with a Trinidad family. One of the pleasures of this life is spending time ashore and understanding more of the local culture and customs. We had a delightful time, Trinidadian style and fortunately for us there was a small grandson to help really appreciate the delights of this time of year. I notice that my Jewish husband truly enjoys the food and gives and receives presents with the best of us. Our hosts were truly a 'rainbow' group. Marjorie was black Afro/Caribbean and John her husband, was white and English. They had met in the UK when she was completing her nursing training in London. Somehow John had managed to get posted to Tobago and their courtship continued and finally, married, they settled in Trinidad. Their two adult children were with us and they were a wonderful combination of the two nationalities. Joanne's partner was Jamaican, and Stephen's wife was a beautiful Irish redhead. The grandchildren were a mixture of all that was good from this combination. A true melting pot.

In Trinidad our New Year's Eve becomes Old Year's Night, but everything else is the same, too much to drink, loads of friends, plenty of music and dancing, and an excuse to kiss everyone. The only difference is that everything is accompanied with the very loud bass drumming which is the background to all celebrations. We were back at the Body Works again so were able to keep up with all these activities.

Eventually time came to lift out and tackle our Big Problem. No sooner did we get settled on land, with the engine hoisted out leaving a huge great gap in the middle of our living area floor, naturally with general confusion around us, than we received a fax from Trevor's number four son, Zhev, to say that he would come and see us next week. He had been incredibly busy all season and needed a break to rethink his career and according to him 'chill out'. To chill out was a new one for us but what could we say but "How lovely, we look forward to seeing you. Bring a paint brush."

The keel bolts were tightened, the gap filled again, the engine went back, 'Boon's' bottom painted and we splashed. Nice to feel the gentle movement of the sea once again, boats never seem right on land. Zhev had been a great help and managed to have some fun time as well. It was build up to Carnival once more and we were in the thick of it. He sailed, met our friends, made some of his own, partied and hiked. As an ex-drummer he was fascinated with the pan drums. Sadly the two weeks flew but hopefully he sorted out his future, and we were on our own again.

What now? Decision time once more. First of all the year 2000 was not too far away and we were still dinosaurs. The computer and printer were still on our wish list. How could we fund it? Finally we agreed. If we sailed back to Venezuela and lived very simply we could buy them. The cost of living was not much different from Trinidad but there were not so many social activities or consumer products to tempt us to spend our pennies, and in the out of the way anchorages there would be little to spend our money on. Zhev's visit had made us realize that it was three years since we had visited home and it would be great to see everyone. Perhaps we could save enough for that too? Just think of the grandchildren, in fact we'd never held and hugged grandson Matthew. We needed to rediscover an older Isabella and we had not seen enough of Jane's ready-made family. Three young ladies needed hugging and some lively boys needed more attention. Let's not forget Ralph a young man in his twenties, Trevor's greatest dread was that Ralph would father a child and then he, Trevor, would be a great grandfather. I was not so keen on going to bed with a great grandfather myself. We definitely needed to save some cash and touch base with them all again.

It was at this time that I finally admitted that in spite of my regular exercise and good diet, I had steadily put on weight, certainly not liking what I saw in the Body Works mirrors. The scales told an alarming tale. These pounds must come off. Upon reflection I realized that over the last couple of years I had enjoyed the cheap beer and even more the inexpensive rum and cokes. I would start by cutting out the alcohol, and what better way than setting sail with a dry boat. Let's see what would happen? There was nothing to stop us, so early one bright sunny morning, we just sailed away.

CHAPTER THIRTY-THREE
PAPERWORK, VENEZUELAN STYLE (OR THE SENORITAS WITH MAGNIFICENT BOOBS)

Once again we enjoyed the gentle Venezuelan weather and had a spinnaker run. I could get to like this. We paid a return visit to our little fishing village, this time prepared with pencils, books and even more biscuits. Then it was up anchor and off to Porto Santos with its smelly fish processing works. We were whizzing along, sailing under full sail and the spinnaker, but two-thirds of the way the wind picked up, so down came the spinnaker. Somehow I managed to get my hand caught in the halyard and suffered a severe rope burn. This was the first accident we had ever had while sailing. I plunged it into cold water until the pain went, probably a couple of hours, but after that it looked horrible but was quite painless. This brought back to us that we had to be Doctor, Nurse and even chemist and must be particularly careful if we were to sail to out of the way anchorages.

We anchored and decided that we would start saving by cutting the costs and signing in ourselves at a little town five miles away. We had been advised to try this as it was easy and much cheaper, and after all as we were in this money saving mode so we'd go for it. But the reality was quite different from the advice – read on.

Next morning we up anchored and moved to the next harbour and at about ten-thirty went ashore. Nowhere to lock the dinghy, so first problem, where to leave the dinghy? Finally we left it with three ancient mariners on the beach. "Dos horas (two hours)" we confidently shouted.

Stage two, find Customs and Immigration. This done we were told that they were having an early lunch and to return in two hours. So we investigated this attractive little town and enjoyed some remarkably inexpensive roadside snacks; got that right anyway.

One-thirty back to the officials and ten minutes later the forms were being completed in triplicate with the assurance that visas were not necessary. Happily our Spanish stretched to all of this. 2,000 Bolivars (local currency) later we were with Immigration; a repeat performance but costing 15,000 B's each. With much handshaking we were directed to the Harbour Master.

By now our Venezuelan cash was depleted but we felt confident that there was little or nothing left to pay to the Harbour Master. We found the good man, at the other end of town of course but he spoke excellent English, and showed us that he could see 'Boon' from his office window. Very re-assuring. I mentioned the dinghy out of sight on the beach. Not so re-assuring. Anyway on with the job in hand. He couldn't find the forms. No problem we first needed the postage stamps. They would cost 10,800 B's. I only had 2,000 left. So 3 pm off to the Bank in town. Long walk, long queue. Finally we left clutching what seemed a fortune in paper money.

Breathlessly we arrived back, now really concerned about our dinghy. Harbour Master was triumphant he'd found the forms. But no, we had misunderstood him, he didn't carry the stamps we had to buy them ourselves; back in town of course.

4.45 off we trudged to the Post Office. Wrong one. More directions, more walking and finally purchasing the stamps from a very frosty faced postal clerk. Back we staggered, now seriously worried about the safety of the dinghy. We collapsed in the now familiar office and were plied with coca cola. All of us, this included the Harbour Master and his deputy, drinking from the same glass.

When we produced the stamps we saw that the very unfriendly Post Office official had sold us two large denomination stamps and two large sheets of small value ones. The Harbour Master roared with laughter and had all his staff assembled to witness this.

5.15 began the process of affecting this special form. He had three very junior clerks; attractive young girls, all wearing very low tops and boasting very large, firm bosoms. All three leaned over his desk exposing more of their charms. Trevor's day began to improve. My mind was more on the dinghy.

One girl, obviously the typist, using one finger and many mistakes, typed the form. Meanwhile a routine was commencing. One by one Trev tore off the tiny stamps, the remaining two girls wetted their fingers and held them aloft with a stamp resting lightly on each digit. Harbour Master removed each in turn and carefully placed them on the form in a precise pattern with only the edges exposed. A true work of art. This continued with interruptions from colleagues, much laughing and more bosom jiggling from the senoritas. I agonized over the dinghy and Trevor had fun.

6.10 job completed. Handshakes all round and we ran to the beach, finding the dinghy quite safe with the three men of the sea still standing guard. More B's and we returned to 'Boon', absolutely exhausted. Next day when we arrived in Margarita we found that using the Agent was much cheaper, far less painful but perhaps not so much fun.

We decided to settle in Margarita for a while and lick our financial wounds. Remember that once we left this area we had to sign out and then in somewhere else again. Now I must be honest and say that there were cruisers who only signed in once and with crossed fingers, sailed around this magnificent country and hoped that they were never investigated. Of course we were only human and discussed this but felt that with our luck, 'Boon' would be the first to be checked out. The fine for such behaviour was beyond belief. So we would spend some time in this island and try to get our monies worth. No sooner did we begin to enjoy ourselves when our Ham/SSB radio died and one of our flexible water tanks split. Murphy again? There was no one on the island who could repair the radio and the Chandlery did not stock water tanks. I guess the computer would continue to stay at the bottom of the list. We felt lost without our radio it was after all our contact with the outside world. Running on just one tank was not a problem on this island as we could have water delivered directly to the boat and the single tank would be OK. Once we started serous sailing again, especially if we were to visit the outer islands, we would need another tank, as water was not available. So earlier than we would have wished, we signed out, paying up of course, and set sail for Puerto la Cruz.

Once there we found that no one could repair this particular radio and it was as if we were mourning a friend. We regularly listened to BBC World Service and of course had contacts with friends via both ham and SSB frequencies. We never realized that we were so radio active! Feeling rather sorry for ourselves we were overtaken by the wonderful friendship of other cruisers. Paul on "Silver Ankh" leant us his spare radio and John on "Half Time" suggested that he take the sick radio with him to Canada for repair. He would not be returning for five months but at least it would save a large postal charge one way and could be sent back via one of the delivery services. We blessed you both.

One problem taken care of, now for the water tank. The local down town Chandlery did not stock any but could get it sent in from the USA, at a fee of course, not forgetting the heavy Duty. We swallowed hard and said, "Yes please, and thank you." If this had happened in Trinidad or even any of the Caribbean islands there would have been no heavy duty. Also Venezuela had a nasty trick of receiving your package in the Customs Department and not informing you for several days. When you came to collect it, you would be informed that as they had held it for over five days, there would be a charge for storage. Surprise, surprise it was always five days before they notified you so we were on a hiding to nothing.

Now all we needed was to find somewhere off the main track where we could lick our financial wounds again and live very quietly. It was necessary to be somewhere where we could buy only basic stores, get free water and live the simple life. We enjoyed some lovely sailing and some glorious anchorages in our search, eventually exploring the Gulf of Santa Fe and finally anchoring off the little village itself. We were the only yacht there and sitting in the cockpit, I could see a long strip of golden sand, punctuated with tall palm trees and little houses. It was quite late in the afternoon so we would save exploring until the next day. One of the joys of this life is the anticipation of what we will find. A few children were playing in the sea and we watched the local fishing men taking their little boats out for the night's fishing. A few had outboard motors but most were rowing. A great number of these men pulling on enormous oars looked too old for this task. We were beginning to learn that in these countries a lot of people looked much older than they really were. Certainly a hard life. The sun began to set and we saw the first of many breathtaking sunsets that were a prelude to night in this particular anchorage. We slept.

Next day we went ashore, chaining our dinghy to the inevitable palm tree and walking bare foot along the sands. Close to it was as attractive as it had looked from the cockpit of our home. At the end of the beach we turned inland and came upon the village and what a surprise, there was a surprisingly large market selling fruit and vegetables with a fish and meat market alongside. It was extremely scruffy and smelly, as it appeared all market rubbish was dumped just outside the open doors and left to fester in the heat and never seemed to be collected, but the road out of the village boasted a chemist, a draper, some basic grocery stores, hardware and a baker with home baked bread. There was a Police Station, two schools and a tiny emergency hospital. Oh yes, there was a newspaper stand, all copies in Spanish of course. What more could we ask for? Shopping done and walking back along the beautiful beach we noticed that there were several cafes and a few very simple guesthouses with little houses nestled alongside.

We came to our dinghy and stood watching some small kids playing baseball, when a man appeared and showed us our dinghy where he had removed the plastic hose feeding petrol from the fuel tank to our outboard. In Spanish and sign language he explained that the hoses were often stolen. (We must get to grips with more of this language). We couldn't believe it, just a simple piece of hosepipe with a plastic fitting each end. Slowly we began to realise that something that was cheap and taken for granted by us could be resold to feed a hungry family. Back on the boat we decided that in future we would row ashore and leave the outboard, hose and fuel tank safely on board.

There followed a delightful month. It was peaceful, friendly and we were able to practice our limited Spanish, try to learn a few more words everyday and most important of all, save money. Our one treat was to row ashore in the evening and buy ourselves a meringada. This is a local drink made from liquidized fresh fruit, ice and yoghurt. It was absolutely delicious. The little café was right in the middle of the beach near a posada (guesthouse) that was popular with backpackers. These evenings

248

became magic as we met many young people and some not so young, who were exploring Venezuela and "chilling out" here before the next mountainous trip or rafting adventure. They ranged from Americans, Canadians, Europeans right through to Israelis. We were fascinated by their travels and they were just as interested in ours. Sitting here at sunset we saw the elusive "green flash" as the sun set. In fact we saw it on three occasions. The only difficulty was restricting ourselves to just one of these lovely drinks per night! I was still not drinking alcohol and found that it was something that I did not miss. Not at all like the nicotine withdrawal symptoms I had experienced many years ago.

We could not believe it when we realized that a month had nearly passed and we needed to revisit Puerto la Cruz to collect our water tank, go to a Bank and check for mail. I MUSTN'T FORGET TO WEIGH MYSELF. The afternoon before we left, two Swiss girls swam out to 'Boon', shared some tea and after a pleasant visit, for us anyway, they left for their Spanish class. Spanish Class where's that? Tell us more. They explained that Senor Vivas gave lessons on his Veranda every afternoon, and more important it was free. He was seventy-three and liked to keep active. Great, this was to be an extra bonus. As soon as we returned we would check it out. So this formed the basis of our year. We would spend at least two to three weeks in Santa Fe, visit Puerto la Cruz for a few days and then sail and explore some little islands or anchorages. We made Santa Fe our base and returning we felt that we were coming home.

We found Jose Vivas and began our Spanish classes. What a delight they were. Usually there was a small group of us, some learning Spanish and some Venezuelans learning English. There were just chairs and a blackboard and lots of fun. Oh yes, there was a stick of chalk that Jose would regularly lose. (As time went on we secretly bought a box of chalk and would produce just one stick when it became obvious that the previous elusive piece was not going to be found).

Each lesson, Jose, our maestro, would write a list of words in both languages along with a new verb. We would repeat these as a group, until we got the correct pronunciation and then singly. When Jose was satisfied we would begin to make sentences. Correcting each other and helping in our respective languages, the hour and a half would fly. We were not learning written Spanish just the spoken word. The day's words must be learnt by tomorrow and on Friday there would be a grand revision. Some days we would arrive and Jose was absent. He was on a mission with some grand plan that he'd thought up in the night. Each of these was to help Santa Fe to develop its tourist trade. In his absence we would drink coffee with La Negra his non- English speaking wife and these conversations were as useful as the lessons.

Jose's dream was that Santa Fe would become a restful holiday resort, small and unspoilt but bringing work and pride to this struggling village. As well as his own Posada, there were three up and running and two under development. Of these two, one was owned by a Frenchman and the other, an American. We met French Michel and Marina his Venezuelan partner but although Jose constantly spoke of the American friend, Jerry, we never met him. We even began to think that he was a figment of Jose's overactive imagination.

Time passed; nothing else broke and the pennies were growing, AND THE WEIGHT BEGAN TO COME OFF. So what did we do with our days? In Santa Fe, we arose at six-thirty and exercised on board, by now we were carrying weights. Of course our boat was too small for us both to exercise below. Needless to say I was gazumped by Trevor and had to do mine on deck. The actual exercising on board did not faze me too much as we were still the only occupied boat at anchor, but being overlooked by all the fishermen as they pulled on their enormous oars to reach their fishing grounds, made me feel incredibly guilty. Here in front of their very eyes was this crazy woman, artificially keeping fit, when the women in their hard lives was struggling to run a home without any extra aids, humping water containers which made my weights look ridiculous, usually surrounded by a huge family, sometimes holding down some sort of job and all with very little money. I must say that I got lots of smiles and waves from these hard working men. We had breakfast in the cockpit, followed by a few chores and by ten we rowed ashore and walked to the Market.

We were becoming known and could practice our Spanish with locals while doing our shopping. Back again, sometimes stopping for a coffee with La Negra or with Michel and Marina. (Jerry was still elusive at this stage), a swim and then lunch. Spanish homework, maybe a little siesta and off to our late afternoon class. This was followed by our meringada, a chat with any backpackers and back home for supper. Some reading, writing letters and the occasional stab at writing another article and then bed by about nine-thirty.

The monthly few days we spent in Puerto la Cruz centred on a visit to the Bank to top up our funds; on principal we never carried much actual cash on board in this country. We were learning. In fact our visit to the Bank was carried out with care. We had stopped using cash dispensers in Venezuela, or hole in the wall as my daughter was want to call it. First of all, interested but no-good observers would know that we were now carrying cash and muggings were becoming a regular occurrence. Secondly, recently there had been problems where one could key in a request for a certain amount of cash and out popped half the amount or less, but it was always accompanied by a receipt for the original amount. This usually happened at the weekend and on Monday, when the irate customer complained; he was assured that only the actual amount received would be debited from his account. Not so, when the Bank Statement finally arrived, and remember with cruisers it was often months away, no such adjustment was actually made. Last of all you only had to observe the security systems when money was delivered to the Bank to realize that crime was only just around the corner. Each armoured van was securely locked and money only passed out when the receiving Bank was completed covered by guards wearing flak jackets, helmets and carrying pistols or shot guns. And even this was not enough. It took a couple of visits before we noticed something strange.

Once again we had badly timed our visit to the Bank; money was again being delivered. We stood outside awaiting the performance to be completed when Trevor noticed several slits in the wall, rather like long letterboxes. Eerily and silently, slim nozzles of shotguns suddenly protruded from these openings; we realized that weapons from the inside were also being trained on the money. For the rest of the morning I felt really uncomfortable carrying money around with us. Anyway we had to shop for unobtainable items not found in our outback life. You may wonder what these unobtainable were. They were things like paper towels, instant coffee, brown flour, washing up liquid and some such exotic items! Then we had our regular trip to the Marina where there was a once monthly Cruisers' Flea Market. You will see that it didn't take much to please me and this was the highlight. A chance to catch up with cruisers' gossip, swap books, perhaps find a treasure and most important for me, to visit the Charity Stall which had second hand glossy magazines on sale. Then off we went on a little cruise where we discovered more tranquil and beautiful anchorages before we returned home, to Santa Fe.

On one of these excursions we met Len, a singlehander with the most beautiful boat. Every morning we would watch him swimming for about a mile. How I envied his easy effortless strokes. He visited one day, complete with hot banana muffins and shared one of his swimming tales. He was anchored alone in Ensenada Tigrillo (Bay of the tigers) working up to his early morning splash when he saw ripples in the water. Was there someone in there before him? He could see the shape of someone swimming in the clear blue water and as he watched he or she came closer to his boat. At last he could see who it was. He saw a large jaguar gliding through the sea and as he came even closer, Len could see the water drops glistening on his whiskers. Time stood still as he gazed in fascination, he did not move and realized that he was even holding his breath. The beautiful animal passed and slowly disappeared into the distance. It was only then that he realized that he had not even taken a photograph. Len did not go swimming that day!

On one of our explorations we sailed to Mochima, pretty little town and met up with a British couple sailing slowly towards Panama. Over a cup of tea and before we left for Santa Fe, they asked about security in this Gulf of Mochima; we suggested that if alone, it was wise to explore the nearby isolated anchorages by day and return to the security of Mochima village at night. We left and several days later, heard on the radio that they had not heeded our advice and spent three days alone in an isolated bay, were boarded, held at gun point and robbed.

We weren't robbed and never saw a jaguar but we did see numerous dolphins. In fact every time that we sailed back into the Golf of Santa Fe the dolphins came to escort us, acting as outriders. In this unbelievable clear water we would see them, even to the scars along their backs. Were these caused by boats' propellers? They certainly played tag with us and I swear that as they dived beneath 'Boon' they turned sideways to look at us making sure that we appreciated their dexterity.

At class one day the elusive Jerry appeared and there began a very lasting friendship. Alone he was converting his properties into an attractive posada and centre for diving. He was struggling with the Spanish language, and the complexities of supervising workmen who really had no concept of skilled workmanship. He was also frustrated with the difficulties of obtaining the right materials and trying to convert his first world methods to their third world minds. For example how do you relay to a local cleaning woman that a guest room has to be cleaned thoroughly and the floor has to be washed, as well as swept, DAILY, when her own abode boasts a dirt floor? Also the painter had to be reminded EVERY day to put a sheet on the floor before beginning to paint. We all managed to convince him that attendance at Jose's lessons would help with some of these problems. So Jerry began regular attendance and we all enjoyed his company and wonderful Spanish with a strong American accent. His American sleeping partner visited while this was happening and he admitted that his Mexican employees in the USA were rocket scientists in comparison with their Venezuelan cousins. This provided Jose with a yet another scheme. He visited the local Tourist Board and suggested a Training Programme for the local residents of Santa Fe. Evening classes in cleaning, waiting at table, kitchen and bar work, reception duties and some basic spoken English. The local Church would provide the hall; people would give their time and skills in training and the trainees would receive a certificate upon successful completion of each section. Hopefully the result would be skilled workers. Local people applied to join and before our year was over the course was up, running and nearly completed. In the meantime he managed to persuade the village that their rubbish dump must change. Before we left that year, bins had appeared and were used (most of the time) and even emptied daily (some of the time).

CHAPTER THIRTY FOUR
CRIME IN PARADISE

Of course not everyone in Santa Fe was nice and friendly. There was a group of about four young men who were the village troublemakers. I guess these young men were bored with life and were looking for trouble. They were between sixteen and nineteen with lots of energy, adrenalin rushing through their veins and no direction. With all four there was no father around. Their petty crimes usually took the form of trivial thieving; sunglasses, shoes or cigarettes left on the beach. Sometimes they would climb through a window and grab a coke or beer. At night they would climb over walls to find any open windows making off with cassette players, radios, etc. The whole village was fed up with their antics. The police seemed disinterested in taking any action.

One day we took our dinghy to fetch a fifty-pound block of ice, so this necessitated our using the outboard and as the wheels had fallen off our ice carrying trolley, we both had to walk the short distance to the ice centre. A few minutes later when we returned, the dreaded deed had been done. Our fuel line had been stolen. My Captain was furious. I guess you would now call it fuel line rage. He questioned a nearby child who said that a young man had taken it, the description sounded like the brother of Opie. Opie was probably the ringleader of these bad lads. Surprise, surprise.

We rowed back, accompanied by Trevor listing what he would do to the culprit. Later that morning we visited Jerry to get some water and I was approached by the brother who told me that he'd seen a small boy take our fuel hose and he, helpful young man that he was, had rescued it for us. It took me a while to work this out as of course it was in Spanish. Trevor then returned and I told him the tale. Trevor turned to the young man, "Thank you" he said holding out his hand ready to take the hose. Of course we were told that we were expected to pay for such a thoughtful act. No way, Trevor was totally aware that he was the thief and told him that he could keep the hose. Now this was not part of the expected scenario. There proceeded a dialogue of he asking Trevor for a small reward and Trevor saying no. It was a case of stalemate when our French friend Michel appeared on the scene. In English he suggested that we would be wiser to have this young man as our friend rather than our enemy, and a small monitory token would end the whole affair. Trevor did not agree. Then of course, I got worried and suggested that we should heed Michel. Trevor was outnumbered and now of course he was cross with me, and against his better judgment and with bad grace, he gave him some money. It did not end there, as our thief was disgusted with such a small amount. He departed mumbling that perhaps we would have more cash on another occasion. Anyway we'd got our hose back.

The following Monday we were lunching in the cockpit when we noticed a small fishing boat heading our way. Remember we were still the only yacht anchored in this beautiful bay. In the bow stood our thief accompanied by Krisandra the fittest and largest of the troublesome gang, a truly big guy. Trevor quietly told me to fetch the flare pistol and he quickly thrust this out of sight. Once the fishing boat was alongside us, the two men jumped into our dinghy that was tied next to the cockpit and the fishermen backed a little way off. The dialogue started with the request for more money and they got the same answer, 'No'. Krisandra flexed his muscles and Trevor did not move. I thought that they would hear my heart thudding. The question and answer was repeated as I looked from one to the other like an umpire at a tennis match. Slowly Trevor produced the pistol, making sure that it was clearly visible and just sat there. There was a great rush of activity as the fishing boat disappeared and now we were left with the two visitors in our dinghy and no transport back to shore. I watched Trevor and he did not blink or move a muscle, and suddenly I knew with utmost certainty that he would use that pistol. I guess the boys felt the same, as without any warning they dived into the sea and swam ashore. A safe distance away, they laughed, waved and never bothered us again. At that point I heartily wished that I had brandy on board, I could have done justice to a very large glass.

As our year progressed we heard more and more of their antics but now it was no longer boyish misdeeds, they were pushing pot and a cheap form of crack to the backpackers and young people in the village. The elders in this little community had a meeting and at last the police agreed to become involved. Fairly shortly after that Krisandra, was arrested and everyone sighed with relief. But that was short lived as he suddenly appeared again; the only difference was that he sported a very short haircut. Gradually the story unfolded. His father, separated from his mother, was in local politics and there was to be no charge made against his son. It says something about the status of the police in Santa Fe when we found out that they did not even have a phone line to their headquarters. Just picture it, in an emergency the fittest person on the scene had to run to the Station for help.

Later in the year, while we were sailing, Opie prowling the market, grabbed a tourist's cine camera and ran. Unfortunately for him two policemen had just entered and one pointed his pistol and shot him in the leg. We had missed all the action but evidently it was quite dramatic as the market was full of people at the time. For a short while peace reigned, but it wasn't long before a limping Opie was back in action again.   One of the problems was that their targets were usually tourists. These visitors did not stay long in Santa Fe and to make a charge, one had to be around for a while and so, in the main, most charges were dropped.

CHAPTER THIRTY-FIVE
ENTER THE WORLD OF COMPUTERS

But our life went on and we heard from our Canadian friends that our radio was repaired, but as we could still keep the borrowed radio it was agreed that we would wait until November and they would bring the radio back with them. Having established that the cost was very low, we realized that we would have enough in the kitty to buy our computer and printer. We couldn't believe it

First of all we did some serious thinking; we wanted to get it right as this purchase was to be a one and only. By now most of our sailing friends had a laptop and it was the obvious choice for a boat. It took up little space and of course used minimum power. We were aware that these computers were not happy living in the cruising atmosphere with the salty air and quite often a lot of condensation and while we were looking at that problem, Trevor moved the goal posts. He decided that he wanted a desk top with a flat (LCD) screen. He felt that this might survive better in our strange atmosphere, and after research discovered that the flat screen used much less power that the full sized monitor. We didn't need portability anyway. Another thing in its favour was that we could buy it here, in Puerto la Cruz at our friendly dealer, Micro Oriente and if anything went wrong we could easily get it mended. We had seen too many people returning laptops to the States at vast expense. Then shock and horror, we discovered that even if we'd wanted to, there wasn't a laptop to buy anywhere in Venezuela or Trinidad. So we were definitely going for the desktop. Then another problem arose; Venezuela did not have a single flat screen for sale. We had entered the world of unobtainable new technology, in Venezuela anyway.

We talked to Angel at Micro Oriente, who fortunately spoke excellent English. Our Spanish was improving but not to the extent of downloading, booting up, formatting and all the rest of it.

Back in Santa Fe, Howard, Jerry's sleeping partner agreed that on his next visit from the States he'd bring a flat screen and Angel could install the mini tower, keyboard, speakers, etc., together with a printer at an excellent price. Now all we had to have was patience. Finally everything came together and Angel even managed to find Windows 98 and Office in English. We hadn't even considered that problem.

Now I want you to shut your eyes and get the picture. We were at anchor at Puerto la Cruz and the shop was in the middle of this busy town, where we had already delivered our LCD screen. We dinghied ashore and almost ran to the shop. There it was, assembled in all its glory. They turned it on and showed us that it worked with our two programs installed and in English. This wonderful equipment was then carefully dismantled and packed into boxes, while we both took a deep breath and paid the bill, carefully pocketing the two-year guarantee. When we next looked, boxes surrounded us. Taxi time and soon the friendly driver was helping us carry our load through the sand to the dinghy. We had taken dustbin liners with us and the boxes were carefully wrapped in these. All aboard and rather wobbly we were off; God smiled on us sending an incredibly calm afternoon, and we climbed on board 'Boon' without any mishaps.

I guess the fun really started at this point. We undid the boxes and were immediately surrounded by packing and what seemed like a mountain of equipment. Sorting ourselves out and putting all the packing on the bed, we were soon sitting side by side at the keyboard, mouse at the ready, with boat batteries full. (Guess who went first?) Trevor turned on the power and pressing the buttons we had Windows 98 in glorious Technicolor. For the next hour, we began to realize what a powerful tool we had and how little we knew. Excel, wizard, fonts and formatting; my goodness that little mouse had a mind of its own. Exhausted, we stopped and decided to call it a day. But how to turn the damn thing off? No button that said stop, close, finish or even end. We tried everything. Eventually we turned it off at the power source, convinced that we had broken everything. In the morning we had the embarrassment of asking on the Net how to turn it off. The answer came over the airways with everybody listening - just click the mouse on 'start' and a panel appears, this gives a few headings including 'shut down'. Oh so simple. But seriously, who would expect to select START to STOP.

Trevor's birthday was in November and of course there was no question of a present for him this year, after all he had the computer and his radio was now returned. Nevertheless we decided to invite our generous friends to a birthday dinner. These were the ones who had lent us their spare radio and the ones who had our old one repaired in Canada. So Trevor's seventy-first birthday began. First of all we attended the monthly Flea market and to our amazement there was a huge chocolate cake covered with candles. Then we hosted a Chinese meal for our helpful friends and when we finally returned exhausted to Santa Fe, Jerry had prepared a birthday feast under the palm trees. We felt truly blessed and I'm sure Trevor will never forget that birthday.

Now we were back in S.F. and as well as our daily Spanish classes we had to teach ourselves how to use a computer. We were told that we should buy the book 'Windows 98 for Dummies', of course we could only find it written in Spanish and we weren't at that level yet, so we taught ourselves. It was frustrating but great fun. In fact we were having so much pleasure, that Christmas seemed to creep up on us. We had got into the habit of taking local friends sailing on a Sunday; we would have a sail and then find an anchorage for swimming and lunch. It always seemed that a group of dolphins would join us and act as outriders making our day even more exhilarating. We had to be careful as many of the backpackers would ask us to take them sailing and they would pay for their day out. This would have been good for our bank balance but we were very conscious that the local boats owners were struggling to earn their living by taking guests to the other anchorages. We didn't want to upset the local economy and to be honest we didn't want to make any enemies, so we would sadly decline while explaining the situation. Taking friends for a free weekend was a different matter.

Suddenly we realized that we were about to spend yet another Christmas on board. Where had the time gone? We dug into our memories to remember exactly where we had been each Christmastide. The first year we were in the Algarve in Portugal, wearing shorts on the great day. Then it was Spain in the Balearic Islands where we watched the three kings arrive by sea, late at night with huge black horses waiting for them at the water's edge. They rode through the picturesque streets throwing packets of sweets to the children.

There followed several Christmases in Greek Cyprus, one with the two of us alone in the Atlantic, and then Christmas dinner in a downtown Diner in Miami. Back in the Caribbean we ate in an elegant restaurant on a sultry evening in St Maartens and heard the news of our grandson's arrival. There was the wonderful occasion shared with a Trinidadian family and friends and now another Christmas had crept up upon us. How were we to celebrate? Could we take friends for a Christmas picnic sailing to an isolated anchorage? Should we host a Barbecue on the sands? Actually we had little time to make any decision when Jose and La Negra asked us to join them in their traditional Venezuelan Christmas together with their family and friends at their lovely guesthouse on the sands. We were delighted to accept. Jerry was going to the mountains in company with Michel and Marina and her student sister was joining them.

We toured Puerto la Cruz to find little gifts with a difference and placing them into tiny stockings or made the packaging like Christmas crackers, hoping to bring a little of our culture to their scene. We duly delivered a crate of beer on Christmas Eve and casually asked at what time we should arrive on Christmas Day. This caused great alarm as the celebrations took place that evening – Christmas Eve. Whoops, we nearly arrived a day too late. The next question was what time should we arrive? Evidently this is a question no one ever seemed to ask. But after much head scratching, it was agreed that 8 pm would be about right. During the rest of the day we were entertained by a variety of music from ashore and an assortment of bangs. Being British and rather correct, we felt we must arrive on time so we promptly dressed in our glad rags, climbed into the dinghy and rowed ashore. On the beach were an assortment of local families and holidaymakers gathering to begin their own celebrations. " Felize Navidad" echoed around accompanied by rather impressive bangs. Rockets, bangers, crackers were obviously a necessary part of Christmas here.

We were the first to arrive; in fact the next guests arrived one and a half-hours later!! No problem, we were enjoying our view from the terrace, the conversation and the delicious smells from the kitchen. By 11.30 there was a full and overflowing house and they patiently explained to us that when they'd said 8 pm, they meant Venezuelan time, not British time. Would we ever learn? We had appetizers and then their traditional Christmas meal. Bowls of salads, bread layered with ham and HALLACA. For those interested in these things, hallaca is a savoury dish of banana leaves spread with a maize dough mix, filled with cooked chopped chicken, red meat, bacon, spices and vegetables. The leaves are made into little parcels and tied with string and steamed. The end result, when unwrapped, is a tasty pastry package, in theory not unlike the Scottish haggis but much more spicy and flavoursome. (Apologies to all friends from Scotland). Cake followed. Drink flowed, friends materialized and from all the other houses the macho Venezuelan males competed to see who could produce the biggest rockets with the loudest bangs. Being a child of the Second World War, I never cease to be taken by surprise and jump. The kids loved it and by now all along the beach everyone had overflowed onto the sand. Presents weren't in great supply but rum and beer seemed to flow. A few houses were decorated with flashing lights and we did see one Christmas tree but every house seemed to have a centrepiece of the Nativity scene. Beautiful little figures of the Holy family, angels and animals and most were carved from wood or made from fine china and pottery. In fact I think it was my first Christmas for a very long time without seeing nasty plastic ornaments, however the inferior and sometimes dangerous children's plastic toys on sale had saddened both Trevor and me over this season. Items that would not have been acceptable in the first world countries.

In the wee small hours we were the only ones who appeared to run out of steam, so amid kisses and handshakes we pulled our dinghy into the sea, sliding away to 'BOON'. The sky was inky black, patterned with twinkling stars and we could hear a background of breaking seas, voices, music, dogs barking and of course even louder BANGS. Another Christmas on board and certainly one to remember.

Our South American year was due to finish at the end of March and by now both Jerry and Michel had their guesthouses up and running. Jerry had become more than friendly with Marina's student sister and life for him in the New Year seemed very happy and full of hope. He was planning the diving side of the enterprise and was going to buy a fast boat for diving trips. The two businesses were quite different. Jerry's built along the traditional Venezuelan lines and activity centred, with Michel's more laid back, ready for tourists to chill out and the furnishings very French.

Life for Trevor and I continued at our gentle pace, we continued with our Spanish, went sailing, made even more new friends and Trevor delved into the wonderful tricks that the computer could perform. I found that I was just content to use it as a sophisticated typewriter. Was I showing my stuffy old age? Anyway I did manage to produce some articles and they looked so much more professional in the printed from with text wrapped around a funny cartoon or picture. A pattern began, Trevor using the machine in the early morning and I had it in the early afternoons. Our Spanish continued but by now Trevor had completely overtaken me. He'd had the head start with his Spanish evening class when we were still in the UK, but if I'm honest he was just better at languages than me. Much as I hate to admit it, he used to try much harder and by this time he could have long conversations with Jose and I was well and truly left behind.

The time flew and one day Jerry swam out to the boat with a broad grin splitting his face in two. He was to marry his Venezuelan girl friend, with the very English name of Daisy. What a wonderful way to complete our year. Over the months we had become special friends with this friendly Californian and we loved Daisy. We mentally searched through our dwindling wardrobe to find suitable wedding finery and then came the decision of a gift. What could we give to these very special people? Finally we decided that it must be something very personal, so I made a pillow which I embroidered with a picture of their beautiful posada surrounded with palm trees, the Venezuela flag, their logo of a toucan and last of all a heart with their names; surrounded of course with daisies. Fortunately it worked and we were very pleased with the finished result.

The wedding was wonderful, more so because the catering was prepared by Michel's French partner who was visiting at that time. So just visualize it, a simple wedding ceremony on a terrace overlooking sand and palm trees, brilliant sunshine, clear blue sea with the most fabulous French catering. Surely a recipe for success. As Trevor and I left that evening I said to them, "Put it together and sell it to the tourists as an away from it all wedding package. You'd have a winner." We sailed away in the morning, our year was over.

Partings were no longer as final as in the past. Email had become part of all our lives and although we could not send e-mails directly from the boat having no phone lines, cyber cafes were popping up like mushrooms where very cheaply we could receive and send news via the free Hotmail, AOL or Yahoo. We would get news of the happenings at Santa Fe wherever we were.

CHAPTER THIRTY-SIX
IT SOUNDS LIKE A PLAN

We had a fairly painless sail to Trinidad stopping only at Margarita and Puerto Santos. Trinidad was exactly the same as when we left her and we realized as we signed in, that it was exactly one year to the very day since we'd left.

We had chosen Trinidad as we could easily fly home and leaving the boat on a TTYA mooring was the most inexpensive method. We still had a little of our hard saved money left and felt that it would be lovely to see all the family again. I think even then at the back of our minds was the niggle that one day we would have to return to reality.

Reunion time in Trinidad again and it truly felt as if we had come home. Our only problem was that the repaired radio did not work. We trudged around recommended workshops but no technician could help us, so there was nothing for it but to take it to the UK with us. This was getting to be a much-travelled piece of equipment perhaps it would begin to earn air miles. We decided we wouldn't book our tickets until the English summer arrived and just enjoy this friendly island once more.

We reunited with lots of friends and I think that we had as many Trinidadian friends as we did cruising friends. The best part for me was the number of people who commented on my loss of weight. On the scales I now stood (first thing in the morning, before anything to drink or eat, naked and breathing out) at eight stones and twelve pounds. About twenty pounds less than when we left. I still hadn't had any alcohol to drink.

We noticed that cyber cafes had sprung up here as well but apart from that, very little had changed. The maxi taxis still went too fast, the music was far too loud, the young girls were still as beautiful, babies never seemed to cry and the humidity was debilitating. The time seemed to fly and departure time arrived.

We flew into London on a sunny Tuesday morning and from that moment onwards we enjoyed the most wonderful six weeks. Everyone was well and seemed pleased to see us. The grandchildren had grown, some beyond recognition. We visited everyone and became acquainted with two-year-old Matthew. My daughter's ready-made family seemed to treat us as an adventure story come to life and I was delighted that they had christened me "Jane's Mumbo". On our previous visit six-year-old Sean had misheard Trevor's name and it was only after we had left, that his father heard him talk about "Treasure". Now Trevor had a new name as well. I, of course, always knew that he was my treasure! My mother had become more frail and sometimes resorted to a walking frame but seemed very happy in her sheltered apartment and I was truly grateful that my daughter gave her so much of her very precious time. Mum was secure in a bright and cheerful flat with all her own treasures, it was self-contained but with a warden on call in case anything went wrong. There was a club nearby where she could meet friends, have lunch and join any classes of her choice. Being over sixty ourselves (well over sixty) we could join her for lunch there and as we united in their lunchtime conversations, I felt that I did not have much in common with them. Upon reflection I guessed that they were a lot older than me. Later during the meal I discovered that it wasn't so. Many were younger than Trevor and I. For a moment I wondered if we would fit in if we returned to the UK to live. But there was too much happening for me to linger too long on such thoughts.

During our stay, there was a heat wave and while everyone was expiring with the heat, we were just comfortable. Our final few days were spent with Trevor's cousins. This was a very special time as she had arranged a reunion of his family's "older generation" and Pauline had researched the family history back to the days of the Czar Nikolai, where their Great Grandfather had been conscripted into the Army at the age of ten and had served for twenty-five years. We discovered that our name is really Nassatissin but was anglicised along the way to make it easier when living in Britain. So we flew back to Trinidad with a repaired radio, books, some different clothes and a family history together with beautiful old sepia photographs to back it all up. 'Boon' was patiently waiting for us and the cruising life began once more.

We were two months into the hurricane season so a decision needed to be taken as to our sailing plans. We couldn't go north as our Insurance wouldn't cover us in that direction. Hurricane Luis had put paid to that; the Insurance companies had lost so much money in claims, the hurricane areas had all been vetoed. We needed to lift out and antifoul and felt that we should leave hot and muggy Trinidad. We finally agreed to make a shorter visit to Venezuela to visit our friends and once the H. season was over to make a long jump from there to Puerto Rico and slowly cruise through the islands. After all we had never been further North than St Maartens. We definitely needed to do something different as the year 2000 was just around the corner. We had made a plan, now all we had to do was action it.

So it was the pattern as before and we were soon squeaky clean and newly bottom painted. There was one more deed to be done and that was a painful one, financially painful that was. Our outboard engine was decidedly elderly and troublesome and Trevor made the mammoth decision that we would not buy a second-hand machine but a new one. He was fed up with things breaking down and the new philosophy was to be, "buy new and be trouble free." How to fund the new philosophy was still a mystery. So we spent our last few weeks in Trinidad running in our new acquisition. Great.

You must be getting fed up to hear that the trip to Venezuela with the wind and current with us was perfect. But it was. We stopped over night at our usual little anchorages and finally had a very quick sail into a windy Margarita and dropped the anchor. The anchorage was crowded with boats and we decided not to venture ashore until the next day. The wind was still blowing hard so we relaxed over our supper and settled down for a lazy evening. Sailing seemed to knock us out these days so we soon found that we were dropping off to sleep over our books, eventually it was an early night for the two oldies. A quick look around to make sure that all was well and we were in the land of nod.

About midnight a big blow, accompanied by a tremendous thunderstorm, swept through the anchorage and we were woken from a very deep sleep with a start. Nothing unusual I guess, it happens from time to time, but on this occasion we dragged or as the Americans say, we drug. In what seemed like seconds, we were bearing down on another British yacht. And yes, you have guessed it, the engine wouldn't start. The skipper grabbed the boat hook while the fast approaching neighbours hung out their fenders and we missed them by inches – well, feet. We let out more scope (anchor chain) and we dug in again. By now we could see the navigation lights of other boats on the move, so we were not alone. A few minutes of generator power and the engine fired and we were in control once more. An hour or so later the storm passed and peace reigned. Finally we were asleep once more.

The next day we were both very tired but we moved the boat, as our jaunt of the night before had left us too near our friendly neighbours. We finally went ashore to begin the process of signing in, with an Agent of course! We found lots of old cruising friends and were surprised to find that because of the growing security problems, a lot of them were spending the whole six months of the Hurricane season in Margarita. I was disappointed to find that I had lost nearly all of my Spanish. Back on board and sitting in the cockpit we began to talk about our sailing plans and how we were looking forward to sailing to Rico. The name alone always made me think of 'West Side Story'. Trevor reminded me that the sail would take several days and it was a long time since we'd spent several nights at sea. In fact it must have been the trip from Bermuda to St Maartens. This triggered a "Do you remember? Where is so and so now?" type of conversation. We were both surprised at the number who had given up the lifestyle or the lifestyle had given them up, because of age or ill health. Before we knew it we were launching ourselves into an in depth discussion on our own future. We certainly could continue for more years but would need to consider maintenance and possible expenditure as parts began to fail on 'Boon' as she got older. We also knew that we were sailing now without a life raft. Not really a wise thing to do. Also we were in the age group where we could encounter more health problems, but these would occur on land as well as at sea. We felt fairly confident that it was the lifestyle that had kept us fit and alert, so we would need to plan an active life ashore if we ever decided to go down that route.

We had only returned together to the UK three times during our ten-year adventure and as these were in the summer months, we had forgotten the diverse seasons and quite frankly, the bloody awful English weather. We did not own any property, so we were not tied to any particular country, but surely we have some ties to eight great kids and their respective bundles of joy. These are truly a joy to us and during the last visit we felt so proud that we had been partly responsible for their being. They are bright, energetic and full of fun. Do we really want to continue seeing them so infrequently? Or is the appeal on both sides because we do not crowd each other out?

At this stage we were just playing with ideas and during that evening we seemed to jump from one idea to another. Most important of all of course, was the need to look at our financial situation and that would govern which country we might choose. Of course we looked at living in Israel and Trevor being a Jew, we would have no difficulty being accepted there. But looking at the bottom line we knew that financially we would not have any kind of life at all, we might just be able to exist. So what did we want from our next lifestyle? We would like to live simply but comfortably; not difficult having lived on a small boat! Have enough money to visit the theatre, museums, and probably take in some courses and maybe travel. We now spoke some Spanish but did we want to have to learn another language again? Security was beginning to cause us some concern and although we knew that we could financially settle in Venezuela or Turkey, would we feel secure and anyway, can one just go and live in these countries? Did we need visas, residential permits or what? We suddenly realized that it was terribly late and climbed into our bed but Trevor had the last word. He did not want to sail until he lost the plot and thought that it would be better to leave the party while we were still enjoying it. With these profound words he was fast asleep. I just lay there with all these million and one thoughts going round and round in my head. What would we be doing next, where and when?

The answer came much quicker than I realized, the next morning to be exact. We had tuned into our early morning radio net. (Oh yes, the radio had been repaired in the UK and was now working perfectly).

We heard the weather report and someone asked for the whereabouts of another boat and then someone asked if Trevor was on the radio. Quickly he replied and transferred to another frequency, then began talking to an old friend in Puerto la Cruz. The long shot was that there was a job available helping to fit out a charter boat in one of the Marinas there; the money was good; too good to ignore and was Trevor interested? Trevor asked a few questions and said, "Yes".

We went ashore to sign out and found that our newly acquired outboard was making a dreadful noise and would only travel at half its speed. Whoops. Ashore Trevor had a quick look and couldn't find anything wrong but decided to change the plugs. This made no difference. Back on board he took it all to pieces but could find nothing. I got quite angry, why was he doing all this? The reason we bought new was to have no more problems as it was under guarantee. Back ashore again and this time to the Chandlery. Yes, they were the Agents for Johnson outboards. But no, they couldn't cover our outboard as it was bought in Trinidad; they would only cover goods purchased in Venezuela. We had forgotten we were in this country with its corruption, rules and version of what could or could not be done. Trevor was furious and I thought he would explode. Eventually we left, he determined that he would not pay anyone to repair the damn thing, we'd run it on stop or slow until we got to some civilized place.

We made a quick visit to Santa Fe and were caught up with lots of reunion hugs and kisses. The Posadas were up and running but no one was making a fortune and the bad lads were still around. Sadly Jose told us that crime generally had increased in this beautiful country. Crime that was now involving boats. More dinghies and outboards had been stolen, boats boarded and more guns were in evidence. No one wanted to be an alarmist and remember good news is no news and bad news is headlines, but things were certainly happening. Because of the job we could only spend one day with them but promised that we would sail back at weekends. When we arrived at Puerto la Cruz we were shocked to find that at the main town anchorage, there were two boats at anchor. Two years ago there had been fifty and last year up to thirty. Crime was certainly having an effect. Fortunately for us because of Trevor working, we could afford to go into a Marina. He had to be near the job that was in a complex of boat yards and Marinas and there were no anchorages nearby. Friends helped us find the least expensive one and soon we were tied up to the dock and linked to water and electricity. Trevor started work the next day and I was left with time on my hands and a dinghy to run which would break down with no warning, anytime, anywhere. Great.

CHAPTER THIRTY-SEVEN
BACK TO NINE TO FIVE ONCE MORE

So here was the situation. At long last we were in a Marina, albeit rather a basic one. I now had water direct to the boat. I could use as much as I liked and laundry became a joy. We were plugged into electricity so we could use all our lights and I could use my computer all day long. AND I had all those days to myself to do whatever I wanted to. So what did I do? First of all I cleaned the boat from top to bottom. Then I started some long overdue varnishing. I did a lot of cooking and Trevor would come home to the smell of fruitcakes, bread pudding, pies and all sorts of vegetarian dishes. The beauty of it all was that I had my own space. When you live in such close proximity with someone in a tiny boat, you have to plan your days around each other's plans. Now the bread maker could spread all over the boat and do whatever she liked, whenever she liked, as long as it was back to normal when the breadwinner returned.

I did however, worry about him, my concern was that Trevor in his seventies, was working again and in such heat. I felt a little reassured when I saw that the boat he was helping to refit was air-conditioned and he seemed to relish in the activity again. Actually it was not as bad as I'd thought, as he only seemed to work two weeks in every three. In all this spare time, I wrote a few more articles and was especially pleased when an item I wrote on the economy in Venezuela, was published in a National Venezuelan newspaper. I'd actually reached the stage when meeting new people was occasionally asked if I was the Ley Liberson who wrote in the papers. Whow!

It was now nearly the year 2000 and this life style had lasted for almost ten years and here was Trevor at 71 back to work again. It set me thinking about our earlier discussions on our future. I realized that in the multitude of sailing magazines and waterside newspapers that I'd read, I'd found there were numerous articles on the joys of this life, how to begin and what it involved, but little if anything, was written on when and why to stop. During the next few afternoons I worked on an article that I entitled, "Shall we go down to the sea again?" Now we had the computer it was great, I could prepare my article, download it onto a floppy disc and take the disc to my friendly Puerto la Cruz Cyber café and send it to a likely Editor. The café was run by two friendly young women, both Venezuelan, who made using their business, a pleasure. Not only were they friendly but also both were incredibly beautiful. It made me realize that in the Miss Universe competitions, a Venezuelan girl was always in the last three. Walking through the bustling streets, one would see these tall, slim beauties. They all seemed to be gracious, hardworking and they all had one other outstanding feature, sorry two; remember the girls when we decided to sign into the country ourselves? Well all these girls had big boobs and they were definitely proud of them.

My article was accepted and from time to time we would still touch on the subject of changing our lifestyle but nothing was decided, and we were horrified when storms further North in the Caribbean, caused terrible floods in this beautiful country. It brought continuous rain and enormous seas with high

281

tides causing mudslides, making homeless and killing so many people. I believe the final death total was over twenty-five thousand. Afterwards we sailed to Santa Fe and saw the effect on the village, particularly the beautiful beach. Water front houses and walls were damaged, some completely washed away, and the sand was pushed up the beach until it rested like miniature mountains against the properties, leaving barren rock where sand should be. Thank God no-one was killed here. We heard via the radio that all along the Venezuelan coastline was tremendous damage and our little fishing community at Punta Pargo was washed away. No one was killed there but the village was no more.

This put everything into prospective; our decisions seemed so trivial compared with the disaster around us. We had a regular pension, a boat we could eventually sell or take home to live on and friends and family who were safe and well. We were truly blessed.

Suddenly it was Christmas again and this one was spent with friends who lived on the outskirts of Puerto la Cruz . Irish Aubrey worked in the world of the oilrigs and with his Polish wife and small son lived in a luxury flat overlooking the sea. With some of their friends, we all enjoyed a fantastic feast, UK style. The house rule was that on alternate years it was Christmas, Polish style courtesy of Kristina, and the other years it was very traditionally British with Aubrey in charge. This year the Christmas pudding has been sent by Harrods and I can honestly say that I have never tasted one so delicious. Baby son, Nikolas was three and made our Christmas even more special.

Upon arrival we sat in a beautiful lounge opening presents, sipping wine and snacking. Came the magnificent meal and we all sat around a beautiful table and slowly ate, drank, talked, had a pause and then started all over again. It was one of those delightful evenings where we never left the table just enjoyed relaxing with special friends.

Trevor's job continued and by now I'd finished the varnishing, was up to date with the cleaning and baking and couldn't think of any more articles to write. One day I was sitting in front of the computer having finished my e-mails. What to do now? Somehow I was loath to turn off the magical machine. I started thinking how easy it was to keep in touch with family and friends now that this new technology was with us. I remembered sitting for days in lonely anchorages waiting for our snail mail to arrive. Would that be of interest to readers? Should I get it down on paper? An article didn't seem quite right. How did we start this strange lifestyle anyway? We'd been toying with the idea of a life cruising and travelling, but how did it actually start all those years ago?

When the dirty /working type skipper returned home I had begun writing a book. What a presumptuous thing to do, I almost blushed at the very audacity of it. It was well into the evening until I could bring myself to mention it. I was persuaded to show him or rather read it to him and his reaction was very encouraging. This didn't mean a great deal as he was always generous in his praise and I really needed genuine criticism and comment. Anyway it was a start.

The year continued and once again the money grew, as did the book; the very unreliable outboard struggled on and Trev's job went on in fits and starts, rather like the outboard. The problem with the job was that the owner lived in the States and a Manager oversaw the refit. From time to time funds ran out and there was a hiccough in the arrival of more dollars. So everything stopped until the cheque arrived again. The delays got longer and longer and warning bells began to ring, until one day the money dried up completely. Never mind we were very happy with our stack. Before we had a chance to plan some more sailing Trevor was offered some casual work and so it continued.

By now my article on stopping sailing was published and this brought about an interesting phenomenon. I had a tremendous amount of feedback, all from women. I was thanked, congratulated and praised for bringing the subject to the forefront. It appeared that a lot of skippers out there would never consider stopping and many reckoned that they would prefer to die at the wheel. They did not want to discuss the matter with their partners and some wives couldn't bring themselves to bring up the subject, but were genuinely worried about their own futures. Now suddenly there was this woman who had taken a stand on their behalf and had put it into print. It was a vehicle for them to bring the subject up for discussion and it appeared to help.

At this time Trevor's new job folded through lack of funds but we were too late into the season to sail to Puerto Rico and get back before the Hurricane season started once again. You must realize that the hurricane season is exactly half of our sailing year. We had just about decided to stay in this beautiful country and spread our wings, or rather our sails a little and take 'Boon' sailing to some of the more out of the way places perhaps to Bonaire, when everything began to happen at once. Crime began to increase with a vengeance. There were many reasons. The new President had made some startling new changes, things that at the time I thought were correct. There was so much corruption in this country he had to try and make changes, and the first thing was to get rid of the Judiciary, possibly a centre of the dishonesty. The Judges were all sacked. The jails were full of untried prisoners; some had been languishing, unsentenced for years. He released them, as reliable Judges hadn't been found, yet alone sworn in. Suddenly we had over two thousand men roaming the streets with no purpose, possible no training and many now homeless. A recipe for crime. The normal criminal fraternities were still with us and these numbers must have swollen by some of those rendered homeless in the latest disaster. I know that I wouldn't hesitate to steal if my children were starving. Although in this country there is a strong extended family ethos, with eighty per cent of the population under the poverty level, one can only extend the family so far. News then reached us that more yachts were being boarded, often trashed with goods and money stolen, again some at gun point. Trevor felt that it would not be long before someone would be killed, one of us or one of them. We sadly decided to leave this beautiful country that was the fourth largest oil producer in the world, could grow enough food for themselves and many other countries, had water enough to sell, produced an enormous amount of minerals and mined semi-precious stones but still had this tremendous poverty level. There is a favourite story here, and it goes something like, 'when a Sage saw all that God had given Venezuela, he questioned it, and God agreed that he might have been too generous. So he gave them Venezuelan Politicians'. No comment.

We began to look at our sailing options for the future. We both agreed that we had no intention of making another big step and sailing into the Pacific. It is a very big a step, going through the Panama Canal, then the huge expanse of the Pacific Ocean, Australia and back to the Med via the Red Sea. At our age it would be too long a time frame; as you will have noticed we don't usually travel in a rush. So we looked at our options; we could continue enjoying the Caribbean or return to the Bahamas and perhaps America again. What about revisiting the Med? Although we had enjoyed every moment of our lifestyle in all these countries, we didn't necessarily want to repeat the whole exercise. This of course brought us back once again, to the idea that perhaps we should reconsider leaving the sailing life and become land based once again.

My head was awhirl with these thoughts when Trevor said that we both really knew that the time was right to stop. It seemed sense to go back to Trinidad and put the boat on the market from there. It was an easy place to live and nothing was written in stone, we could always change our minds. So we did not make our trip to Puerto Rico but had a gentle sail back to Trinidad and began talking to everyone about selling boats. Remember this would be the first time that we had actually sold one. The other two had somehow slipped through our fingers!!!

CHAPTER THIRTY-EIGHT
HOW DO YOU SELL A BOAT?

We were back in the world of calypso, pan music, liming, theatre, good book swaps and quite often forgetting that we were supposed to be selling a boat. When we did get back on track we found that there were two schools of thought. One was to put the boat on the market immediately and not waste any time, as boats aren't easy things to sell. The other option was to make sure that we had the boat in excellent condition before we advertised her. The second did actually make sense, as 'Boon's' decks badly needed repainting. People viewing her could so easily be put off before they had even stepped on board. That threw up another question, should we do it ourselves or let the professionals loose on her? Much head scratching and watching both the professionals and the amateurs doing the job, we decided that we could manage that ourselves. Then yet another decision, should we do this in the water or on the land? Before we had even got our heads around this particular conundrum it began to rain and yes, we were into the rainy season. Rain in Trinidad is unbelievable. It comes down in torrents, thick, fast and furious. It usually lasts for about an hour or an hour and a half, often accompanied by some strong gusts. Strangely it seems to keep to a strict timetable and occurs between mid-day and two o'clock. So a hefty job like the deck couldn't be tackled in this season.

We rationalized that the one thing that we had plenty of, was time, and using some of Trev's hard earned money, we decided to visit the UK but wearing different eyes this time. We would be looking at costs, rents, weather and locations. So we did just that. I won't bore you with all the details as you've read it all before, but once again we had a fantastic time and it didn't cause us to change our tentative plans. There was one small fly in the ointment and that was other people's attitudes to our campaign. Both amongst our sailing friends and now UK landlubbers, the general consensus of concern was and I quote, "Won't you miss the life you've had over the last years? You won't find people in England so friendly. What will you do with yourselves? You'll be bored in three months. AND WHAT ABOUT THE WEATHER?" We got seriously tired of hearing this but managed to grin and bear it. Didn't they realize just how often we had asked ourselves those same questions?

One of things that we did as soon as we returned to Trinidad was to buy a little gizmo which when linked to our computer and through ham radio, gave us our own e-mail system on board. Now we had instant contact with friends and family all over the world. Since we started this sailing life the world had certainly shrunk. It brought back memories of all those days spent in ports waiting for snail mail to arrive at local post offices. Also those expensive minutes while we listened to the answer phone speaking to us or distances trudged to phones only to get no reply at all.

Any way eventually the rain stopped but the humidity was still with us. Common sense prevailed and we lifted her out and had 'Boon' perched firmly on the ground and began the tedious task of repainting the decks. First of course, we had to rub it down and clean every speck of it. Then mask off all the fittings, ports, toe rails, etc. Then clean it all over again as our industrious neighbours were scraping, sanding and grinding. You name it and they did it and then we had to do our own work all over again.

In the meantime we had sent e-mails to Yacht Brokers in the islands and the USA. We gave them details of her and our suggested price. We had decided to include everything in the sale, as after all we had no need of all her goodies. So the final package looked good on paper. We hoped that all the electronic aids, computer, printer, onboard email, dive bottle, generator, radios, etc., would make up for the fact that she was, although in good condition, elderly. I wondered if I could say the same about myself?

We were surprised that we only had replies to half our e-mails to Yacht Brokers, but those gave us their terms and quoted that if we were interested to let them know, and they would download their contract. We were surprised to read that they wanted our fax number for this purpose. Still not sure why, when everyone else was using E-mails? Legality perhaps, as of course they would need our signature, anyway we gave the fax number of the boat yard we were using. The last Agent informed us that they were about to open a branch office in Trinidad and in fact it was to be situated at our current venue. Sure enough we found the office and saw that it was to open the following Monday. In the meantime the other Agents did not fax us the contracts.

A wise cruiser suggested that we get the Agent to look at Boon's decks before we got any further with the paint job. Reason? They would see the condition of the deck before it was completely covered. Some people do a cosmetic job with paint to cover up cracks and imperfections. Good thinking. We definitely weren't streetwise or should I say boatwise?

Monday came and we visited the Broker and found a very friendly but very inexperienced lady in charge. At this stage she knew less about selling boats than we did. During the week she came on board and looked around, asked questions and then went off on a training course and came back and asked a lot more questions, took photographs, inspected the deck on our suggestion and we signed a contract. We continued with the task in hand and we were using brushes not the spray on method. The logistics of it were a problem. Remember we were living on board and once the deck was painted we had to stay below until it dried. Also we had to work to a very careful plan. We started in the bow, Trevor on one side and I on the other. We slowly worked backwards, trying to keep a 'wet edge,' as in this heat paint dried quickly. We had to be careful not to rub up against any sides and we applied the paint with a bristle brush and then flicked over with a foam one. We had to begin very early, as in this heat one could not continue much beyond 10.30. Unfortunately with the humidity, everything was very damp at dawn and although we wiped it all down it wasn't dry enough to start until about eight-thirty. So it was truly a race against a limited time.

Eventually the day came when we could apply the very last coat. We anxiously listened to the Weather forecast and it was exactly the same every day and had continued so for the last few weeks, 'sunshine with possible showers around mid-day'. We looked at each other and decided to go for it. Breakfast and the pattern as before and donning our old shirts and with our paint spattered hats, we were on our way. Nearly eleven and we were finished and standing in the cockpit surveyed the finished effect. It looked good, in fact quite dazzling and we'd got a good finish. We collapsed over a cold drink. About half an hour later the skies darkened and looking through the hatch we could see menacing black clouds approaching. Let's hope they passed us by, if they didn't perhaps the paint was fingertip dry enough to escape damage. There was nothing that we could do anyway.

The drumbeat of the rain announced its arrival. Half an hour later and it was all over. Once more we tentatively put our heads outside. We touched the nearby side decks; they were touch dry and unharmed. Slowly Trevor worked his way forward. One side was perfect but on the portside where the wind had driven the rain, the surface of the paint was marked and damaged. I could have cried. We would have to rub it all down and do the last coat again and worse to come; we would probably need another tin of paint. Dejectedly Trevor went to the Chandlery but came back without the paint. Our friendly shopkeeper had advised Trevor to speak to the professional painter on site before he launched into any more costs. We felt embarrassed to do this; after all we had chosen not to use the professionals. Nevertheless we decided to give it a go. Trevor came back with the man himself and after a quick look at the damage, he announced that no more paint was necessary, just a lot of hard work. We were to rub down the damage with a very fine rubbing compound, then buff it with a finer compound and polisher. It would come up unscathed and with a lovely finish. We did, and it did.

Our Agent came back and took photographs then arranged for adverts in several publications. We ran off our own flyers and placed them at strategic places around the Marinas and Boat Yards. Sailing friends leaving would take copies to place around the Caribbean. If we managed to sell it ourselves, we could save the ten per cent Agency charge. So there we were with our pristine decks, gradually doing a little varnishing and waiting for prospective buyers to arrive. We waited but no one came, so we got on with our lives and finally our first newspaper advert appeared. We looked in horror as we saw that the Yacht Broker had put in a higher price than the one we'd agreed. A quick 'phone call and she told us that she thought she had to add the Brokerage fee of ten per cent, not realizing that she had to take it off our original price when a sale was concluded. We looked at each other with similar thoughts. What chance did we have if she hadn't got the basics right? Well, we'd just have to wait and see and try even harder ourselves.

We enjoyed our waiting time; at least with very little sailing on the agenda, we were able to get used to our future lifestyle. But first of all we had to sell the old one. Time passed. We got heavily involved with our writing and by now Trevor had joined me as we were writing a children's book between us. We attended the Cruisers' Writers' Group and we suddenly realized that perhaps the actual writing was the easier part. We discovered frightening facts and statistics. The world was full of 'wannabe' writers and the advent of computers had more than doubled their numbers. Publishers weren't interested in unknown authors and one must use Literary Agents. Who and where did we find them? Even if we did find them, there were strict rules to be followed, and I quote. 'Write a query letter including a C.V. of one's writing background, prepare a synopsis and then submit two or three sample chapters of your book and don't forget the most important detail, enclose a self addressed, stamped envelope.' Oh yes, I nearly forgot further advice given. 'If you are not receiving at least two or three rejections each week, you are not trying hard enough.' A final statistic, "every single Agent usually receives about three thousand submissions each year. From these they generally choose three hundred manuscripts to actually read and if they are successful, they manage to get a Publisher to print three.

Back to the serious matter in hand that of selling 'Boon'. We still hadn't had a single sniff. The advert had reappeared with the correct price, but Trevor thought that damage had been done. Everyone seemed to tell us that they had a friend who wanted to buy a boat, they even asked for flyers, which we rushed to them along with photographs, but we never seemed to hear anymore.

With our bright sparkling boat we took ourselves off on a mini-sail along the Trinidadian coast sporting a huge hand painted sign. As soon as we anchored we would hoist it and wait for interest. Nothing happened. Nevertheless it was fun and some Trinidad friends with their boat joined us. We finally anchored in a little bay near a Yacht Club. We intended staying there for several days but once ashore we discovered an infestation of vicious daytime mosquitoes. The Commodore of the Club was devastated, as they loved welcoming visiting cruisers. They had cut back all the undergrowth and the local pest controllers had sprayed every inch of the place, twice, but to no avail. The Club members very seriously assured us that these mosquitoes were 'a vicious Venezuelan breed' and they seemed convinced that this was some dastardly plot on the part of nearby Venezuelans to send these wee beasties their way. Their coast was only a few miles away. Anyway this meant that even smothered with repellent, we were bombarded once ashore and I must admit these bastards were huge but I never discovered if they spoke Venezuelan or Trini English.

We all had to rush back to the boats where for some reason, the mosquitoes never came. Once back we did had fun, in fact it is impossible not to have fun with a crowd of Trinidadians. We ate, drank rum, fished from our stationery decks, some brought instruments, so we sang and Trevor and I learned a lot about this island from the old calypsos sung until the wee small hours. Never the less every time we ventured ashore we were attacked once more. Back on board, cell 'phones were produced and urgent calls made to local friends who soon appeared with cooked chicken legs, ice-cream, supplies of mangos and of course six-packs. Once the helpful friends were on board the next party started and more tales were exchanged. Trini's love liming, I think it is the thing they do best. I should have mentioned that our friends' boat is identical to ours and by nightfall it was loaded with happy people. The next day we discovered that most of them had stayed the night. Where on earth did they all sleep?

I guess all good things have to come to an end and without being able to go ashore, we felt the need to stretch our legs. Our friends had to go back to work, we all set off and had a magnificent sail to our usual anchorage, which thank God, was almost mosquito free.

CHAPTER THIRTY-NINE
PIRATES IN VENEZUELA

I have a strong suspicion that you are beginning to wonder what has happened to the mis-adventures that I used to have. It seems a long time since I was in the middle of a storm, lost at sea or Trevor landed me in undesirable overnight accommodation. Perhaps I was getting more experienced or maybe it just was someone else's turn. In fact I was glad that it wasn't my turn as other people's adventures were beginning to sound horrendous.

We heard over the SSB radio of a Dutch boat that was anchored in Puerto Santos. Remember the Venezuelan harbour with the dried fish factory? Well with his female partner he was anchoring overnight en route to Trinidad, when during the early hours they were boarded. They were held at gunpoint, tied up and then everything on the boat was loaded into a small fishing vessel. Unknown to the raiders, Jack was fluent in Spanish and he heard them discussing whether they should kill them both. Finally they decided to tow the yacht out of the harbour and once at sea, sink it. No sooner said than done. Once out of sight of the village they took a hammer; and adding insult to injury using one of Jacks, begun to attack the hull. What the thieves did not realize was that this boat was made of concrete. In fact it was called 'Dutch Concrete'. They must have got tired of this game as they finally left, leaving the boat drifting out of sight of the harbour, and the couple very much alive and the boat still intact. They managed to get untied and headed straight for Trinidad. Once there, they were well looked after and between us we managed to replace their stolen goods. The cruisers were wonderfully generous and provided clothes, food and electronic goodies including radios, a GPS and even a generator.

Safely tucked up in Trinidad we had hardly got over the shock of this incident when the next horror happened. A German couple, again returning to Trinidad from Venezuela, but this time were nearly at the Trinidad coast, when a motorboat hailed the skipper and by sign language indicated that he wanted cigarettes and booze. The captain shouted 'No' and with no warning the man pulled a gun and shot him in the stomach. The boat was quickly boarded and stripped of all goodies and money and it wasn't until they left, that the wife was able to tend her husband who was lying bleeding in the cockpit. She raised help via the radio and eventually both the Trinidad and Venezuelan Coast Guard came to their aid. Once in Trinidad the skipper had a seven-hour operation but I'm pleased to say that he recovered and more amazingly, the couple have gone sailing over there again.

You can imagine that this had a devastating effect on all the cruisers planning to sail west. Few wanted to risk visiting Venezuela and those having to sail in that direction to reach other cruising grounds, began to go in groups or at least with a buddy boat. The Caribbean sailing lifestyle was taking a pounding and many cruising plans were changed. But back to us, what were our plans? We'd had two people seriously interested in the boat; both from our own flyers but in each case raising the money was their problem. One man had to first sell his second house and the other couple had just launched down the house purchase route and felt overextended. We still had heard nothing from the Yacht Broker and so far had received no response to our own efforts.

Remember 'Boon' had pristine decks; some glossy varnish and we'd repainted the anti-fouling and felt ready for anything, so we decided to go cruising. We'd take our huge for sale notice with us, hand out and post flyers everywhere and any prospective buyers could come and find us. It was definitely time to take 'Boon' sailing again and the three of us have some more adventures.

CHAPTER FORTY
THE ANCHORING DANCE

We sailed through the Boca de Monos late one sunny but windy afternoon. Before we really had time to get our sailing act together, we were flying along with a steady thirty knot wind. Because of the proposed night passage we already had a reef in the main. Darkness descended in its usual early and rapid Caribbean way and by seven o'clock in the evening we were well underway and in a sailing mode once more. Like learning to ride a bike one doesn't forget how to do it. We'd had our main meal at lunchtime, so we sat together in the cockpit, munching cheese sandwiches and apples, washed down with lemon tea. It was too cloudy for any stars and ahead looked so very black. Even though it seemed a long time since we'd had a night crossing I'd remembered to make up a 'night watch box'. This time it included peanut bars, fruit and chocolate digestive biscuits. As far as Trevor is concerned, chocolate digestives are an absolute must on night watch. Thankfully in Trinidad we were able to buy them. With the Caribbean daytime temperatures it's impossible to nibble at these delicacies during the day, but with the cool of night they don't melt and are perfect for watch keeping, according to The Captain anyway. Typing 'The Captain' reminds me of a friend, who looking at our watch keeping rota saw the two headings. My watch times were headed 'Ley', and Trev's headed T.C. She looked at it silently and then said, "Does he really like to be called The Captain?" I thought for a moment and then realized what she meant. "No, T.C.

doesn't stand for The Captain, but his Christian names Trevor Cecil."

We kept to our watch-keeping timetable, but neither of us, while off watch, really slept well. I guess we were out of the habit, or perhaps not yet tired enough. This would soon change as we had decided to travel through the islands, just stopping overnight until we felt we liked the look of somewhere and then drop the hook. The overall plan was to travel as far as possible and then slowly sail back, stopping as and when the fancy took us. It's easy to do daytime trips through these islands and is not necessary to travel at night, as there is always a friendly anchorage somewhere.

By dawn we were well within sight of Grenada and could see Prickly Bay clearly on the computer. Yes, you did read that correctly, the computer. We now had electronic charts. While in Venezuela we'd been given charts on discs. In fact they covered the whole of the Caribbean islands. We still had our tatty old paper charts complete with coffee stains, but now we had two other choices. Before our journey we could either print clean, little copies of our passage or bring up the computer from time to time, and actually see where we were. Linked with our GPS we can also have a boat icon and actually watch ourselves as we sail along. Oh, the wonders of new technology. Who would have thought back in the eighties, when we were sailing 'Sea Mandala,' using a sextant along with a fat book of air navigation tables to find our way, that one day it would by pressing a button on a computer screen. Of course tucked away at the back of a deep locker, we still have the old tools, but neither of us is certain that we could use them without a refresher course. Let's hope that on this trip, we don't have to find out.

We spent the day and night in Grenada, while wandering around we were delighted to see one of our flyers prominently placed on a notice board. One of our friends had done us proud. The next day we sailed to the island of Carriacou. The wind was still boisterous, the sky and sea brilliant blue and we were able to sail all the way. It was a bit bouncy and producing food or drinks was a little tricky. We anchored just as it was beginning to get dark, then ate, fell into our bunk and were ready to move on bright and early the next morning. I must say that looking ashore we were sorely tempted to stay and explore. But we had a plan; let's for once stick to it. The next leg of our journey took us around and through a lot of little islands, including the fabulous Tobago Cays. It was getting towards late afternoon when we saw Mustique. Now this is really the exotic island for the rich and beautiful, the holiday homes of Mick Jagger and Princess Margaret. I was tempted but we sailed on as our destination that night was the island of Bequia.

It was nearly dark when we rounded the cape into her big bay. Gosh, what a lot of boats were anchored here. We'd visited her several years earlier and headed to a familiar point, only to find that mooring buoys were scattered over the area. Warning dollar signs began to flash. Our new pilot book told us that, (a) these moorings were expensive and, (b) they were not well maintained, so one should dive on them to check that they were OK before tying on. No way, so we moved and began to realize that things had changed and nearly half of the Bay was taken up with these moorings. Eventually we found ourselves a space and anchored.

By now it was quite dark and although tired, we had to make sure that our anchor was well and truly IN, as from experience we knew that a katabatic type wind blew down from the mountains, particularly at night. We went astern and the anchor wouldn't bite; we tried again and the same thing happened. By now we were uncomfortably close to another yacht. Oh well, up came the anchor and we moved again. Finally we managed to set it and collapsed into the cockpit.

We looked at each other and silently agreed that after all this effort we'd stay here for a few days. After all, isn't sailing supposed to be fun? In the middle of the night it no longer became fun. I was awoken by the sound, and feel, of a strong wind hitting us on the bow. We could hear it whistling through the other boats' rigging and feel the jerk of our anchor chain; we remembered only too well how windy Bequia could be. Why does it always happen in the night and before one is absolutely one hundred per cent certain of the anchor? Of course T.C. went straight back to sleep and I sort of dozed worrying if we would drag.

Sun up and we still had the strong wind with us but we were safely in the same place. Funny how everything looked and sounded so much safer in the light of day? We sat, cups of coffee in hand, and looked around. Yes, apart from the moorings everything was as we remembered. We were in a deep horseshoe shaped bay with a buoyed passageway through the centre. As we watched, the St. Vincent ferry trundled up to the dock. There was a crowd bustling around waiting for the unloading. We couldn't wait to get ashore. To our right we could see beautiful sandy beaches, and dotted all around the circumference of this Bay were little, mostly one story buildings. We knew from experience that they were quaint and many were gingerbread houses. I think that the word 'quaint' really sums up this little island.

By the time breakfast was over, even I was satisfied that our anchor was well and truly secure. If anything the wind was even more blustery. Pumping up the dinghy, passports and documents in hand and we were away. I must explain that unlike many other islands, Bequia is well aware of the value of the visiting yachts. It does everything it can to make them welcome and more important, persuade them to stay awhile. It also provides holiday packages with a difference for tourists and as we walked ashore we could see these holidaymakers at their early morning coffee. Some were just elderly and enjoyed the slow pace of Bequia, others were here for the diving and many of the long-term visitors, came to paint.

We tied the dinghy at one of the many dinghy docks and picking up our bags of rubbish, set off. We followed the narrow winding path around the Bay, my mouth watering at the smell of hot coffee drifting on the air. There were tables and chairs in the tiny gardens that fronted the few small hotels and the coffee drinkers watched us with as much interest as we watched them. We arrived at the centre of the town; I say town although it really was one shop lined street around the bay with perhaps a couple of side roads that looked interesting. We dumped our rubbish in the only skip available and ran the gauntlet of the aggressive Rastas who ran the greengrocery market then arrived at the Custom House. Whow, that's a new addition.

Official once more, we explored and realized just how spoilt we'd been in Trinidad. Here we were back again with very simple stores and limited produce to buy. Fortunately 'Boon' was full to the gunnels with all the goodies that Trinidad could supply and she could hold. Anyway we still needed some fresh fruit and vegetables and of course bread. Along the docks were roadside stalls and there we found large brown loaves and a few vegetables. The produce had been delivered from the fertile island of St.Vincent, sister island to Bequia. With the advent of Bequia's tourism the locals had stopped growing most of their own food. They preferred to run taxis, boat trips, work in hotels, bars, etc. This is quite common in the majority of these islands. Enough of the Economy lecture. I bought a loaf, and finding most things extremely expensive, took the locally grown much cheaper plantains, bananas and tomatoes together with some dark brown eggs.

On our way back, we passed a Bar and I spotted the magic sign 'book swap'. Inside the ramshackle, dark interior, we found four sagging shelves loaded with dusty books. With big grins we agreed to come back, with our own swaps tomorrow morning. On board we cut into our new loaf and I waited for T.C's reaction. Several bites later, he announced that it was

305

OK but not the best he'd tasted. That afternoon we dinghied to Princess Margaret beach and joined some of the yachties and the beautiful people, at play. For the record it is always possible to identify each type. Beautiful people lie on magnificently bright beach towels; ours are dull, thin and skimpy. They have pristine holiday type paperbacks, and their beachwear is exotic and of the latest fashion. Our books are battered and torn and I will leave our beachwear to your imagination. Nevertheless we all managed to have a great time. Time to leave and we pile our bits and pieces into the dinghy, and do my eyes deceive me? Did I see a look of envy from a beautiful person as she scrambled her belongings together and began the trek uphill to her hotel? Surely not?

During our four-day stay we met up with many sailing friends and visited the office of the Caribbean Compass, our friendly Caribbean waterside newspaper. There, we were reminded that as we both had articles published over the last twelve months we were invited to the annual brunch to be held at Easter, this preceded the annual sailing regatta. Gosh we'd nearly forgotten all that. Anyway we couldn't stay here until Easter we really intended to travel this time.

So four days after we'd dropped the hook, we up anchored and set off again. With sails up but with engine on, we negotiated our way through the masses of yachts thinking how on earth would they all fit in, when more arrived for the Regatta? Once clear and the engine off, we turned towards sta'board, ready to clear the end of the island and then sail towards St. Vincent. We were both in the cockpit when the

Bequia blast hit us; the strong wind came swooping down the mountain as a final goodbye. We violently heeled and T.C. speedily spilled the wind from the main. The Captain had everything under control. Not so the Mate. She's forgotten to double lock the china cupboard. The crash was devastating. All over the cabin floor lay broken china.

The skipper said nothing and I went below, and on hands and knees began the job of clearing up. Head down anxious not to miss any, was not exactly the ideal position in a bumping sea. I finished and just got back outside again when the feelings of nausea overcame me. Whoever said that sailing was great? Not me.

We'd intended making for St. Lucia but as we made our way along the coast of St. Vincent the wind began to drop, and soon we were sailing much more slowly, but oh so much more comfortably. From the cockpit we could see the rich growth on this big island, no wonder they were the vegetable and fruit providers for the area. Soon we were passing more deserted areas and could see little tiny fishing villages nestled in clumps of trees. As we passed one village we saw a tiny wooden fishing boat coming out towards us. As it got closer we could someone straining over two huge oars just managing to make headway through the sea. This was really hard work. At last he was near and shouted that we could go inshore and he'd help us tie to a tree. Sadly we said we were going further on, but perhaps another time.

Our pilot book had told us that along this coast the water was too deep to just anchor but one could go ashore and finding the tiny little shelf that was shallow, quickly anchor and that there would be plenty of volunteers to tie ones stern to a tree. What a hard living these people had? As we slowly headed towards the end the island we looked back and could see another yacht behind us and yes, our friend was rowing out again to try his luck once more.

We reached the end of St. Vincent and could see St Lucia in the distance, probably some nine miles away. Once we began the passage between the two islands, the winds blew up and we made an extremely exhilarating passage, with of course, the cupboard doors securely closed.

Although we made this extra speed it was obvious that we were not going to make our target of Rodney Bay, situated at the far end of St. Lucia before darkness. Should we go into the harbour in the dark or continue on to Martinique and arrive in the early daylight hours. We decided to make our decision as we got closer. The wind began to drop dramatically so we agreed to go through the night, as it was obvious that we wouldn't reach Martinique until morning and that would tie in nicely. The day before, via the SSB radio, we'd told friends of ours that we expected stop in St Vincent and that we would see them in Martinique a day or two later. At least we'd give them a surprise when they woke up and saw us arriving in Martinique.

The night sail was pleasant and at first light we were off Fort de of France and as we approached we could see the long docks awaiting the cruise liners who were regular visitors here. Beyond that was the area where yachts could anchor. From our position we couldn't see it yet. Gradually it all came into view and we saw once more that it was quite crowded. Now anchoring is a fine art and the actual spot where one finally drops the anchor, causes more tribulations between cruising couples than anything else. Eileen Quinn the Canadian singer and songwriter, expresses it superbly in her song, "The anchoring dance". You watch next time you are near an anchorage. You will see one person go into the bow, the significant other stays at the wheel. He points this way, she points the opposite way, they finally seem to settle on a spot and hand signals come into play. He points to the right, she prefers to go to the left, he indicates ahead, she slows down, he indicates again, then very agitatedly mimes go astern and she returns with drop the anchor signals. It truly is the anchoring dance. Remember the name, Eileen Quinn and look for the C.D. it's great fun.

Anyway our anchoring dance completed and we look around for our friends' boat. Too crowded to see, we'll check by dinghy later. Cup of coffee time and tune into the SSB Net. Sitting back, cup in hand when we hear Dorothy on the radio. Surprise, surprise they moved to St. Lucia to be there when we arrived, where are we? Would they believe that we are in Martinique to give them a surprise? Stalemate, but I'm glad to say that we are still friends.

CHAPTER FORTY-ONE
A MAGICAL CRUISE

Crazy as it sounds, I always feel that Martinique is more French, than France. Both Trevor and I love all the French Caribbean islands. Now we are in the capital of the largest one. We have some breakfast and a snooze and then after lunch decide to go ashore. Just in time we remember that this is France, and most of the shops are closed for the extended, obligatory French lunch break.

Once ashore we find the laid back Immigration Officer who handles our arrival with a single form, no cost and many French gestures. We can sail freely around the various anchorages, sign out wherever and whenever we desire and if it's a Sunday just pop the departure form in the letterbox and go.

We pass a chandlery and of course have to browse. There we find the slickest torch that we've seen in a long while and can't resist it. In fact we went mad and bought two. We are trying to find some Yacht Brokers but discover that although this is the capital of the island, the sailing centre is in fact Marin near Ste. Anne and that is where the Brokers hang out. Finally loaded with baguettes, French cheese, peaches and of course some pate we head back to the boat. We spend four more days enjoying street cafes, museums, art galleries and more besides. We are slowly beginning to realize that we are natural city dwellers and make a mental note of this fact for when we decide where to put down our roots.

On the Sunday morning we decide to sail back a

short way and find Marin and hopefully some interested Yacht Brokers or at least some notice boards for our flyers.

It was a great sail but once again it was getting late by the time our destination was in sight. Actually we could clearly see Ste. Anne and a very tenuous channel leading to Cul-de-sac du Marin. We decided to make for Ste. Anne and leave Marin for daylight. It looked a magnificent bay and certainly a large number of boats seemed to agree with us. Once again we dropped the hook and over drinks viewed our latest resting place. The sea was azure blue, the sands golden and the setting sun magnificent. After Bequia it was the most wonderfully peaceful anchorage with not a breath of wind. By now you will have realized that all things associated with sailing have double standards. If it's nice and calm, your wind generator doesn't put any power into the batteries, and if it's wonderfully dry one can't fill the water tanks with the rain. Oh well, such is life, you win some, you lose some.

Next morning ashore, we found the most delightful village. Of course very French and to T.C's delight we found a bakery with multi-grain baguettes. There was a tremendous range of fruit and vegetables but very expensive. Over the next few days we realized that they weren't in fact so expensive, as every item we bought was carefully scrutinized by the vendor before she popped it into the bag often giving us a few extra ones. There certainly wasn't any waste or damage and the extra cost was often balanced by the low cost of the beautiful cheese and bread.

We filled our days with hiking, exploring, swimming and even playing boules. We met up with many friends and enjoyed the company of the plentiful French tourists. I particularly loved our morning walk along the long sandy beach between Ste Anne and Marin. This is where we found most of the French visitors, who with typical French determination were laid out or walking the length of the beach, dedicated to building up their suntans. This was a topless beach and everyone seemed to sport the most gorgeous coffee colour. Most of the women were in miniscule bottoms or tiny thongs whether they were seventeen or seventy. The older women seemed completely unconcerned that their tanned breasts drooped or their nutmeg coloured stomachs were badly in need of tummy tucks. The French seem to handle everything with such panache. I loved it when beautiful sales girls, carrying huge baskets overflowing with brilliantly coloured wisps of fabric appeared on the beach. These baskets were overloaded with bikinis, sarongs, swimsuits and exotic flimsy cover-ups. Each girl would model one of the items and the sales seemed fast and furious. Cautiously I checked the prices, woops, I hurried away in shock. Never mind after all I had the edge, they were on a short holiday and I could stay here just as long as I liked.

We made our way through the channel into Marin and treading, or rather sailing very carefully, we inched our way through to an anchorage and went off to hunt Yacht Brokers. Although Marin seemed larger than Ste. Anne and boasted a huge Marina it was nowhere near as pretty. We found two Yacht Brokers and also found that they were not interested in us, our boat or our flyers. They had no one who could speak English and didn't want to work with us with our limited French and a dictionary. We were dismissed with the usual, very French shrug of the shoulders. We could have returned with French Canadian cruising friends but felt that it was not worth the effort.

While in Marin we visited the one and only Cyber café in the area. We joined a long queue and eventually it was our turn. I must explain here that although we receive and send e-mails via our computer and ham radio, we are only allowed to do this for personal use; any business must be conducted over the Internet hence the need for the café. So we have become very expert in finding friendly cyber cafes. This one was very friendly but extremely busy. Never mind, it was fun chatting to all the others and we quickly caught up on news, sights to see, things to do and of course the best places to shop. Our turn, and still no news from our Yacht Broker but I did receive an e-mail telling me that I had an article in next month's Caribbean Compass and a reminder saying 'please try and make the brunch.'

Back on the boat and over our French style food, the conversation turned once more to the sale of 'Boon'. We were in a catch twenty-two situation; we had to stay with her until she was sold as we needed the money for our next lifestyle, we didn't have a house waiting for us in the UK. We conducted a sort of brainstorm pulling out all the options, even if they seemed crazy. Auction her, raffle her, it got really silly and we had to stop in case we hurt her feelings.

313

Eventually sanity ruled and we became serious and realized that if we went to Bequia for the brunch we would (a) have a wonderful free lunch and (b) be in the right spot for the Regatta that started the next day. AND of course, there would be hundreds of sailors and more to the point, 'would be sailors' on tap. Delighted with the idea we checked our diaries and found that we had another week to enjoy Martinique and then it would be off to Bequia and all those would be sailors. It sounded like a plan.

We made the most of our last week and even decided that when we were no longer boat owners, we would come back to this lovely island and stay at the little campsite that ran parallel with Ste.Anne's gorgeous beach. The future looked more promising.

The Martinique week over, we paid a quick visit to St. Lucia, which was getting far too touristy for us and then had a very exhilarating trip to Bequia. We were surprised to find that there seemed fewer boats than on our earlier visit. Never mind, it was easier to find a good spot. We needed to anchor somewhere where 'Boon' would be SEEN. We chose our spot and anchored firmly and began to look forward to a great time.

First of all the Caribbean Compass Brunch was absolutely wonderful and we were greeted at the gate by Sally Erdle, the Editor. We mingled with people who had only been a by-line in her paper to us; now they were becoming flesh and blood realities. There were huge jugs of fresh orange juice, coffee and margaritas. Up until now I still had not had an alcoholic drink, not for any particular reason except that I hadn't put my extra weight back on and wasn't fussed about having a drink. Food was served and being a French restaurant I can only şay it was absolutely delicious. Food, drink and conversation flowed. Of course, as most people there were writers, the chat was fast, fascinating and fun. As usual, quite a few people didn't look as their names suggested they should. And at last I met Eileen Quinn. Eileen is Canadian and writes and sings her own songs, accompanied by her own guitar. I had heard of her over the last couple of years, but missed her gig in the Bahamas, was just too late to hear her in Grenada and my friend had forgotten to lend me her promised CD's. Well, here she was in the flesh but not to entertain, just to enjoy herself. Never mind I discovered she was going our way and I was sure to hear her eventually.

Speeches were made, nothing too serious and finding my glass empty of orange juice, went for a refill. The jug was empty, but there were still plenty of margaritas. What the heck I'd have one, after all this was a special occasion. Back with the crowd I took a sip and whew this was wicked. I nearly lost the top of my head. Then I began to feel a glow reaching right down to my toes. Fortunately a refill jug of plain juice appeared and I topped up my glass but even with constant additions I still felt on a high. Finally the party ended and I managed to walk to the dinghy still six inches off the ground.

That night we slept the sleep of the well-fed but were rudely awakened by an enormous bang. Jumping out of bed we rushed on deck and to our horror saw that another boat had dragged down onto us and was caught on our bow. By the bright searchlight that the owners had provided we could see that they were sorting things out. Trevor helped and no damage seemed to be done. With many apologies they drove away and it was only then that we realized we'd been lit up like a Christmas tree in just our skin. The regatta was tremendous fun and several people looked over our boat and one couple was on holiday and guess from where? Yes, Trinidad. Well they were leaving the next day and would like to talk more when we got back there. Email addresses were exchanged and they departed.

There followed a wonderful period of cruising in and out of little islands, golden sands and incredibly blue sea. We discovered the Tobago Cays – just a group of tiny deserted islands surrounded by a huge reef. We had to tip toe between sandbanks and reefs, that's if a boat can be described as tiptoeing, until we found ourselves behind the reef and in paradise; paradise both above and below the sea. Diving here was the best in the whole of the Caribbean, for us anyway. We stayed as long as our water lasted and reluctantly left, again cautiously creeping out.

We loved the island of Carriacou. It was rather old fashioned but with an incredible history. It was while we were finding out more about the slave trade, old customs including their fantastic wedding ceremony that we met the two youngsters who ran the Tourist office. How courteous and confident they were. They explained if any young people were fortunate enough to attend a University they had to go to Grenada or Cuba to study. The boy explained that he had only had a secondary school education. My silent thoughts were that if our British secondary schools could turn out bright confident young people like these two, we would be very proud of the system.

Finally we reached Grenada again. No rush to get back to Trinidad as this island was just out of the Hurricane belt and actually it was June again. We at last met up with Dorothy and Brian, the friends we lost between Martinique and St. Vincent. These were friends from way back in the Mediterranean days and like us had lost their boat in Hurricane Luis. We certainly spent some quality time with the two of them. Reading 'quality time' makes me realize just how indoctrinated I'd become in American expressions "You guys, apartments, let me share this with you, sodas, movies and cookies". Fortunately here in Grenada, the situation was being rectified; we were making friends with British and European cruisers who had just made their Atlantic crossing. Several said that they thought we would have no difficulty selling 'Boon' in the UK. Prices were higher that side of the water and they felt that 'Boon' would be a bargain over there. Food for thought.

This trip I had a magical evening, finally listening to Eileen Quinn sing her songs under the stars, next to the water with the scent of nutmeg in the air. A wonderful way to end our Summer cruise.

Time flew and at last we set sail for Trinidad. The promised light winds turned into a very boisterous thirty to thirty-five knots; so with a lumpy, bumpy motion we continued on our way. This time we took it in turn to doze in the cockpit and over a cup of coffee at about the halfway mark 'Boon' very dramatically veered off course. Trevor grabbed the

317

wheel while I quickly switched off the autopilot. Swinging on the wheel, TC found there was no response and 'Boon' continued on her way, quite determinedly in the wrong direction.

"The steering's gone," called the Captain. "Get the emergency tiller." Off I shot and diving into the overcrowded pilot berth, I tugged on the protruding tiller and it slid out smoothly and when I got back, TC had the cockpit floor lifted and the hole exposed waiting for the tiller. Once in place he swung on it and the boat went smoothly back on course and we were off again.. The only problem being that our self steering was designed to fit a wheel and so we had to hand steer our course for Trinidad. Easier said than done. The winds and sea were still high and so it was quite hard work. Probably these two sailors were out of practice and of course by now were rather tired. So on we went and had half an hour on and half an hour off. As we got nearer, the wind began to drop and of course the sea became calmer. In fact as we made the entrance through the Boca, we found an outgoing tide, little wind and so our entrance was very, very slow. Never mind, what was the rush?

CHAPTER FORTY-TWO
SEPTEMBER 11th

Upon our return we discovered that our interested couple in Trinidad had bought another boat in our absence. We still had two separate people seriously interested in the boat; both from our own flyers but in each case raising the money was their problem. One man had to first sell his second house and the other couple had just launched down the house purchase route and felt overextended. We still had heard nothing from the Yacht Broker. In fact our six-month contract had almost run out.

In our explorations we discovered a local Cyber Café who would produce a 'Boon for sale' website, using our own pictures and dialogue but giving us whatever help we required. Everyone could see 'Boon' and all her assets in glorious computerized technicolour at the press a button. This could run for one year at the cost of £30. This was more like it. We included our email address and it had a running total of hits so we could see how successful or not we were. A pattern began, we printed more flyers but this time we were able to say 'visit our website'. We were able to put tiny, cheap adverts in magazines and newspapers, again with the magic words 'visit our website'. Then we decided to see what would materialize and continue to enjoy what Trinidad could throw at us.

This season we didn't fancy another spell in Venezuela, as security remained problematic although Trinidad was beginning to experience similar troubles. Not on such a grand scale but there were too many muggings and recently there had been a spate of hold ups along the road between the various Marinas and Boat Yards. These were occurring in the evenings and with too much regularity for comfort.

Once more we were in Trinidad's iron grip and back at the Keep Fit Centre we were given a great welcome and once again I struggled to get fit once more. After a long absence it is always purgatory to get into shape. So you would see us three times a week jumping on a maxi-taxi and bumping along to the Bio-Fitness .Centre. Actually with the speed these maxis travel and the condition of the roads, we were more in danger of damaging ourselves en route than while actually working out. Once inside the Centre our ears are battered with the throb of the music. Remember this is Trinidad man and everything is accompanied with music, loud music. It can be soca, rap, reggae or calypso just as long as it's loud.

We change into our trainers and socks and once in old shorts and tee shirts leap onto a walk master. Whoops, we're off. I walk very fast getting nowhere, while Trevor runs even faster, getting nowhere even quicker. To stop us thinking of the futility of the whole thing, there are numerous TV's to watch. All silent of course, as sound may interfere with the music. A few have captions but others don't. The sport programmes are fine but you try watching the news or a movie without sound. I must warn you I'm beginning to excel at lip reading. So be careful what you say if I'm in your vicinity!

The whole room is mirrored and we can see others and ourselves. Faces look back at me. Everyone is sweating like crazy, but why, oh why, do black skins look so alive and healthy when wet while our white ones look so dull and tired. We are a mixed bunch – housewives, businessmen, the young and fit and of course the body builders and we two ancients. By now Trevor is really sweating, I'm just damp, I guess I'm not trying hard enough.

We progress into our programme; today it is legs. We move between the machines and start some serious working out. By about four o'clock the beautiful girls from the Banks and Business Centres begin to arrive. They join us in their skimpy sports wear and looking at them I think that getting older is one of life's dirty tricks. My slightly chauvinistic skipper is horrified to see the enormous weights some of the girls lift and this spurs him on.

Trevor's despondency increases when the "big" fellers enter. Actually they all seem to make a definite 'entrance'. Attired in designer sportswear and don't forget the designer trainers and even socks, they wander around the room greeting each other with high fives and lots of laughter. Of course they constantly pause and pose in front of the mirrors. Then it gets interesting as they lift, pull and push using the most incredibly huge weights, often accompanied by grunts, groans and even shouts. The labour ward in the local Maternity Hospital has nothing on this.

Trevor's confidence was restored when he watched one of the really big guys doing pull-ups and making seriously hard work of the whole exercise. Trevor looked smug as he nudged me to watch, then his face fell as he saw the 150 lb weights hanging from his feet. Oops!

We continued to enjoy the local theatre, pan yards, fetes, and all the wonderful things that are so essentially Trinidadian. We thrived on the typical Yachtie entertainments of Pot Luck Suppers, weekly videos, book swaps, Trivial Pursuits, and of course musical evenings. It's amazing how many sailing folk have talent. We of course had Eileen Quinn, then Robinson Crusoe who specialized in Rock and Roll, jazz groups and our regular entertainers Mood Indigo, who gave us Blues and Jazz and always managed to fill their stage with local and cruising entertainers. We had our regular Writers' Group and one way or another this International group seemed to fill every spare minute. How boat work, cooking, laundry, correspondence and more, got done is still a mystery.

All this time we were meeting up with British cruisers who had just crossed the 'pond'. They were very welcome for several reasons; we needed first hand news of home and the Mediterranean, and as I said earlier definitely wanted an influx of spoken English. A spate of "gosh, you chaps, how jolly or even frightfully" was very welcomed. They were still telling us that we should advertise 'Boon' back in the UK, again higher prices were mentioned. Back on the boat we would discuss it but nothing seemed to get done. We did however, have responses to our website but in the main these were from the Caribbean and Venezuela, this seemed to prove our point that anyone living further away is unlikely to travel to Trinidad to see our old lady. There were lots of hits and email enquiries but nothing definite happened.

One evening we dined with very special friends, they too were selling their boat and making a frantic dash to the UK on business. Of course our joint concern regarding selling our respective boats took up part of the evening, and the outcome was that they agreed to place a small advert in a British Yachting magazine for us. Comfortably replete and relaxed after beautiful Chilean wine we promptly put it to the back of our minds.

September arrived very bright, sunny and oh so hot. The humidity was like something else. Would we ever get used to it? But more important, would we get used to colder weather if and when we finally retired? By now we had agreed that for starters we would go back to the UK. We both felt a need to re-establish our bonds with the kids and I felt that I definitely need to surround my mother with lots of TLC. We would take everything in easy stages and just 'suck it and see'.

We watched the rise of the number of hits on our web site and replied to the few e-mails that resulted, and then a Scandinavian friend called to say that she had some Swedes flying over to look at yachts in our price range, should she include ours? Yes please.

On September 11th we had a mammoth clean up until everything sparkled and the next morning we turned on the VHF to wait for their arrival. They would give us a call from the Bar and we'd pick them up in the dinghy. The bartender gave us the call and as T C climbed into the dinghy we gave each other a high five and he shot off. In those few quiet minutes I looked around me, we were anchored in an idyllic bay with a few boats gently swaying around us with a back drop of trees. The occasional pelican swooped

323

for breakfast and if the venue had anything to do with it the viewers wouldn't be able to resist.

They arrived and climbed on board; fortunately it was just the interested couple and not our friend as well, and even then we were looking like a crowd, not a good start. As we climbed into the cockpit I realized that this couple were incredibly tall; they seemed to tower over Trevor and me. In fact 'Boon' seemed to shrink as we talked; we were always aware that the awning was low but this looked ridiculous. I showed the woman around and then Trevor went below with her husband and began to discuss engines, generators and electronic charts and as they leant together over the chart table the VHF crackled into life again. A fairly agitated female voice announced, "Turn on your TV or radios, a plane has just hit the World Trade Centre and there is devastation." We were horrified and immediately tuned in to hear that a further plane had crashed into the second tower and it looked like a terrorist attack. We were all stunned, especially our visitor; as he explained to us, earlier that year he was actually working in the tower on the twenty-eighth floor. He of course would know many of the people involved.

We all went ashore and watched the rest of the terrible happenings on the Club's big TV screen. More and more cruisers began to arrive and silently all of us sat transfixed.

As I sat stunned, I watched a couple come through the gate and stop by the gazebo and casually glance at the screen; at that moment they were showing a re-run of the first plane. "What film is this?" the woman carelessly asked. I realized that it looked exactly like that, a disaster movie set in New York. But no, this was life and this was the terrible world that we all lived in.

Selling boats was no longer of interest. By now we'd heard of the third 'plane crash and the whole terrible scenario began to unwind. Along with everyone else we seemed to spend our time either in front of the TV screen, or back on the boat listening to the world service. Of course with our close proximity to so many American cruisers we became more involved, as many of them had lived, worked or had friends and family in New York. Then of course we realized that it was an international disaster as we all heard of the numbers of our own countrymen and women who were involved. We watched in horror as we saw Palestinians dancing in the streets, dancing with exhilaration at the attack on America and the Western world. To me the whole world seemed to have gone mad.

In the middle of all this we received an e-mail from the UK asking for more details of the yacht 'Boon' which the enquirer had seen advertised for sale in the Yachting Monthly. He asked some very in depth questions and ended with the magic words 'this is a serious enquiry.' Whow, in all the drama we had forgotten that our advert was due to appear. With great care we replied to his e-mail.

Very quickly we received more questions from the same man and we fired off more answers. Our lives suddenly seemed to run along two parallel courses, one, was the ongoing fury over the disaster, then we heard Bush announcing retaliation and all that was involved. And we were receiving the news that we'd been waiting for and now were too numb to fully appreciate it. Before we had time to sort out our conflicting emotions our prospective buyer made arrangements to fly over and see the boat for himself.

I guess it was, to us, the most important thing to happen but of course tinged with regret and sadness.

We drove to the Airport with the statutory placard bearing his name and watched all the new security processes. Passengers were relieved of all those objects that were now suddenly classed as 'life threatening'. Which sailor would ever travel without his ever present knife or Leather Man tool? These now were no longer acceptable.

The passengers began to slowly appear, they emerged in ones or twos and all seeming to look around in a bewildered fashion as if they'd just come out into the light. I guess most of them were grateful to have arrived safely as aeroplane disasters were still too fresh in everyone's minds. Suddenly my own mind jerked into action as I saw a man of enormous proportions, both upwards and outwards. God, he'd never fit into 'Boon'. I shared this with Trevor and for the next ten minutes we watched every man with anxious scrutiny. Finally a very pleasant, and thankfully, short man, appeared with a small overnight bag and wearing an anxious look. He appeared to look right through our placard and then looked again and came cautiously towards us. Introductions were made and then over the next few days followed the sale, or buying of 'Boon', depending on which side of the fence you stood.

Although an epoch making occasion, seeming to take long in gestation, it was all over so quickly and painlessly. Graham saw the boat, made a thorough examination and the next day he and Trevor went sailing. Evidently a good time was had by all and according to the retiring Skipper, 'Boon' behaved impeccably. Fate had a hand in it as the weather was superb and Murphy never appeared once. We received the price that we'd asked for and a rigging survey showed just a couple of faults, which we were quite happy to pay for. Graham seemed to enjoy his week and joined in with the usual activities and before we knew it we were reversing the procedure and waving him off to the UK. All we had to do was wait for the cheque, exchange a bill of sale and it would all be over. We both felt that we were putting 'Boon' in two very capable hands.

The next day we had three more serious e-mails enquiring about the boat we had to sell, and another from Trevor's cousin Michael. In it he wrote and I quote "What a mess this whole Osama Bin Ladin thing is. Actually I think you two have got it right, you're probably much safer over there sailing in your third world countries. Have you got any room for two more, Pam and I might just join you?" We just looked at each other in silence.

CHAPTER FORTY-THREE
THE PARTY'S OVER

We departed Trinidad leaving behind our floating home and numerous friends. All we took with us were three medium sized travel bags and a million memories. Memories of a magnificent eleven and a half years and I still cannot express my feelings at this moment in time. All I know is that I would not change any of it. The sinking and the hurricane happened, we survived and I like to think that I appreciate life so much more because of the experiences.

The people I have met have been outstanding. The full time sailing community is so very special and I salute every one of you. This period of my life is something I shall never forget. If you think of becoming one of us, or should I now say one of them, I can truly recommend it.

What the new life will bring, I do not know. I imagine it will be a lot fun. One thing I can say, and that is whatever I have done since meeting Trevor has never been dull. Being an adventurer he already has lots of plans so time will tell. I am the more cautious one in this partnership but I will definitely finish my book and have decided to call it "The Mis-Adventures of a Sea Wyfe." Although I am Trevor's wife, I feel that during this time of my life, part of me was also married to the sea. I never felt that I was looking for an adventurous life but somehow mis-adventures did seem to come my way. This manuscript may never see the light of day and just languish in a drawer, or should I say on a floppy disc. Nevertheless I could dust it off from time to time and relive some of my memories. Or of course, it could get published, now wouldn't that be the start of another adventure.

Ley Liberson in Whitstable, England.
January 2002

AND THEY LIVED HAPPILY EVER AFTER.................

It is now April 2008 and I can honestly say we are living happily and are both well. I am 73 and Trevor is approaching his 80th birthday.   So what happened? We settled in Whitstable in Kent. A very small flat in a very small fishing town. Small of course is relative, after all anything is large after our boats. We found our families had managed very well without us, but it was great fun discovering them all again and hope of course that they enjoyed us once more.

How did we fill our time? First of all we brought ourselves up to speed with computing. We joined some local courses and Trevor went on to pass his European Computer Driving Licence. I chickened out of this one as it involved six exams. We enjoyed all those crisp new books from the local library; we went walking and camped from time to time. The weather was a surprise as we didn't feel cold, but of course Global Warming is now with us.

Trevor wanted to discover more about the scientific changes that had occurred during our absence, so signed up for an AS Level in Human Biology. I reworked my book but still had no luck with an interested Publisher; I could have papered our toilet with rejection slips/letters. Over a delightful dinner party at my cousin's I found myself answering questions about our life-raft experience and one guest mentioned that it would make a good talk. Food for thought.

We kept in touch with some of our closer sailing friends and had a great holiday in France with one couple. But it reinforced the fact that we felt comfortable in England and didn't need to chase the sun anymore. However the one thing we did miss was living out of doors. On the boat we seemed to spend a great deal of time in our cockpit and in the great outdoors.

I visited my local Women's Institute to view the speakers and decided to give it a go. But before I had an audition for WI's, I had a request to be the guest speaker at a Ladies Luncheon; talk about being dropped off at the deep end. So in a delightful restaurant, with good food and wine, I did my stuff and it seemed to go down well. Trevor produced some flyers and by word of mouth it took off.

By now Trevor, with his AS level under his belt, applied to Christchurch University to be considered for a place on the Bachelor of Science Degree Course in Bioscience. He was accepted and whow he became a student and like the cheese was seriously mature. He had three wonderful years and got his degree.

During this time I had five different talks to offer and I averaged three to five a month. I did join the Women's Institute and after a year became the secretary of our Whitstable branch. I made lots of friends but most of important I had two lovely years with my Mum. Sadly she died but I was so glad that I was there for her. At her funeral the Minister asked if I would speak about her. I was horrified; I knew that I would break down. Then I thought of how she was so proud of my talks and loved to hear about them, surely I could speak for five minutes about my beautiful mother. I did.

So our lives have been filled. With Trev's student friends we have been kept on our toes and one of my proudest moments was sitting in Canterbury Cathedral watching him get his degree. But of course you know Trevor is a rebel and never does things by halves, so he applied for a place at Kent University to do his Masters in Biotechnology. He was accepted and given a bursary for this one year course. That year is now over. What next for him?

In 2006 we decided to self-publish this book via Lulu.com and when I held the first copy in my hands it was like my baby. I sell copies at my talks and it is in my local library. Recently we have re-read it and realise that as the professionals were not involved, there are far too many errors. We have corrected these and added this postscript.

I guess it started with the sailing and must end that way. We do not own a boat but number one son, Max does, so Trevor gets a sailing fix now and then. Me, well my sailing days are over, it was part of my life which I will never forget but I have no desire to continue. Trevor always tells me not to look back but forward. So I will. I wonder what comes next?

ley liberson